Relationality

BEYOND THE MODERN
Series editors: Clive Dilnot and Eduardo Staszowski

In the face of the scale and intractability of the multiple compound problems that threaten to engulf us there are two urgent demands. The first is to seek to encompass—to give measure—to the unrepresentability of the complexity which confronts us. The second—working against the seeming impossibility of so doing—is to establish the possibility of being able to effect transformative shifts in the causes (economic, technological, ontological) of disaster.

These tasks are made difficult by the continuing limitations of inherited patterns of thought and action. Neither models of (technological) acting, which eschew reflection in favor of immediate efficacy, nor the human sciences, which still maintain their distance from generative action)—are adequate to what is required. The engineered blindness of the first is mirrored by the limitations of critique and fear of intervention in the second. Neither adequately comprehends the dysfunctional destructive relationality of the world as-is. One consequence is that both lose sight of the immanent possibilities of acting-otherwise that are also objectively present in the world. Yet envisioning the latter, and bringing these to articulate consciousness and possible realization, must be the real subject of thought and practice today.

Working at the intersection of thought and practice, this series focuses on teasing out the possibilities of what is immanent within what now is. Grasping the significance of remaking and operating in a third space of "praxiological" thought and action—one that acts without illusion but with the necessary political conviction that the seemingly impossible can be overcome—they explore, at a variety of levels, configurations of thought, material and social practices and models of politics which can potentially realize transformative possibilities in the world. In so doing, they begin to offer snapshots of a different journey, a different narrative, politics, and praxis for the world; prefigurations, in relations, in political imagination, in the sense of what is possible for ontological and economic shifts in the trajectory of the world.

Forthcoming titles

Relationality: An Emergent Politics of Life Beyond the Human,
Arturo Escobar, Michal Osterweil, and Kriti Sharma

Contrapractice: Practice and Defuturing Now,
Tony Fry and Dulmini Perera

designing Politics,
Anke Gruendel

The Possibility of the Artificial/The Urgency of the Possible,
Clive Dilnot

PRAISE FOR *RELATIONALITY*

"The world is a story, but the planet? The planet is an interdependent field of infinite possibility. This book is a guide, not only for how we may evolve, but for how evolution beyond the story of scarcity and separation is already happening all around and through us. This book is an invitation into a scale of being where our actions can be part of an unimaginably beautiful future, if we let them. Read this at the smallest scale, let it ring in the tiny matter making up your cells. Read this at the largest scale, remember your responsibility as a universe."

ALEXIS PAULINE GUMBS, author of *M Archive* (2018),
Undrowned (2020), and *Dub* (2020)

"Perhaps there is no story more scandalous to the modern than the idea that we do not live on our planet, or in it. We live with it. Imbricated with its desirous flows, yearnings, and gestures. In a time when the feverish drumbeats of civilizational trouble are louder than ever, this book takes that unwieldy proposition of relationality seriously and alchemizes a capacious politics. A welcoming politics. A politics that releases us from the traps of thinking we are alone and that the future is left entirely to us. Read it. Share it."

BAYO AKOMOLAFE, author of *These Wilds beyond Our Fences:
Letters to My Daughter on Humanity's Search for Home* (2017);
Chief Curator, Emergence Network

"Because of the radical nature of what it offers us, *Relationality* requires careful reading; it forces us to stop and think about how to deal with it in the search for new ways of being and doing. This beautiful book confronts us with the fact that designing relationally implies radical choices, to be pursued systemically starting from where you are. I fully agree with the authors that a life-centered ontology of inter-existence is what we need to give hope of life to Earth, and to us within it."

EZIO MANZINI, author of *Politics of the Everyday*
(2019) and *Livable Proximity* (2022)

"A path-breaking call for the principle of relationality to be placed at the center of all our worldmaking practices, and for the myths of modernity to be replaced with new relational stories that will guide us in the protection of our planet's social and ecological fabric. This book is essential reading for educators, researchers, practitioners and activists working for systems level change."

TERRY IRWIN AND GIDEON KOSSOFF, Transition
Design Institute, Carnegie Mellon University

"This book situates itself within the scholarly critique of modern/colonial world systems, with particular gravity towards pluriversal politics and expanded biological thinking. I find much strength and purpose to the book's emphasis on designing as inspiration for bridges and portals for other possible ways of worlding. The proposed task of restor(y)ing life is highly engaging for anyone working in the arts and humanities, as well as for all expressive and poetic media as reflections of interdependency."

RACHEL HANN, Assistant Professor of Performance
and Design, Northumbria University, Newcastle;
author of *Beyond Scenography* (2019)

"This is a deeply personal and intellectually stimulating book. It is an invitation to hope, but it does not frighten, cajole, or scold the reader. Instead, it offers crucial insights into the current world, while showing us that other ways of living are not only possible but already very real. It performs a rather unique task, made concrete by the variety of voices from different places the authors mix together—from the scholarly and theoretical to the activist and indigenous, all held together by the joyful effort to create a common voice for themselves."

LAWRENCE GROSSBERG, Professor of Communication and Cultural
Studies Emeritus, UNC, Chapel Hill; author of *Under the Cover of Chaos:
Trump and the Battle for the American Right* (2018)

"A rigorously intellectual yet heart-led exploration of the dominant story that has made us inhabitants of an impoverished One-World world, but also a compendium of stories that point towards ways we might remake ourselves. *Relationality* speaks to that feeling that leaves us paralyzed between, on the one hand, a proliferating yet uncaring (when not lethal) world, albeit dressed up in all kinds of 'realistic' garbs, and, on the other, the aspiration of something kinder and livelier, the promise of genuine relations. The way out of this impasse, the authors show us, is by slowing down to connect with the myriad ways of relating that are proliferating in the cracks of what appears as the one and only 'reality.' This is necessary nourishment for those wishing to undertake the mighty work of transitioning away from the stories of life many of us live by."

MARIO BLASER, Professor of Archeology, Geography and
Anthropology, Memorial University of Newfoundland; author
of *Not about the Anthropocene: An Essay of Political
Ontology for Life Projects* (forthcoming)

"A book that is seeking ways toward affirmative futures while fully acknowledging the depth and extent of defuturing is an ambitious, almost impossible undertaking, yet one that is absolutely necessary. Escobar, Osterweil and Sharma take on the challenge in this emotionally intense work that is part manifesto, part conversation, part exposition. In the face of escalating crises, they refuse pessimism, and insist on the possibility of *designing* life otherwise, drawing inspiration from the world-making practices of social movements and communities of resistance. Here, they mobilize design as prefiguration in a social and cultural sense rather than as a delimited instrumental practice, and they are especially alert to the designing power of narrative, arguing for, and experimenting with, narratives of relationality and commonality."

"*Relationality* is a profound critique of the conventional understanding of the story of life that simultaneously appeals to intellect and affection, sketching uncharted pathways to the future. Going well beyond the notion of 'network,' the authors arrive at a powerful conceptualization of relationality that draws multiple readers into an enticing ecosystem in which only an active engagement from each of us can remake the circle of design. The evolutionary behavior of seagrass, which transitioned from the ocean to the land and back, is always present in the background as an inspiring conceptual leitmotif."

"*Relationality* engages with the risks of a designing that *makes life*, practices that do not passively consume life but that actively and emergently enact it. This is an unusual book about design, 'a different story, told in a different tone, from a very different starting place,' a book grounded on the experience of being loved, supported, inspired, and interconnected. Escobar, Osterweil, and Sharma gift us with a sense of what is possible and their loving commitment to the future."

"This beautifully composed book is a highly inspiring and original contribution to understanding anew the nature of worldmaking in the context of the planetary crisis we all face. *Relationality* is a great text to assign to younger students but also a brilliant entry point for anyone seeking an introduction to the approach of relationality from the deep wisdom of the multiple movements, traditions and communities on which the authors ably draw."

"Poetic and passionate, this book gathers a host of voices into a chorus that proclaims 'another future is possible!' … but only if we re-story our world *now*. Readers are urged to unmake the selves we have inherited by stepping into contact zones where design praxis transitions us from one story to another.

Embracing uncertainty, Escobar, Osterweil and Sharma navigate a course that rejects progress and enmeshes us in a world of hopeful relationality."

"Finding a book that offers radical hope in the theory and practice of relationality is a much-needed gift. Escobar, Osterweil and Sharma guide us through a pluriverse of stories, calling on us to counter modernity's dominant narrative of *homo economicus* with new and better stories of life. As a teacher and scholar-activist I will be using this book to encourage my students and communities to recover the notions of well-being required for life-worlds built on flourishing relations with humans and more-than-human others."

"Escobar, Osterweil and Sharma gift us a bridge that enables us to transition from the naturalized idea of a One-World World to the recognition that other civilizational narratives are possible and necessary. Poetically, they share an alternative vision based on relationality as the foundation of life, where all living beings are participants in worldmaking and designing what we all do to make life. By doing so, they illustrate the coexistence of many worlds and stimulate the emergence of new ones."

"Osterweil, Sharma and Escobar have written an inspiring book that helps us account for the necessity of hope in the future while trusting our concrete doings in the present. Rather than ask readers to focus so much on the myriad things that need to be done, they confront us with the questions of what it means to 'do' today, and how we could make relationally. As a designer I found the proposal unsettling and full of possibilities."

"If you despair about the present polycrisis, read this book. If you don't despair (yet), read it as well. The authors provide a persuasive roadmap for rethinking and remaking our world through design stories that support relationality, pluriversality and the creativity of life. This book is a timely wake-up call that brings together a stunning diversity of voices—from biology, philosophy, anthropology and design to activist and indigenous movements—all pointing towards relationality as the key to a new ontology."

TON OTTO, Professor of Anthropology, Aarhus University, co-editor of *Design Anthropology: Theory and Practice* (2013) and *Impermanence: Exploring Continuous Change across Cultures* (2022)

"In this book, Escobar, Osterweil and Sharma navigate through the interstices of contemporary monocultures, envisioning paths from terricide to *terrigenesis* while lovingly embracing the numerous nows reverberating at the interface of denied, but still livable, pasts and foreclosed but possibly emerging futures. The political activation of relationality, they argue, is essential to reinventing ourselves through other myths that enable us to perceive anew the webs of relations that make us and the wisdom of caring for them. *Relationality* is a purposeful drift into the uncertain terrain that throbs between transitions in place and the place of transitions in life. This book is a disobedient call to make life outside the restrictive trajectories of modernity."

ALFREDO GUTIÉRREZ BORRERO, Professor of Design, Universidad Jorge Tadeo Lozano, Bogotá

"Every action impacts everything and everyone else, any time everywhere. Activating this notion is a treasure that changes the way we work and live. This is a timely book that asks us to make radical choices about what to (re) make and unmake."

SOPHIE KRIER AND ERIK WONG, co-curators of *In Search of the Pluriverse* (nieuweinstituut.nl)

Relationality

An Emergent Politics of Life Beyond the Human

Arturo Escobar, Michal Osterweil, and Kriti Sharma

BLOOMSBURY VISUAL ARTS
LONDON • NEW YORK • OXFORD • NEW DELHI • SYDNEY

BLOOMSBURY VISUAL ARTS
Bloomsbury Publishing Plc
50 Bedford Square, London, WC1B 3DP, UK
1385 Broadway, New York, NY 10018, USA
29 Earlsfort Terrace, Dublin 2, Ireland

BLOOMSBURY, BLOOMSBURY VISUAL ARTS and the Diana logo
are trademarks of Bloomsbury Publishing Plc

First published in Great Britain 2024

Cover design by Andrew LeClair and Chris Wu of Wkshps

A catalogue record for this book is available from the British Library.

A catalog record for this book is available from the Library of Congress.

ISBN: HB: 978-1-3502-2597-8
          PB: 978-1-3502-2596-1
          ePDF: 978-1-3502-2599-2
          eBook: 978-1-3502-2598-5

Series: Beyond the Modern

Typeset by Integra Software Services Pvt. Ltd.
Printed and bound in India

To find out more about our authors and books visit www.bloomsbury.com
and sign up for our newsletters.

Contents

ON ANOTHER PANEL ABOUT CLIMATE, THEY ASK ME TO SELL THE FUTURE AND ALL I'VE GOT IS A LOVE POEM[1]
by Ayisha Siddiqa

What if the future is soft and revolution is so kind that there is no
end to us in sight.

…

How rare and beautiful it is that we exist.

What if we stun existence one more time?

…

Been born from so many apocalypses, what's one more?

Love is still the only revenge. It grows each time the earth is set on
fire.

But for what it's worth, I'd do this again.
Gamble on humanity one hundred times over

Commit to life unto life, as the trees fall and take us with them.

I'd follow love into extinction.

[1] Excerpted with the author's permission, Ayisha Siddiqa, "On Another Panel About Climate, They Ask Me to Sell the Future and All I've Got Is a Love Poem," On Being, June 10, 2022. Full poem available online: https://onbeing.org/poetry/on-another-panel-about-climate-they-ask-me-to-sell-the-future-and-all-ive-got-is-a-love-poem/ (accessed June 26, 2023).

Preface

This is a book about the future and is dedicated lovingly to the future. It is about how we imagine, relate to, and therefore act for the future in the present. As climate, environmental, economic, and political crises continue to escalate, and the complexity of their interrelations makes them ever more difficult to comprehend and address effectively, many of us are deeply concerned that our species, along with the rest of life and the earth herself, will face escalating upheaval in the coming decades and centuries. Given the dominance of the current destructive and extractive mode of life, it is easy to lose hope—especially because so much contemporary analysis, while helpful in illuminating what is going wrong, does not offer adequate understanding of what is possible. Relationality—and designing relationally—offers us a different move, a different story, a different affect.

We opened with the moving poem by Ayisha Siddiqa—a young Pakistani-born New York-based activist—because, in their expression of such a loving commitment to the future, her words capture this sense of possibility. It is a commitment at the heart of the project of relationality. Importantly, this commitment does not come from some sort of naïve or romantic ignorance of all that ails us, but is, on the contrary, a deliberate choice to "gamble on humanity" in full awareness of the mess we are in. Readers imbued in political realism, and demoralized by the state of things, might read this poem and these opening words with cynicism. We understand this cynicism and even sympathize with it; yet we insist with Siddiqa that the future remains radically free and filled with possibility.

The well-known design theorist and philosopher Tony Fry calls our current extractivist, industrialist, and modern capitalist mode of life "defuturing", a way of life that actively erodes the possibility of a livable future. This calls for a commitment to what the future should be and is not yet, to love and to humanity, a realization shared by many people, particularly those who, like

Siddiqa, have been through so many apocalypses, small and large.[1] Such a radical commitment to possibility often comes from those who have borne the brunt of past and present attempts to foreclose the future, because (as we will show) love as well as grief and loss are often portals to relationality, and to designing relationally.

We say this early on because we want to be honest from the outset, both about what this book is, and what it is not. While this is a book about crises and it strives to contribute to changing the world, it is not a solutionist book. At this time, solutions cannot help but remain stuck in the same paradigm or story as the problems they describe and presume to be real.[2] Instead, this is a book about *the possibility* of designing and making life otherwise, which as we say early on, requires a different story, told in a different tone, from a very different starting point. This also asks something of you, dear reader. There is a lot of bad news out there. Our nervous systems are primed for dealing with despair and fear with reactive responses: fight, flight, freeze, and appease. Yet these reactive responses not only don't get us very far, they are also products of the same story and reality we are so terrified and angry about. As such, rather than simply reacting, resorting to either our analytical or nervous-system default settings, we can take a breath, pause, and choose to remember and to recognize all the things that have gone right and continue to go right on this planet. We can do this while also knowing that this journey will take us to grim places. We will definitely wade into "the mess," filled with problems that are deep and tragic and painful to recount. But, or rather *and*, we revisit these problems because we believe that lovingly facing the tangled history of how we have gotten here is crucial for living otherwise into the truth and therefore into the future.

When we say, "dear reader," we don't use the term "dear" perfunctorily. You are dear. Someone who really matters. A being connected to others by love, a designer making life every day. Perhaps this feels a little uncomfortable to hear; after all, hardly any of us have been treated with the care we each deserve. We understand, as we too were made and swim in the same water. The same culture in which kindness, affection, and love must be earned and are generally reserved for the private sphere. Where cynicism is considered smart, and optimism naïve. Still, we invite you to remember that you are dear and to remember those you hold dear as you read these pages.

Love and care are important to understand what we mean by designing and by relationality. As a noun, design is often thought of as a professional practice

---

[1] Nick Estes, "Indigenous Resistance Is Post-Apocalyptic, Interview with Nick Estes," *Dissent*, July 31, 2019, available online: https://www.dissentmagazine.org/online_articles/booked-indigenous-resistance-is-post-apocalyptic-with-nick-estes (accessed November 2, 2022).

[2] Bayo Akomolafe, "What Climate Collapse Asks of Us," The Emergence Network, August 17, 2019, available online: https://www.bayoakomolafe.net/post/what-climate-collapse-asks-of-us (accessed November 10, 2022).

and a primarily intellectual endeavor in which we use our analytical capacities to assess what is possible, then work to manifest our visions. In this design mode, we can argue with one another and persuade one another that certain designs are possible or impossible, realistic or unrealistic, and so on. However, in this book, we do not think of designing in this way. This book is certainly not about object-oriented professional design, although it has significant implications for what goes on under the banner of design.

We prefer to speak of design*ing*: always a verb, a process, an open-ended imagination concerned with making life, and potentially, a modality of active caring. Designing *relationally* means creating with the awareness that we are in inextricable relationship with one another, with the earth, and with numerous nonhuman entities. And that, moreover, we ourselves are constitutively relational. We are complex webs of relationships comprising minds, bodies, hearts, communities, knowledges, and so forth. We are webs that are in relationship with the future, the present, and importantly, the stories we tell about them.

The experience of being loved, supported, inspired, and interconnected opens up our entire sense of what is possible. As Black feminist poet Alexis Pauline Gumbs put it, "when I remember how loved, supported, inspired, interconnected I am and we are, it really shifts what is possible. I really believe that it is as necessary as oxygen to the brain."[3] A loving future begins in a loving present. From this place, we expand our capacity to face the tragedies of past and present and expand our imagination to possibilities worthy of the future. Joyful and fulfilling possibilities, imagined with tenderness and respect, so that the future may decide to stay.[4]

This book thus emerges in the space demarcated by care, designing, relationality, and possible futures. It is from this sense of possibility that we invite you to enter this book and to begin to continue making life relationally. All of us have the potential to be designing in this way. Perhaps many are already.

A LITTLE ABOUT US AND OUR PROCESS

This book is the result of a long process of learning to write, think, and know relationally. A process between three people with great affinity and numerous differences, including all the networks of people and experiences that in turn comprise each of us. While it is impossible to list these differences *in toto*, we can point to some: we were each born in different countries (Colombia, Israel, Canada), raised with different languages (Spanish, Hebrew, English), religions

---

[3] Alexis Pauline Gumbs, "Our Labor Has Become More Important Than Our Silence: Writing Workshop for Rogue Intellectuals in Honor of Audre Lorde," Sangodare, Online workshop, September 1, 2022, available online: https://sangodare.podia.com/our-labor-has-become-more-important-than-our-silence-writing-workshop-for-rogue-intellectuals-in-honor-of-audre-lorde (accessed December 21st, 2022).

[4] See Siddiqa, "On Another Panel About Climate."

(Catholicism, Judaism, Hinduism, Buddhism), and professionalized or trained in different disciplines. Kriti holds a doctorate in biology and spends a lot of time gazing through a microscope at minuscule organisms from the bottom of the ocean. Michal and Arturo are both anthropologists but arrived at the profession at very different times, from very different questions and places. Arturo by way of development work and engineering originally in Colombia. Michal through the pathways of activist-scholarship in the United States. We hold overlapping but different political commitments and political communities. Each of us has what we consider a contemplative or spiritual practice, but our experience with it is quite distinct and evolving.

These differences became a fertile and formative ground for one of the key ingredients of the text before you: the ability to see commonality, resonance, affinity, without effacing specificities and difference. As the poet Walt Whitman once put it: "Do I contradict myself? Very well then, I contradict myself. (I am large, I contain multitudes)." Tension, paradox, difference are not problems in a relational worldview, they are generative. We each learned from the differing areas of expertise and life experiences in our process of co-authorship, deferring to each other at times, raising queries when things were not clear or seemed problematic.

There are numerous ways one could tell the story of this book's development. From its emergence as a research question and hunch to its material manifestation, largely during the pandemic years of uncertainty and lockdown beginning in 2020. The book arose out of a transdisciplinary seminar entitled "The Carolina Seminar on the Theory and Politics of Relationality," created and led by Arturo and Michal at the University of North Carolina at Chapel Hill, beginning in 2011. Kriti, who was then finishing her book, *Interdependence: Biology and Beyond* (2015), was one of the participants from an early date.

The Relationality seminar was itself an outgrowth of the Social Movements Working Group, active at Chapel Hill between 2003 and 2011, of which Arturo and Michal had been core members. One of the shared insights of this transdisciplinary group was the recognition that social movements were in and of themselves important knowledge producers and theorists of the present. This is important because the examples and definitions used in this book tend to privilege social movements, or at least lived realities and worldviews, rather than abstract theory or philosophy. We progressively visualized the emergence among social movements of a broader field we came to call "the political activation of relationality." A similar concern was steadily arising in some social science and humanities fields, often under the guise of "relational ontologies," and also on the margins of unexpected fields such as management, planning, and social work. Parallel to launching the seminar in 2011, Michal and Arturo began co-teaching a course called "Social Change in Times of Crisis: Knowledge, Action, and Ontology."

We bandied about the idea of a book for several years. It was always clear that if we were to write it, it had to be all three of us. We shared commitments to social and epistemic justice. To living coherently with our principles and beliefs, including care and generosity as an ethos of intellectual work. Our areas of knowledge and life experiences felt aligned. The entire endeavor was animated by our intuitive observation and evolving understanding that while there were numerous differences in the practices that we started to call relational, there was also something shared: a core resonance, something that worked against the dominant story of discrete objects and subjects, or of politics being limited to the State and capitalism, and which evinced an affect of possibility, love, and connection.

We do not provide an analytical overview of relationality in academic literature, an endeavor that would require hundreds of pages and would likely leave us confused. Our notion of relationality is philosophical and theoretical, yes, but more than that—it is a vision of life. As much as from theory, if not more, the sources and the inspiration for our stories of relationality come from social movements, projects, practitioners, and communities where relationality is key to a vision and practice of living and making—messiness, contradiction, and all. The difference between such a praxis and theoretical reflection alone is something we hope the following chapters will elucidate.

Finally, we never assert or claim *one* definition or version of relationality in large part because relationality requires specificity and context. There is no such thing as relationality as an abstract or universal concept, and yet this book is in many senses an effort to put into words the story of relationality. This tension, of wanting to put into a book something that we know exceeds conceptuality, animates the project: ultimately this is a book about reality.

We will conclude by sharing one of our core questions and desires: can we be for you, dear reader, what the experiences that moved us to create this book were and are for us? So that the reader too will be moved to create relationally? This would mean capturing the lived notion of relationality in its flow and to arouse a steadfast determination to reconnect with the stream of life.

Acknowledgements

Given the nature of this collectively authored project, it almost seems impossible to write a bounded set of acknowledgements. We strongly feel this book is itself a deeply relational and collective undertaking; both in terms of the ideas shared, as well as the material networks of support that made it possible for each of us to devote the time to writing and reflecting. As such, the following will necessarily be incomplete—which is also to say that this work reflects the thoughts and politics of far more friends, colleagues, and influential fellow thinkers than we could cite or acknowledge here.

First, we are deeply grateful to Clive Dilnot and Eduardo Staszowski for welcoming our book into this series and for their unfailing support of the project. Clive's detailed commentary on the entire manuscript was incredibly helpful throughout the writing process; we could not have hoped for a better editor, and the result is a much more compelling and well-structured work. We also thank the various readers who offered extended commentary on the first full draft of the work: Matthew DelSesto, Tony Fry, Rachel Hann, Ezio Manzini, and Anne-Marie Willis. Their comments were very helpful for refining our arguments and being more rigorous with some of our positions.

The work of a number of friends and fellow travelers have been particularly important in our reflections and evolving understanding of the various dimensions of the book: Bayo Akomolafe, Kenneth Bailey, Mario Blaser, Marisol de la Cadena, Alexis Pauline Gumbs, and Ezio Manzini. And while we have not met Sylvia Wynter personally, our thinking has been deeply influenced by her work, as readers will discover throughout the various chapters.

We are also deeply grateful to the participants in the "Carolina Seminar on the Theory and Politics of Relationality" at University of North Carolina at Chapel Hill (2011-20) where many of the ideas for this book germinated, and where Arturo and Michal reconnected with Kriti. We want to thank Sunny Osment whose work as a research assistant and whose thesis work on spirituality and social change were invaluable to early phases of the book project.

Many other friends and colleagues have offered support for our project in various ways, sometimes even without explicitly seeking to do so (or even knowing they had). We would like to mention in this regard Herman Greene, Larry Grossberg, Charlie Hale, Claudia Horwitz, Terry Irwin, Geci Karuri-Sebina, Sophie Krier, Gideon Kossoff, Renata Leitão, Steffano Maffei, Matt Meyer, Lesley-Ann Noel, John Pickles, Peter Redfield, Orin Starn, Virginia Tassinari, and Erik Wong. The material in Chapter 4 was written while Michal was teaching classes on social movements and prison abolition at UNC Chapel Hill, and she is indebted to her students not only for their lively engagement but also for their recommendations of resources. Particular thanks to Samantha Davis who has been a potent interlocutor in this regard.

The book has an important Latin American dimension. Our gratitude goes out to Lina Álvarez, Andrea Botero, Patricia Botero, Andrés Burbano, Pieter de Vries, Claudia Garduño, Diana Gómez, Alfredo Gutiérrez, Laura Gutiérrez, Enrique Leff, Xochitl Leyva, Moira Millán, Tatiana Roa, Cristina Rojas, Rita Segato, Erik Vergel, Astrid Ulloa, and Ignacio Valero. Two Latin American groups that have been important for this book's writing are the Latin American Ecosocial Pact of the South (https://pactoecosocialdelsur.com) and the transition design project for the Cauca valley region in Colombia. *Nuestros agradecimientos* to the friends belonging to these two groups, and to the Global Tapestry of Alternatives (https://globaltapestryofalternatives.org/), a transnational initiative devoted to fostering transformative alternatives with their main bases in India, Mexico, Colombia, and Southeast Asia.

Special thanks to Fernando Flores, Terry Winograd, Don Norman, and B. Scot Rouse. Their periodic meetings, in which Arturo participated—with the purpose of reassessing the arguments put forth in *Understanding Computers and Cognition: A New Foundation for Design* (1986) in light of today's social, philosophical, technological, and political challenges—were an active presence in the collective conversations we, authors, regularly had about our book.

We have presented aspects of the book at various venues over the past two years. The three of us jointly presented chapters of the book in progress at the Graduate Technological Union in Berkeley, the "Global Epistemologies and Ontologies" Group at Wageningen University, and a session organized by the Design Studio for Social Intervention and Bennington College. Our thanks to Rita Sherma (GTU), David Ludwig (Wageningen), and Kenny Bailey (DS4SI) and Susan Sborgati (Bennington College) for coordinating these events and to all the participants for their constructive feedback.

Finally, we want to express our immense gratitude for the generosity of spirit and practice that has underpinned so many of the projects and ideas that have taught and inspired us—both in the writing and in terms of how we go about the material and messy work of making and storying life in these difficult yet generative times.

Introduction: The dominant story of life is not working

That which we have made, we can unmake, then, *consciously*
now, remake.
SYLVIA WYNTER[1]

Most people guard and keep; they suppose that it is they themselves …
that they are guarding and keeping, whereas … what they are actually
guarding and keeping is their system of reality and what they assume
themselves to be. One can give nothing whatever without giving oneself –
that is to say, risking oneself. If one cannot risk oneself then one is simply
incapable of giving.
JAMES BALDWIN, *THE FIRE NEXT TIME*[2]

Mira, let me tell you something about stories. Stories can make you bigger—not
on the outside, of course, but on the inside. They can stretch your mind
and heart. But a story can make you smaller if it takes up all the space in your
mind and heart. When new people or new ideas come along there is no room
for them. *Whenever you hear a story you must ask yourself: What is this
story doing to me? Is it making me bigger or smaller?*
LAURA ALARY, *MIRA AND THE BIG STORY*[3]

---

[1] Sylvia Wynter, "Human Being as Noun? Or Being Human as Praxis? Towards the Autopoetic Turn/Overturn: A Manifesto," unpublished essay (2007), 75, emphases in original.

[2] James Baldwin, *The Fire Next Time*, reissue edition (New York: Vintage, 1992), 85.

[3] Laura Alary, *Mira and the Big Story*, illustrated edition (Boston: Skinner House Books 2012), 17.

1

INTRODUCTION

Something is terribly wrong. An anguish at the heart of modern living. The phrases "existential dread" and "fear of the future" come up every day in conversation. We are being actively defutured, for as we rush to secure our individual short-term futures under capitalism, we erode the possibility of a longer-term future for all. We write this book because we believe that the foundational story that led us to this existential dread—a story of separation, hierarchy, ontological dualism, objectivity, and unlimited growth and development—is a large part of the problem. A different story, one we call relational, holds promise for addressing the defuturing the currently dominant story enacts.

North American ecologist and theologian Thomas Berry opened his text *The New Story*, with the following startling but formidable proposition:

> It's all a question of story. We are in trouble just now because we do not have a good story. We are in between stories. The old story, the account of how the world came to be and how we fit into it, is no longer effective. Yet we have not yet learned the new story.[4]

The prevailing story, he added, the one we moderns inherited from the long history of the West, whether in its Christian or its secular versions, has become "a dysfunctional cosmology." It functioned well for a long time. At least ostensibly for its supposed beneficiaries, "but it is no longer the story of the Earth. Nor is it the integral story of the human community. It is a sectarian story."[5] Hence, we are in dire need of compelling new stories. How do we understand and help usher us into these new stories? How does one exist in the in-between and go further? Being in between stories is not an easy place to be. And yet it is where we are.

In writing about relationality, we are not saying that the world is not full of separation, struggle, and scarcity. It is this way. Our wager is that it does not *have to be* this way. The tendency to "guard and keep," to experience the self as separate, small, struggling, and insecure—this is not, like gravity, a necessary, predetermined fact of existence. Rather, it is a *mode of existence*, a particular pernicious habit and way of being that has come about and persisted due to mutually reinforcing historical and contemporary causes and conditions, which have created particular "stories." These stories work themselves out through dominant narratives, partial truths, ideologies, theologies, opinions and even evasions and outright lies, all of which legitimize the state of things.

---

[4] Thomas Berry, "The New Story," in *The Dream of the Earth*, 123–37 (San Francisco: Sierra Club Books, 1988).

[5] Berry, "The New Story." Berry finds sources for a new story in Native American cosmologies, as well as in "the story of the universe" unveiled by contemporary science. His ideas have been rendered into a beautiful film by Brian Swimme and Mary Evelyn Tucker (*Journey of the Universe*, 2006).

We do not recognize these stories as stories because they are treated as facts, "the way things are." In the modern era, certain "facts of life" are routinely considered universal and ahistorical: that desires are endless and public resources scarce, that people are fundamentally selfish and will fight each other for what they need, that the pursuit of rational self-interest for the small separate self maximizes benefit for all, and that life is largely a zero-sum game characterized by competition where the victory of one is mostly won at the expense of another. But, these facts are not baked into nature or natural law. They have *become* facts of life due to the self-reinforcing workings of modernity and capitalism.

It is particularly ironic that most people, even many supposed beneficiaries of these facts, have come to agree that these assumptions make for a pretty miserable existence. If egoic self-gratification and self-defense could bring about happiness, we would all be happy by now. If parsing the world into property and the pursuit of rational self-interest could bring about prosperity, we would all be wealthy by now. If our economic system could bring about the bright future it so loudly advertises, we could realistically envision a livable future for generations. If scientific objectivity, allegedly validated by technological achievement, was about bringing us in touch with the real world it could offer solace from alienation and suffering. If "the truth is what works,"[6] then we contend the dominant truths under which the modern world is operating are simply not working.

Or are they? How do these stories work, and what do they do to us? When we speak of the current dominant story, it is easy to be perplexed: "What do you mean it is a story? Surely the millions of lives lost to capitalism and colonialism cannot be attributed to a story or countered by another one." Force, violence, genocides—no one can deny that the history of modern capitalism has been materially violent and destructive. It has been, and we are not denying this. What we are saying is that necessary for this violence to take place were versions of reality that helped maintain a status quo that otherwise would have been untenable. If force were enough, why are there so many colonialist representations, theories, and stories? The modern era is characterized not only by violent oppression but also by the *naturalization* of oppression. It is not enough to win resources or power: that "victory" must be seen as natural, even as good or civilized.

We can easily begin to see the historicity of this story by drawing a contrast with those often espoused by Indigenous activists. As Sioux activist-scholar Nick Estes writes in a piece entitled *Freedom is a Place*:

> Capitalism is not merely an economic system, it is a social relation. In contrast, Indigenous social relations—premised on radical relationality— offer a revolutionary different way of relating to other people and the world. For capitalism to live, the Indigenous world has to die, and vice versa.[7]

---

[6] A motto of the Pragmatists in the tradition of American philosopher John Dewey.

[7] Nick Estes, "Freedom is a Place Versopolis," *Versopolis.com*, available online: https:// www.versopolis.com/times/reportage/842/freedom-is-a-place (accessed June 29, 2022).

In other words, one can describe the dominant story as the making of non-, or anti-, relationality, given that it banishes profoundly relational life-worlds and knowledges to the margins or death, while simultaneously enshrining an ontologically dualist worldview in which either/or, subject/object, good/bad, spirit/matter, body/mind, and so on, not only dominate but seem natural. It is important to recognize, however, that in those very gestures and stories, there is a kind of relationality. This double maneuver, which involves denying, hiding, and/or annihilating relationality, on the one hand, and making dualism seem natural, inevitable, and universal, on the other, is what we call the *active production of nonrelationality*.

CAPITALISM, THE INDIVIDUAL, AND THE ONTOLOGY OF SEPARATION

There is a tight relation between the production of nonrelationality and the historical processes of colonialism, capitalism, slavery, and the genocides that accompanied them and that separated people from their territories, cultures, and communities, destroying and subjugating collective lives to logics of markets and development. Nonrelational ways of being, knowing, and making were progressively deployed through violent forms of primitive accumulation and the instantiation of patriarchal and white supremacist orders.[8] Primitive accumulation in Europe and elsewhere forced people to abandon commons, where they collectively worked land and maintained a more relational life, to go to the cities to sell their labor as individuals; the witch hunts that accompanied the enclosures of the commons devalued women's bodies, turning them into machines of reproductive labor.[9]

These processes were essential to the breakdown of relationality and to the *making of individuals* operating in something called a market economy; they fostered a vision of the human as separate: separate from society, from nature, and from (and often better than) other categories of human. This apparent separateness does look like a-, or even, anti-relational, and it does correspond quite clearly with the concept of the self-made individual of modern liberal capitalism. However, and this is the punch line, all these apparent nonrelationalities depend on a lot of relationships, historical and ongoing, to appear as such. The production of the idea of the autonomous individual continues to be reinforced by practices of modern education, advertising, health care, and the economy,

---

[8] This understanding of capitalism as inherently anti-relational is informed by the concepts of Racial Capitalism from Cedric Robinson and the Black Radical Tradition, more recently popularized by abolitionist geographers such as Ruth Wilson Gilmore, a key intellectual in the prison abolition movement we describe in Chapter 4. Feminist Marxists such as Silvia Federici, and Indigenous Scholars such as Glen Coulthard, have contributed to expanding the traditional understanding of primitive accumulation. See also Jodi Melamed, "Racial Capitalism," *Critical Ethnic Studies*, April 1, 2015, available online: https://epublications. marquette.edu/nglish_fac/345 (accessed February 9, 2023).

[9] Silvia Federici, *Caliban and the Witch: Women, the Body and Primitive Accumulation* (New York: Autonomedia, 2004).

among many other domains. This ongoing effort to convince us of the intrinsic existence of the individual is often done in tandem with the cultivation of a fear of anything collective.

That so much effort goes into concretizing the notion of the individual should at the very least give us pause. We suggest that beyond pause, it also underscores that *there is no such thing as an intrinsically existing individual*. Individuals are always embedded in webs of relationships, systems, places, landscapes, communities, and so on. There is no such thing as an individual; rather it makes more sense to speak of persons in relations. We will explore this theme further throughout this book but suffice it to say for now that one of our wagers herein is that the belief in the existence of "the individual" has been one of modernity's greatest foundational narratives. You might recognize the following version of the myth of ourselves as individuals, since it is widely available and practiced:

> *I am an individual; I was born in a family from two parents, having a particular sex. I am a unique human with a personality, a life cycle, choices to make, options to take; I am not nature, nature is "out there." Given that scarcity is the iron law of life, my options and choices will be determined by the state of the economy and the resources, commodities, properties, and opportunities I might be able to command in the market (food market, education market, job market, health market, house market, religion market …), which is where I find all the tools and elements for making my life. So, I better listen to the economists and the scientists for information and guidance; even if they might get it wrong sometimes, their knowledge is the only reliable way to know the world and plan ahead. This is what being rational, secular, and realistic is all about: adopting as my own the picture of the world given to us by science, a world that is always external to us, which moves around us without our participation in it, really, because we live within a single world and objective reality, even if different societies might have different beliefs about it, or differ-ent "worldviews." And if there is one real, then there surely must be one possible, or at least a preferable possible, which it is the best we, rational people, can do to control the conditions of our lives … because science is true, and true is the fact that we live in market-driven societies, and that we are individuals endowed with rights and choice who live in national societies with their institutions and laws, which we can opt to change through a democratic process ….*

This is the "song of myself," to borrow from Walt Whitman, that many of us tell ourselves daily; this song creates the singer, an atomized individual work-ing diligently and rationally to secure their individual well-being, forgoing the essential collective dimension of social life. Tony Fry underscores the fatal contradiction at play here. "Living unsustainably," he writes "is mostly enacted as unconsciously living the error of a striving to gain, or retain, 'the quality of life of a standard of living' …. Error here thus means living in the belief that one can secure the *individual* means of future well-being *independently of the care for the general condition"* (emphasis ours).[10] Indeed, modern heroism largely consists of turning oneself into a perfect, crystalline object, mastering and disciplining oneself into a glorious individual even as the world falls apart— as greed and war consume everything. Our last consolation as the web of life frays: at least we, ourselves, were perfect objects, higher animals, remarkable "individuals."

And yet, we cannot pretend that the damage is not already done, that we do not experience ourselves as atomized, neoliberalized individuals. So, we have to attend to that individual, mythic as she may be, from precisely the situation—one might say, the mess—that we are currently in. We might go further and suggest that this mess is replete with the possibility of *portals* and *bridges* to different worlds—including the possibility of a self beyond individualism, a self that has a different kind of agency, one who does and knows differently.

The move to relationality entails a new, or different, ontology of the human. Thinking ontologically about relationality and transitions is a crucial premise of this book. In the last instance, one may say, it is all about ontology, that is, about thinking differently about what is real and, hence, about what is possible.[11] The appeal to ontology will accompany us throughout the book (see the Appendix for a discussion of our use of this concept). For now, we want to stress that today's challenges are not just about politics, economics, culture, or even just about epistemology (how we know); while these are important, the challenges summon us to reconsider what we think about reality, about the contemporary modes of being human, about the relation between being, knowing, and doing (with no separation among them), and about the philosophical architecture of modernity, all of which have to do in one way or another with ontology. This fact is part of what renders the transition so challenging; after all it is not just about moving between descriptions of values, goals, and so on, but our very understanding of what is real and possible.

RELATIONALITY AS A RE-EMERGENT FOUNDATION OF LIFE

Though the dominant civilization is premised on the radical separateness of objects and subjects, of selves from the environment, relationality is *a different foundational story of life and reality,* and hence a different point of departure. Yet, it has been known and practiced widely. At its heart, relationality points to the radical interdependence of all things. The South African principle of *ubuntu* declares, "I am because you are, I exist because everything exists." Pat McCabe,

---

[10] Tony Fry, *A New Design Philosophy: An Introduction to Defuturing* (Sydney: University of New South Wales Press, 1999). Republished as Tony Fry, *Defuturing: A New Design Philosophy* (London: Bloomsbury, 2020).

[11] Arturo Escobar, *Pluriversal Politics: The Real and the Possible* (Durham, NC: Duke University Press, 2020). This book deals with how prevailing notions of the real and the possible change when we adopt a relational ontological perspective.

Dine and Lakota elder, writes that relationality means the understanding that "every action we take affects every other being sooner or later."[12]

Buddhism is one of the oldest and most influential philosophies and practices focused on the relation between mind, self, reality, and interdependence. This tradition continues to inspire a great deal of scholarship on this question. As the Buddha said:

> When this is, that is.
> From the arising of this comes the arising of that.
> When this isn't, that isn't.
> From the cessation of this comes the cessation of that.[13]

Buddhist teacher Thich Nhat Hanh defined this as *interbeing*—a foundational principle of existence. As he wrote centuries later:

> If you are a poet, you will see clearly that there is a cloud floating in this sheet of paper. Without a cloud, there will be no rain; without rain, the trees cannot grow; and without trees, we cannot make paper. The cloud is essential for the paper to exist. If the cloud is not here, the sheet of paper cannot be here either. So we can say that the cloud and the paper inter-are.[14]

We have gathered here accounts of life, reality, and the world that center the inextricable mutual interdependence of all beings and things—contra the dominant story of our time, which is that objects, subjects, selves, and environments have separate intrinsic existences of their own. In gathering these accounts, we do not aim to elide differences between them. We do not call them the same thing or seek to put forward a totalizing proposal for what relationality is. Relationality cannot be turned into object or property—certainly not intellectual property.

It is, however, useful to understand what we do not mean by the term. Philosopher Andrew Porter cautions that interdependence is not necessarily by itself an ethical or political value.[15] Being related does not by itself entail being responsible, careful, or kind, as is evidenced by many of our family relations, and by the coercive relations through which we are bound to employers, property,

---

[12] Pat McCabe, "What Could Possibly Go Right?: Episode 63," *Resilience*, December 7, 2021, available online: https://www.resilience.org/stories/2021-12-07/what-could-possibly-go-right-episode-63-pat-mccabe/ (accessed February 1, 2022).

[13] Assutava Sutta, Samyutta Nikaya, 12.2, trans. Thanissaro Bhikkhu. Quoted in Barbara O'Brien, "Interbeing: The Inter-existence of All Things," *Learn Religions*, March 6, 2017, available online: https://www.learnreligions.com/interbeing-3866931 (accessed July 19, 2023).

[14] Thich Nhat Hanh, "Clouds in Each Paper," *Awakin*, available online: https://www.awakin.org/v2/read/view.php?tid=222 (accessed August 2, 2022).

[15] Andrew Stone Porter, "Spookiness, Sea Sponges, Stardust, and the Sacred: The Ethics of Quanto-Bio-Cosmic Ontological Interdependence," *Journal of Religious Ethics* 49, no. 2 (2021): 382–411.

and the market. The ideas of "connection," "interdependence," "communication," and "network" that have been so popularized and exploited by twenty-first-century capitalism are premised on a very thin notion of relations as a network of transactions. An ethic of true mutuality can never take root in such shallow soil, where the words "relations" and "relationship" mean the management of transactions between capitalists, workers, and consumers, or the creation of "value chains." If the use of "relation" has become so brittle and thin, then "relationality" cannot properly convey the depth of mutuality, shared destiny, gratitude, care, and responsibility that we share as beings alive together in this world upon which we necessarily depend. Part of our work in this book is to amplify and help restore the meaning and gravity of relation, of what it means to be related and what ethical responsibilities ensue.

There is an important difference between relationality understood as a fundamental condition of existence and reality, on the one hand, and the notion of connection between already existing entities, on the other. Said differently, the words interconnectedness and relatedness often presume separation, then a subsequent relationship. But we can think of relatedness differently: I am not *related to* my right hand—I *am* my hand, it is me, and we were never two separate things that were subsequently bound by relation. The degree of mutuality we mean to evoke in the word "relationality" is an intimacy with our relations that is as immediate as our own limbs. Another way to put this is relationality, or interdependence comes first. Nothing preexists the relations that constitute it.[16]

The ethical implications of relationality are that the term means not only relatedness but also *openness*. Definitionally, this means things can go many ways, toward greater suffering or its alleviation. Consider both the hopeful and the ominous valence of the phrase, "Anything can happen." Contra the foreclosure of a future offered by dualism and determinism, relationality offers not a guarantee but a possibility.

If the world is not already finished, if it is not already out there, if it depends on our participation for its continued creation, then in every moment, there is always the chance of change. No matter how habitual, entangled, and addicted we are. No matter how deep the canyon, no matter how long the tires have been spinning in the mud. Our species may have been doing the same thing for millennia, passing on intergenerational trauma as culture, and still there is the chance of another way. The ant trail shifts left instead of right; the land-adapted ungulate tests out the waters. As long as there is life, there is hope, there is possibility.

The only reason this bears stating at all is because of a remarkably narrow and fatalistic view of the future and of life that seems to have settled over the modern world like a chilly fog—sometimes even over those most committed to

---

[16] For a thorough explanation of this difference, see Kriti Sharma, *Interdependence: Biology and Beyond* (New York: Fordham University Press, 2015).

transformational change. It passes as "realism" but is instead a two-dimensional simplification of reality. The interesting and tricky thing is that this current narrow story of realism is so powerful, we rarely recognize that other stories are possible. One of our main contentions here is that a belief in the predetermined, radically externalized world is precisely one of the moves that habitually replicates the same kinds of selves and worlds. It is a way of giving up in advance on the possibility of a different future. This is a core feature of dualism.

In a dualist worldview, the external world is a place to be discovered outside of oneself. From a relational perspective, the "external" world is not an outside place but an act of participation. Cognition, as biologists Humberto Maturana and Francisco Varela wrote, is not "a representation of the world 'out there' but rather … an ongoing bringing forth of a world through the process of living itself."[17] We are not self-made, not unentangled, and not ahistorical. A living being is a participant in the world's creation, a being whose perception of the world actually constitutes that world. Therefore, we are responsible for the world we create with others.

In splitting the subject from the object and placing the external world radically outside of the subject, rational thought hoped to save human beings from the self-centeredness of thinking that they were mighty creators rather than humble discoverers and co-creators of the world. Ironically, putting the world outside of us has led to a great deal of self-centeredness. Yet, even as relationality restores agency to the self as a creator of its world, relationality also means that the very subjects who bring forth the world by their participation in it are themselves constituted by that world. Therefore, the self is not some sort of solipsistic, detached, unmoved "prime mover," rather, it is a creator who is brought into being by creation—we make each other's worlds; our most private perceptions and emotions do not arise without one another. Restoring agency to the self, lessening the sense of being buffeted around in an uncaring universe, gives more a sense of fundamental safety.

Relationality then is a particular way of knowing, being, and doing—it anchors a distinct *onto-epistemic formation*, or as we prefer to describe it in this book, it is the key to a new story of life. It is challenging to write about precisely because it entails the conditions of and for an *emergent* reality, rather than already existing or known entities or concepts. Our current language as well as our theoretical frameworks are simply not capacious enough to account adequately for this emergence, largely because relationality is about life; no theory or concept can adequately capture it. As Chapter 2 discusses, the very limitations of modern social theory have a lot to do with the assumption that one can intellectually arrive at a genuinely relational living, knowing, and making practice.

---

[17] Humberto Maturana and Francisco Varela, *The Tree of Knowledge: The Biological Roots of Human Understanding* (Berkeley, CA: Shambhala 1987), 11.

REMAKING THE MAKING OF LIFE

When that one *outsources the work of life*, the whole world falls apart.[18]

Leanne Betasamosake Simpson

Although many years in the making, our serious writing began during the years of the COVID-19 global pandemic. This was not an insignificant coincidence. The global pandemic brought into sharp relief the reality of interdependence in both its beauty and its danger, making clear that each and every one of us depend on—and indeed are largely made by—myriad parts of the web of life for our existence and on the labor performed by millions. The chaos we felt as millions of workers were unable to do their work made the reality of our interdependence palpable in ways that might have been more abstract just a year earlier.

The virus laid bare the fact that the pandemic was only a catastrophe because of the intricateness of relationships in which we are ineluctably enmeshed—as if these relationships were "preexisting conditions," including the destruction of ecosystems, runaway capitalism and rampant socioeconomic disparities, and racism. It also made clear the limitations of efforts aimed at addressing these crises not by taking into account the larger and more complex story of how we got there, but by focusing on one linear and simple cause: a pathogen. For us, the pandemic also poignantly raised the question of what it means to consider our radical interconnectedness not only in times of crisis—when your action might detrimentally impact your elderly neighbors or parents—*but all the time*, when your actions, or someone else's, intrinsically enrich your life. Sadly, so far and despite interesting exceptions, the pandemic continues to be a tragedy because political and economic interests dictate "solving" the problem in global, technical terms.

Finally, the pandemic was also a stark reminder of how much we have *outsourced the work of making life*. This awareness became one of our organizing motifs. In a moving speech at Duke University in 2019, Anishnaabe scholar and writer Leanne Betasamosake Simpson, described the profound difference between practices that simply reproduce or passively consume life, and those that actively, meaningfully, and emergently make or build it:

Making maple is a lot of work. It's not the kind of work that takes place Monday through Friday, 9-5 and that you get a paycheck for. It's not White Man's work. It's the kind of work you do that makes a life. We [Anishnaabe] have a lot of stories about the kind of work that makes life. And, every once in a while, we get one in our community that gets ideas of outsourcing the work of life. "Oh, I'll get so and so to make my moccasins, I'll buy maple

---

[18] Transcribed from the presentation: Leanne Betasamosake Simpson, "As We Have Always Done: Indigenous Freedom through Radical Resistance," Duke University, January 29, 2019, available online: https://www.youtube.com/watch?v=vEgQLhoosTI (accessed December 10, 2020).

syrup from the Farmer's market, I'll order the commercial hide on the internet instead of learning how to tan hides with brains ... then I can just sit at my desk and do my important computer work for the University of Minnesota Press. I'll just consume the world instead of producing the world and I'll get lots of grants and book contracts and a nice big long CV as a reward." Well, in every single one of those stories when that *one outsources the work of life*—rendering life into consumption—the whole world falls apart for the Anishnaabe.[19]

It should be clear that design has greatly contributed to outsourcing the work of life. Modern inventions have of course eased the life of many, sometimes even contributing to the very survival of those living in the peripheries of the world economy. As critics are quick to state, modern technology has significantly increased life expectancy and the quality of life for many. We will have more to say about this throughout the book. Let us say for now that it is also true that the power for making life and constructing worlds have been wrested away from common people since modernity has entrusted the production of collective life to experts; this process has been organized by the State and intimately entangled with capitalism. The increasing awareness of this fact brought into prominence for us the idea that the present is an exciting moment for designing—where designing is understood not as an expert or professional practice, but as what we all do to *make life*. This strengthened our conviction that designing, expert and otherwise, is slowly emerging as a crucial domain for thinking about the production of life and the making of worlds, at least in some of its critical and experimental renditions. This in no way means just more professional opportunities for designers but rather understanding designing as a process based on a varying set of capabilities for remaking the making of life.[20]

In her remarkable book, *The Body in Pain: The Making and Unmaking of the World*, Elaine Scarry speaks of the dialectic of making and unmaking at play in many or most human events; "torture and war" she says:

> are not simply occurrences which incidentally deconstruct the made world but occurrences which deconstruct the structure of making itself; conversely, western religion and materialism suggest that the ongoing work of civilization is not simply making x or y but "making making"

---

[19] Transcribed from Simpson, "As We Have Always Done," emphasis ours.

[20] In the Preface to the 1984 edition of his book, *Designing Designing*, John Chris Jones describes moving away from a notion of design "as the specialized activity of paid experts who shape the physical and abstract forms of industrial life which we all as consumers accept or adapt to. That notion cannot possibly last forever—it's too limited, too insensitive to the reactions it provokes. It's too inert. Designing, if it is to survive as an activity through which we transform our lives, on earth, and beyond, has itself to be redesigned continuously." See the recently reprinted version of the book, *Designing Designing* (London: Bloomsbury 2020), lvi–lvii.

itself, "remaking making," rescuing, repairing, and restoring it to its proper path each time it threatens to collapse into, or become conflated with, its opposite.[21]

She offers these interpretive categories as a means to understand traumatic events, "whether arising on the unreachable ground of a distant past or on the more important (because reachable and repairable) ground of an approaching future." Think of climate collapse as the tragedy and you will realize the crucial importance of *remaking making*; this is a political task of a highest order, for, as she goes on to say on the same page, "achieving an understanding of political justice may require that we first arrive at an understanding of making and unmaking."

Retrieving the relationality and place-making potential of designing is a task that needs to be undertaken in earnest. It is here that we find the deeper meaning of designing relationally and pluriversally: in recuperating humans' ability to make life more autonomously by weaving ourselves back into the tapestry of existence to the greatest extent possible. This also means that designing, too, needs to construe itself as a practice of transitioning between stories—from the expert-driven ontology of separation to a life-centered ontology of interexistence. As Daniel Wahl put it in his advocacy for a regenerative practice of design, designing is central to the transition from the narrative of separation to that of interbeing. A change in narrative, he argues, will change "*how, what, and why* we design"; moreover, "we need to examine the extent to which the 'story of separation' (scarcity and competition) has also colored our perspective on life, biology and ecology."[22] Such change requires drawing on the multiple "beautiful experiments" in the political activation of relationality that can be seen throughout the world.[23]

DESIGNING AS TRANSITIONING BETWEEN NARRATIVES OF LIFE

Our book is predicated on the premise that the dualist story of separation is being undone by the planetary crisis, to begin with, but also by the incredible array of new ideas and practices being tried out all over the world to get out, implicitly or explicitly, of the toxic loops of existence such a story has deployed. To resort to Gramsci's oft quoted idea, "the crisis consists precisely in the fact that the old is dying and the new cannot be born; in this interregnum, a variety

---

[21] Elaine Scarry, *The Body in Pain: The Making and Unmaking of the World* (New York: Oxford University Press, 1985), 279.

[22] Daniel C. Wahl, *Designing Regenerative Cultures* (Axminster: Triarchy Press, 2016), 20, 191.

[23] We borrow this evocative expression from Saidiya Hartman, *Wayward Lives, Beautiful Experiments: Intimate Histories of Social Upheaval* (New York: W.W. Norton & Company, 2019).

of morbid symptoms appear."[24] While the morbid symptoms are out for all to see (climate collapse, pandemics, persistent racial and wealth disparities, and the war in Ukraine to cite the most prominent at present), the myriad beautiful experiments conducted by people to heal and reconstitute the web of life are also becoming increasingly widespread, diverse, and tangible. These experiments have inspired this book and are the realities we hope to get our readers to be able to not only witness but also believe in. In other words, today the new could be born, if we consider that the planetary crisis is creating new conditions for thought and the possibility of other modes of relating, oftentimes lurking beneath capitalist modernity. Perhaps we are less fated than we think; our worlds could be otherwise.

As much as this is a book about making life relationally, it is also a book about the challenge of moving between stories, about being in transition and becoming otherwise. The pull of the known, including the categories and default settings we did not even realize were there, are so powerful that it is common to slip back into the old ways. Even those actively working to create, author, and weave new stories slip back into the old story. However, while these *slip-pages* are both common and often pernicious, they can reveal potential points of ontological passage into other stories, as we will argue in detail in Chapter 3. In fact, much of what we ended up puzzling through was how to write this book to generate ideas for finding and building bridges and portals to new narratives and practices of relationality, while being mindful of the slippages in which we, and many movements, often find ourselves.

Writing about relationality in the context of transitions presented several challenges. If it were about making a logical argument that is intelligible and persuasive to a liberal Eurocentric modern subject, we could try to do that—though there are of course limits to persuasion; after all, many people have long attempted to make this type of man listen to reason, so to speak, using the language he ostensibly ought to understand. And, if it were about speaking to and thereby adding to the collective field of courage, life, and love that some Black and Indigenous feminists, environmentalists, and others are already creating at the shoreline of reason, we may not be writing in academic prose at all. Adding to the challenge is that relationality is not fully comprehensible as a concept. And even if it were, how would we even describe it using the languages and concepts from the old story? Moreover, unlike the modern telos of progress inherent in most transition narratives, the ground of relational transitions is much more tentative, pluralistic, and subtle; they do not necessarily go in one way. Transitions are not completely knowable—at least not in the form of knowing to which we moderns are so accustomed.

Our sources for writing about relational ontologies are very diverse, a reflection of the fact that many peoples and collectives know and have known that survival and thriving is not individual, but interdependent, and have practiced

---

[24] Antonio Gramsci, *Selections from the Prison Notebooks* (London: Lawrence and Wishart, 1971), 275–76.

this knowing in manifold ways. Again, we aim to gather these approaches and offer patterns based on our noticings, without eliding differences between them, and certainly without claiming authorship or authority over them. Our sources range from Western philosophy and modern social theory to Indigenous ways of knowing; from social struggles to instantiations of the sacred and nondualist spiritual traditions; from biological theories of complexity, self-organization, and emergence to renewed attention to ancestral traditions; from Black and Latin American feminisms to grassroots environmental struggles waged on the basis of caring for the earth; and from nondominant ontologies within the West ("alternative Wests") to emergent networks of relational initiatives in the Global South.

We follow these sources and pathways as they surface in a variety of domains of practice: science, politics, social struggles, prison abolition and other anti-racist movements, sacred activism, food, cities, and designing. Throughout the book we choose to work more closely with and through some inspired thinkers and practitioners of relationality who serve as relevant guides for our journey; we do not make any claims that they represent the totality of possible sources or expertise on relationality—and in fact we represent only some of those that guided us.

Notably, many of the examples of relationality we explore are non-Western or come from the "global majorities"—those marginalized within the dominant old story. This is not an essentialist argument but a recognition that those on the margins and those who have been oppressed generally—women, people of color, Indigenous peoples, urban marginals, the poor—have more access to understanding the limits of the dominant, as well as to seeing alternatives, due to historical circumstances. While many important sources of relationality come from Indigenous and place-based cultures that were violently overtaken by patri-archal capitalism, ours is by no means a romantic call toward the halcyon days of the past, and we do not believe relationality is something that only existed or exists among "pre-" or "non-modern" cultures. This is not about a "return to," but rather an active retrieval in the present of the history and worldmaking potential of these worlds and cultures, and a reflection of their ongoing efforts at imagining new ones.

We want to acknowledge, however, that the work of making relationality visible and comprehensible may run into the dangerous territory of essentialism, romanticism, and cultural appropriation. We understand this and that real harm has been and continues to be caused by doing so. We believe that if relational worldviews are sought after without a material ethic of relationality—one in which accountability, respect, and placedness are considered vital—or with unexamined ideas of the atomized individual without recognizing the relation-ships and the annihilations that went into making it even possible to imagine oneself as self-sufficient—then there is not only trouble, but we run the risk of falling into the colonizing projects we have been trying to interrupt. Rather than avoid this conversation, we consider it a practice of relationality to address the risks head on, with accountability, compassion, humility, a willingness to make mistakes, be corrected, and learn as we go.

This book is a basket of noticings we have gathered at this particular juncture. We offer patterns we have observed, the way someone listening to the ocean can offer a song based on the rhythms she hears in the waves. The ocean is never predictable—just about anything could happen there given the confluence of the right conditions—yet listening for hours at the shore, it becomes easy and intuitive to pick out a steady beat that makes it feel like one could make a guess at when the next wave will arrive. It is like that: neither definition nor prediction, but guesses made of listening and patterning. Another way to understand our role is that we are scribes, translators, relaters of the wisdom of myriad brilliant relational innovators. This does not mean we do not take responsibility for our role. We chose what and how to interpret; we simply want to reiterate that we neither claim sole authorship nor authority over these ideas.

We love books and have been touched by their transformative power and are delighted and humbled to be writing this one. We do so with an awareness of one of the dangers of writing books under capitalism, which is that they participate in the usual circuit of objectification (turning ideas and practices into things), appropriation (i.e., turning those "things" into property), and commodification (buying and selling such property). In such a circuit, it is quite easy to imagine a book called *Relationality* being published in 2024, and an entrepreneurial group of Relational Designers™ emerging in 2025. Objectification, appropriation, and commodification enable co-optation, which means that the radical potential, the beating collective heart of relationality, would be cut back up into thousands of pieces to give individuals yet another thing to individually own and add to the individual song of ourselves. By doing so, we would be slipping back into the project of attempting to "secure the *individual* means of future well-being *independently* of the care for the general condition."

Similarly, principles meant to undermine the stronghold of the ego can be used to reinforce the ego—another form of slippage.[25] This process has occurred multiple times as profound and radical traditions encounter and are co-opted by capitalism: yoga, meditation, Indigenous practices of healing, for example. This does not take away from the potency of the principles and practices themselves. It means that when these principles and practices are filtered through capitalism and through egoic self-serving, we end up experiencing the smallest fraction of their true transformative power. This is particularly tragic because we need the full potency of that transformative power so much now.

It can be said, as a heuristic, that personally and collectively each person and group moves along a spectrum in between the old anthropocentric story of the individual and a variety of newer stories infused with relational practices. For those immersed in the individualizing world, the challenge is to commence the journey toward relational and healing existence through awareness of

---

[25] See Chögyam Trungpa, *Cutting through Spiritual Materialism*, ed John Baker and Marvin Casper (London: Shambhala, 1973).

being trapped within Man's norms (many are already underway, such as those engaged in transformative personal or collective anti-patriarchal, anti-racist, nonbinary, and re-earthing praxes). For those coming from the side of relational and communally oriented living (such as many ethnic groups, peasants, and the urban poor), the challenge is to prevent the further erosion of their constitutive relationality by resisting the pressures of ontological individuality. For those interested in redesigning designing, reflecting on where we are along this spectrum becomes essential for designing relationally.[26] As we will suggest, if our narratives are designed, and if our designed narratives design us, then the question of re-storying is a central task of designing. Overall, our goal is thus to provide a clearing for inquiring about other possible narratives and categories in the making of our worlds.

AUDIENCE, AUTHORSHIP, AND CHAPTER OUTLINE

This book is neither an anthology nor a monograph but somewhere in between. It is something like a chorus of different voices—one voice sings the melody in one chapter or section, and others sing harmonies or percussion, then the voices switch. And of course, our voices then interweave with the voices of the thinkers and practitioners we cite. It is this larger chorus that is making living relationally a reality. We hope the differences in the tones, styles, and approaches we take means that the needs of multiple readers or multiple parts of the reader can be met. We have let consonances and dissonances rest side by side without perfect resolution. True to relationality, contradictions are not resolved, and loose ends are not tied up but remain open for further weaving. However you read is a good way to read: all the way through, or bits and pieces of each chapter, or sticking with particular sections the whole way through. There is some repetition and recursivity since we speak to similar themes in different ways, but we believe that these are useful in deepening understanding and in understanding at different levels.

And so, for whom and how do we write? For, and from, the hybrid. That is all of us, variously mixed, in proportions and degrees. Sylvia Wynter speaks of us as hybrid and has compassion for the fact that the norm of the Western bourgeois subject has shaped us all, whether in adopting the ideal or rejecting it. Throughout the book, we move between styles, between prose and poetics, to speak to the hybrid beings we are: we who have been produced by the dominant onto-episteme as liberal rational bioeconomic subjects and who are in the transformative process of becoming otherwise.

---

[26] Andreas Weber, *Sharing Life: The Ecopolitics of Reciprocity* (Delhi: Heinrich Böll Stiftung, 2020), 29. Andreas Weber provides a useful heuristic for moving toward the relational story; this includes the premises of working together, reciprocity, everything being alive, understanding life through participating in its aliveness, and to keeping the world fecund.

The book has three parts, corresponding to Wynter's refrain that we must remember, choose, and remake. Part One, Chapters 1 and 2 describe the dominant story of life, as solidified by the natural and social sciences, inviting us to re-member (put back together), the elements that made this story seem so immutable and real. Part Two, Chapter 3 (and part of Chapter 2) describes the political implications of these stories and, moreover, why even when we attempt to choose something different, we often find ourselves back in the dominant story. Finally, Part Three, Chapters 4 and 5, point to emergent social change projects that can be understood as initiatives for remaking life and redesigning worlds.

Chapter 1, "Bio-Graphies: Relational stories of life within and beyond the natural sciences," examines biology as one of the preeminent modern discourses on life. It underscores how we create stories about life and about who we are, how we live within the stories we create, and why then the question of re-storying is a central task of designing. Chapter 2, "Modern thought and the active production of nonrelationality," revisits the role of modern thought in shaping the worlds in which we live and hence its limitations to give us compelling accounts of relationality. Our aim is to provide a reinterpretation of what theory has done to shift the terrain of understanding from liberal secular humanism toward relationality as a horizon for life. In Chapter 3: "The political activation of relationality: Ontological slippages as portals to relationality," we move to the terrain of social struggles over making life. These struggles reveal the coming into being of a series of relational practices and worlds, but also the slippages into the dominant mode of politics. By examining the ontological dimension of the political, we underline the possibility of shifting from slippages to portals to relational worlds.

Chapter 4, "Autonomy, abolition, and sacred activism: Bridges to remaking life," explores the kinds of practices that help transform slippages into portals to other worlds. It identifies five principles of relational politics (contingency, emergence, radical uncertainty, non-normativity, and heart-based epistemology) out of three core examples (Zapatista autonomy, prison abolition, and a variety of forms of spiritual activism). Chapter 5, finally, "Designing relationally: Envisioning paths toward pluriversal transitions," discusses the political activation of relationality as a praxis of making and restor(y)ing life, drawing both from design literature and from broader inquiries concerning commons, food, and cities as portals where practices attuned to relationality are emerging. By describing an emergent relational narrative of life from Latin American social struggles, we substantiate the idea that designing could be reimagined as a praxis of transitioning between stories.

SEAGRASS: ANOTHER STORY OF TRANSITION

We close this Introduction with a homage to seagrass, a powerful embodiment of transitions. Kriti's biological research has brought her to fields of seagrass living submerged in ocean waters off the coast of California. An article offering a reading of the genome of the seagrass species *Zostera marina* pieces together a story of a remarkable plant. In the telling of life's history given by evolutionary biology, all plants evolved from algae in the early oceans, who adapted to land to become part the massive and diverse family of land plants we know as angiosperms. Seagrasses then became some of the very few land plants to return to the ocean, living submerged under saltwater. To do this, seagrasses have modified some of their terrestrial features to better suit life in the sea, turned back to ancient marine adaptations kept in their genomes from the time of ancient algae, and invented novel adaptations found neither in ancestors nor close terrestrial kin.[27] On top of this beautiful and complex history, today seagrasses sequester a remarkable amount of carbon dioxide, breathing in the greenhouse gas and delivering it to the ocean floor where it can remain buried and undecomposed for long time periods.[28] To this carbon-sequestering hybrid ancestral-descendant shapeshifter cousin, from whom we have learned and can learn so much, we pay our respects:

Lab notes: What the seagrass said

You mix up different times, where the future is the past, where progress is regress, where ancestral is descendant. You loop time in a genome that circles, you interrupt forward and back. Life is not like that, you say, not a linear bursting forth from the Big Bang. Life is on and off, memory and forgetting, a place where things don't get better or worse but different. And even then, perhaps not that different. The algae within you, the chloroplast genome, the ancient endosymbionts you hold close to your surface to touch the living olds, to know them? Intimately inside and indistinguishable from self still the impulse is to say "I am here, I remember." Remember our kinship, algae and land plant? "I'd say remember, there is something called love. There is something called freedom."[29] Tangled tree, remarkable rhizome. Freedom. You escaped into water. Escaped? No more airborne pests. Left your former enemies behind, they say. Made a new place, a revolutionary place, a never-done-before deed, a sacred space-travel space. You felt ocean and said home. "I'd say remember, there is something called love. There is something called freedom."

There were problems there too. Not things to be solved. Just different conditions. How would you speak to each other? You were used to breath and

[27] Jeanine L. Olsen, Pierre Rouzé, Bram Verhelst, Yao-Cheng Lin, Till Bayer, Jonas Collen, Emanuela Dattolo, et al., "The Genome of the Seagrass Zostera Marina Reveals Angiosperm Adaptation to the Sea," *Nature* 530, no. 7590 (2016): 331–35.

[28] Carlos M. Duarte, Hilary Kennedy, Núria Marbà, and Iris Hendriks, "Assessing the Capacity of Seagrass Meadows for Carbon Burial: Current Limitations and Future Strategies," *Ocean & Coastal Management* 83 (2013): 32–8.

[29] Sung by Sangodare Akinwale in Mobile Homecoming Sunday Service live Zoom event, reading from *Undrowned: Black Feminist Lessons from Marine Mammals* by Alexis Pauline Gumbs.

air. How would your embryos find shelter in seed? You had relied on the air currents to carry pollen. How would you find light below the attenuation of water? You were used to the full spectrum, the bright rainbow light, though it aged you with ultraviolet. How would you? How would you? If you had thought it through, you would have never begun. A hundred million years ago you listened to Toni Cade Bambara and said, "The most effective way to do it is to do it." You made why into how into now. Tangled the reason with the means, the need with the adaptation, the knowing with the doing, the ancestral with the future. And stepped root-first into the ocean.

At the shore of the rising sea, in response to the massive socioecological shifts we are facing and the evolution it requires of us all, we offer no firm answers, and certainly not a totalizing systematic view of the crisis and ways out. We listen to those who may have some knowledge about great transitions into the unknown or at least barely remembered—perhaps our seagrass kin.

Our kindred seagrass live bravely submerged. Their ancestors knew something about twoness, hybridity, borderlands, living between worlds. There comes a time when the Known and the Real—the world of land overlain with the only air we thought we could breathe—must be abandoned. But it does not happen all at once. It comes in waves. There are times in between. It can feel in turns or simultaneously like new life as well as total death. This is not easy. Our hearts, too, are beating fast. To do a thing with heart is called courage—literally from *coeur* or heart. In moving toward a brave transition, it helps to remember that we are not alone, and that we do not know who will reach back for us, which elders are ready for us to make the leap saying, "Welcome, welcome. Make yourselves at home."

PART ONE
Remember

1   Bio-Graphies: Relational stories of life within and beyond the natural sciences

1   May we remember that scarcity, separation, and supremacy are myths
as we recreate relationships and systems sourced in deep care for
ourselves and each other.
KIM CALHOUN[1]

2   If you're going to tell yourself a story,
why not tell yourself a story of freedom?
MATTY WEINGAST, FROM THE POEM
"UPACHALA—THE SECOND SISTER"[2]

3   and if i said i could make you from anything, replace or add anything,
roll you out any thickness, cut your edges any curve, then what? what
would you ask for?
ALEXIS PAULINE GUMBS,[3] WITH REFERENCE TO THE FOLLOWING QUOTE:

That which we have made, we can unmake, then,
consciously now, remake.
SYLVIA WYNTER[4]

---

[1] Kim Calhoun, AbunDance Healing Arts email, August 5, 2021.

[2] Matty Weingast, "Upachala—The Second Sister," in *The First Free Women: Original Poems Inspired by the Early Buddhist Nuns* (London: Shambhala, 2021), 87. This book is an anthology of poems loosely based on the Therigata, the first record of the first community of Buddhist nuns in 500 BCE.

[3] Alexis Pauline Gumbs, *Dub: Finding Ceremony* (Durham, NC: Duke University Press, 2020), 175.

[4] Wynter, "Human Being as Noun?" 75.

In this chapter, we elaborate on one of the key concepts for this entire book and project: the concept of restor(y)ing. More specifically, we expound on what we mean by "restor(y)ing life."[5] We engage Sylvia Wynter's definition of human beings as *homo narrans*—the ones who narrate ourselves—to examine how people create stories about life and about who we are, and how we live within the stories we create. From this perspective, changing the story of life changes the lived experience of life. We examine biology as one of the preeminent modern discourses on life—one that is not experienced by modern subjects as "story" so much as the real world of limited capacities within which we live. If our narratives bring out some of our capabilities and obscure others, and if our designed narratives design us, then the question of re-storying is one of the central tasks of design. A most urgent task—both through the remaking of infrastructures and through the "restorying" of our founding myths—is to make ourselves into the kinds of beings (individually and collectively) who no longer relate with life as a scarce commodity to be guarded and hoarded.

In alignment with the quotes above, this chapter is organized into three sections. The first is remembering. The second is choosing. The third is designing. Or, said otherwise, with the help of Wynter:

1   Remembering: "*that which we have made*, we can unmake ..."
2   Choosing: "... then, *consciously* now ..."
3   Designing: "... remake."

REMEMBERING: "*THAT WHICH WE HAVE MADE*, WE CAN UNMAKE"

May we remember that scarcity, separation, and supremacy are myths as we recreate relationships and systems sourced in deep care for ourselves and each other.[6]

This quote conveys beautifully and succinctly what we understand "designing relationally" to mean: to remake relationships and systems centered in care and not in the myths of scarcity, separation, and supremacy. First, there is remembering. We live immersed in a situation that presents itself as immutable reality: the story of life as scarcity, separation, and supremacy. Yet here we are called to *remember* that scarcity, separation, and supremacy are *myths*. Wynter's quote emphasizes this in italics, as if to awaken us from a powerful, enchanting dream: "*that which we have made*." In dreams, we often feel buffeted around by situations external to us. Waking up, we see that the entire situation is our creation: "*that which we have made*." Wynter and Calhoun call on us to wake up within the dream. To remember.

---

[5] An earlier version of the book's title was *Relationality: Remaking and Restor(y)ing Life*.

[6] Calhoun, AbunDance Healing Arts email.

The forces that limit our lives and life itself in the modernist, capitalist context are very real. Yet they gain their power and substantiality *just because* they are stories: myths that we as modern subjects have made. How can the forces of scarcity, separation, and supremacy be both *powerful* and *mythical*? A simple answer to this question is that myths *are* powerful, some of the most powerful forces shaping human existence. A longer answer—which spans this chapter—explores (a) the complex valences of the term "myth" and its supposed antonyms ("fact," "truth," "reality," and "science"), (b) how myths exert their power, (c) how to work with the power of our ascendant myths, and to live within the tensions and obstacles they pose deeply enough to find resolution and integration, and (d) how we might find, create, and live within new and newly remembered myths with unseen horizons.

This chapter addresses what we mean by the neologism "restor(y)ing life" that is so central to our project. Modern lives and living are saturated with expert discourses or stories. The stories we live by are powerful, stemming from the most "expert" of disciplines including the natural and the social sciences. Understanding our foundational stories is key to recognizing how we have gotten here, being able to choose differently, and remaking ourselves as humans.

Bio-mythology

Sylvia Wynter calls human beings *hybrid* beings: progeny of both biology and narrative, both *bios* and *mythoi*.[7] The biologies of human beings—our bodies, communities, and ecologies—support consciousness, awareness, language, sociality, storytelling, and myth. The communicative, creative, artistic, story-telling, and meaning-making activities of human beings in turn create lived worlds and lived selves. Wynter read and drew inspiration from the findings of Chilean biologists Humberto Maturana and Francisco Varela to draw this schema of humans as, in a sense, circular beings: as creators of ourselves and our worlds, and simultaneously as creations of the worlds we bring forth. The closest visual metaphors for the strange situation in which we find ourselves may be M.C. Escher's surrealist drawings, wherein object and subject, creator and creation, self and environment, foreground and background entangle in infinite loops within which one aspect cannot be picked out as primary, fundamental, or original. Rather, object and subject, creator and creation, self and environment are depicted as mutually constituted, arising simultaneously and interdependently. Maturana and Varela took Escher's surrealist artworks to be more apt illustrations of reality than any photograph, and they used these

---

[7] Sylvia Wynter and Katherine McKittrick, "Unparalleled Catastrophe for Our Species? Or, to Give Humanness a Different Future: Conversations," in *Sylvia Wynter: On Being Human as Praxis*, ed. Katherine McKittrick, 9–89 (Durham, NC: Duke University Press, 2015), 16.

pieces liberally within their books to help illustrate their central point: that the world of the living being is not strictly external to the organism's body, but rather, organisms *bring forth* their worlds.[8]

Whereas Maturana and Varela applied these concepts to all organisms—exploring, for example, how the visual systems of frogs specify the worlds that frogs inhabit—Wynter examines how humans, specifically, bring forth our worlds.[9] Not only do visual systems bring forth, for many, a world saturated with color, but our myths, narratives, stories, and poetics bring forth a world saturated with meanings. We make myths and these myths make us and our world: our limits, our capacities, our longings, and our sense of self. We tell ourselves who we are.

What happens, asks Wynter, when a mythmaking species actively forgets that it is making myths? What happens when it places its creator radically outside of its own creative activities? "We keep our authorship and agency opaque to ourselves,"[10] she writes. Cultural geographer Katherine McKittrick, in conversation with Wynter, writes that modern, secular, rational human beings are *"storytellers who now storytellingly invent themselves as being purely biological."*[11] In inventing ourselves as *purely*—only, solely—biological beings, we occlude the fact that we are *also* storytelling beings. We are the ones who tell ourselves the story of biology and of what it means to be "purely" biological beings.

What is this ascendant *mythos*, the dominant story of human beings and human nature within which secular, modern humans now live? First, it is universalizing. Human beings are narrated as a single species related and defined by biology rather than as peoples who are related through practices, discourses, and culture. The rules of biology and the laws of nature thus become universally applicable laws and principles governing and subjugating peoples *globally*. Second, it is economistic and materialistic, narrating life as primarily a quest, task, or struggle to accumulate matter and energy for survival and reproduction. Third, it is hierarchical, a schema wherein the fit and unfit are sorted out justly not by social practices but by the extra-human force of natural selection. The subject in this story lives in a scarce world, rife with competition to acquire and consume ever more. The war against scarcity is never won, but scarcity is temporarily kept at bay through work, productivity, growth, and expansion. Moreover, the desires of this subject for power and gain are narrated as natural and beyond question—as if power and gain were *intrinsically* delicious and

---

[8] Maturana and Varela, *The Tree of Knowledge*, 11.

[9] Wynter and McKittrick, "Unparalleled Catastrophe," 27–8.

[10] Sylvia Wynter, "Unsettling the Coloniality of Being/Power/Truth/Freedom: Towards the Human, after Man, its Overrepresentation—An Argument," *CR: The New Centennial Review* 3, no. 3 (2003): 257–337, 315.

[11] Wynter and McKittrick, "Unparalleled Catastrophe," 11. Emphasis in original.

desirable to all human beings. Fourth and finally, there is no mention of the storytelling being who narrates her own story; there is only the material, biological animal who is subject to natural laws. The god of this story is nature: the extra-human agent who determines the constraints and possibilities within which human beings live and against whom it is less than useless to file a complaint. It is, we say,—either cheerily or wearily—what it is.

Wynter's thesis is that just as our biologies (our bodies, communities, and ecologies) give rise to our stories (insofar as they make possible the capacity for language and myth), our stories in turn also act on our biology. That is, our stories work on us biologically—physiologically, neurologically, neurochemically. They activate us at the level of synapse and hormone, of gut and marrow. For example, we live within the myth that it was ultimately nature who sorted humanity into the housed and the houseless, into the tiny few hyper-securitized behind gates and the vast many precarious and always on the edge of death. Natural selection was made into a law that exists outside of humanity and has the agency to sort us justly into fit and unfit.[12] The story is repeated, familiarized, spoken with great confidence and authority, and therefore it becomes so convincing—so scientific and universal, so reasonable and unassailable— that we viscerally in our bodies feel that we will die if we violate the laws we ourselves have created. We feel that if we do not "win" by making enough money or being "fit" enough to survive by the standards of our society, we will die. Our bodies tremble horrified at the prospect of abject poverty, exile, and social or physical death.

So even if we say that the law is in a sense fictive, we can hardly say that it is not effective. The law becomes real—it actually works. The laws we make work not only on our individual bodies but also on others. In our fear and revulsion at the violation of the law, we react in disgust and indignation when we see others violating the law, and therefore we make it true that they will die materially and/or socially if they violate the law. If someone else is deemed as somehow deviant or unfit, we will place them outside the circle of social care, and we will say—with no hint of dishonesty—that it was not us who did it but the law of nature. Hence, "we keep our authorship and agency opaque to ourselves."[13] Cognitively and physiologically, once we create our creators and place them radically outside of ourselves, they truly become agents, and we can no longer afford to see ourselves as agents.

In the dominant story of biology, biology means the set of material laws within which all living beings, including human beings, live. In Wynter's view of biology, biology means the material conditions that *give rise to* the human capacity for mythmaking and are in turn *responsive* to myths that are made. In the post-Darwinian, modern era, biology is also the name of one of the dominant myths. That is, seen from Wynter's critical standpoint, Biology-the-Discipline

---

[12] Sylvia Wynter, "'No Humans Involved': An Open Letter to My Colleagues," *Forum N.H.I.: Knowledge for the 21st Century* 1, no. 1 (1994): 1–17. Wynter discusses natural selection and eugenics in many pieces, but most explicitly in "No Humans Involved."

[13] Wynter, "Unsettling the Coloniality of Being," 11.

is the dominant, expert discourse on life in the modern era. Human biology in this sense (a) enables the creation of myths, (b) is the substrate that is responsive to myths, and (c) today, is a dominant myth to which human beings are responsive. Said otherwise, humans as bio-mythological beings have created a story about ourselves as predominantly biological beings, and this story (which is called, simply, "the field or discipline of biology") works on us biologically and cognitively.

What does this thesis accomplish? What possibilities does this critical Wynterian view of biology raise? Wynter is using the force, power, familiarity, and cognitive consonance of "the natural" to both describe our current reality and to point beyond it. She is mobilizing nature—the powerful *myth* of nature—to move away from meaning constraint and toward meaning possibility and agency. As "moderns," we are people for whom nature, science, biology, and the natural carry great weight—even if we are skeptical of them or yearn to think otherwise. We are formed by these myths both by adoption of them and in reaction to them; they are the current ascendant founding myths. If we are to take a next step, to get to another place, it will be from here, from where we are. By suggesting that we are biologically, naturally storytellers who tell ourselves who we are, Wynter both affirms this dominant myth and expands it to mean that we are not trapped by biology or nature but rather made creative and powerful by them.

Wynterian biology[14] thus becomes a *bridge* for those of us who narrate ourselves as modern, secular humans: a means to get from here to there, from this ground to elsewhere, a transition. Wynter's phrase "human being as praxis"[15] suggests that human being is not a noun, an entity with properties and features that are basically static and able to be dissected by mechanistic explanation. Rather, being human is an active practice. *"That which we have made*, we can unmake, then consciously remake." This offers the possibility of a different kind of biopolitical project: to change the embodied experience of being alive from one of scarcity, supremacy, and separation to one of ease, generosity, and belonging.

Again, we write for the hybrid, the transitional, for whoever around us and whatever part of us is on a journey toward becoming people who do not live scarce, small, disconnected, insecure, and scared. To get to a livable future, something has to change. That something is us: the part of us that is viscerally convinced that survival means scarcity, struggle, and supremacy. As many have noted, it is not the generic "human" who has brought about the so-called Anthropocene, but a specific mode—or "genre" as Wynter puts it—of *being* human that has laid to waste and put at risk so many and so much.[16]

---

[14] The term "Wynterian biology" is, as far as we know, introduced in this piece.

[15] Wynter and McKittrick, "Unparalleled Catastrophe," 23.

[16] See, for example, Janae Davis, Alex A. Moulton, Levi Van Sant, and Brian Williams, "Anthropocene, Capitalocene … Plantationocene? A Manifesto for Ecological Justice in the Age of Global Crisis," *Geography Compass* 13, no. 5 (2019): e12438.

We do not underestimate the central importance of wresting material resources back to collective stewardship and liberating the commons.[17] Simultaneously and interdependently, it is also necessary to take on the central task of undoing scarcity, supremacy, and separation at the level of gut and marrow. Indeed, if, as Wynter suggests, our narratives are *designed* to bring out some of our capabilities and to obscure others, and if our designed narratives design *us*, *then the question of re-storying is a central task of designing*. A most urgent task—both through the changing of infrastructures and through the changing of our founding myths—is to make ourselves into the kinds of beings (individually and collectively) who no longer relate with life as a scarce commodity to be guarded and hoarded.

The obstacles to these tasks stem not from "human nature" but, as McKittrick writes, from "the processes through which the empirical and experiential lives of all humans are increasingly subordinated to a figure that thrives on accumulation."[18] The belief that it is human nature to want everything endlessly always (or indeed, that it is the nature of life itself) is the overrepresentation, as Wynter says, of a certain vision of "Man" as if he was all humans,[19] all that was possible and desirable for all people and peoples. The overrepresentation of Man as *homo economicus*—"a figure that thrives on accumulation"—becomes a limit on what we think (and therefore enact) as possible for the human species; what is even worse is that this story also becomes the limit of what we think is possible for life itself, for all living beings. As if the current capitalist frenzy to accumulation is all that life in all its vibrancy could dream, desire, or create.

The story of life is big—we are simply caught in a tiny story. What is life capable of? The sheer plenitude of the world means there is no drying up of findings, metaphors, and interpretations of natural phenomena. The "data points" that make up our known world are relatively few, even in today's much-touted world of "big data." Given how much could be theoretically observed, measured, or even simply experienced, we have collectively gathered just a fraction. Of all the scientific experiments that could be done to elucidate various causal relations, only a tiny number have been (or may ever be) done. Yet the scientific model of reality can nonetheless feel rather airtight and complete—as if science and the entire enterprise of knowledge production was more or less finished and we were just working out the last minor details. It is like seeing constellations within a smattering of stars: given just a few data points, we fill in the rest with theory, image, or story. Life is far vaster than any one idiom, valence, or explanation. Understanding life (even if one restricts oneself to equating the term "understanding life" with a technoscientific explanation of life) is necessarily using story to pattern sparse pieces of evidence with rich and myriad possible

[17] See, for example, J.K. Gibson-Graham, Jenny Cameron, and Stephen Healy, *Take Back the Economy: An Ethical Guide for Transforming Our Communities* (Minneapolis: University of Minnesota Press, 2013).

[18] Wynter and McKittrick, "Unparalleled Catastrophe," 10.

[19] Wynter, "Undoing the Coloniality of Being," 262.

interpretations. In short, it is a work of art. In a world such as this, where *bios* and *mythos* are inextricably interdependent, how has biology come to mean the fixed, the unchangeable, the limits of our dreams and possibilities?

Heretical re-storying

Modern subjects live in a very heavy world. Phenomena are freighted with the weight of being immutable, constraining, universally perceptible, and incontrovertible (that is, limited to single interpretations and explanations). As Gustavo Esteva explains, such faith in the Real—which neoliberal and scientific rationality present as both *prior to* reason and *discovered by* reason—can never be experienced by believers as *faith*, but only as *reality*:

> Reason became a substitute for God, without my knowing it; it became the ultimate referent, valid in and of itself. This new consciousness, typically Western for both believers and non-believers, presupposed a trust in reason that assumed it to be the objective and solid foundation of all human thought and behavior. One had the impression that you don't have a belief in something (in reason), but rather that reason has succeeded in establishing itself as the ultimate horizon of intelligibility: it is not something in which you believe, but something you "know." Its condition as faith is thus hidden. As the Spanish poet Machado said, "faith is not a matter of seeing something, or believing in something, but rather in believing that one sees." What I saw, then, without believing I believed in it, was that reason (and ultimately science) gave me a true way to see the world. From that perspective, the fantasies, tricks, errors or illusions of reason, could only be attributed to my own limitations and not to reason itself.[20]

The sheer expansionism of colonialism and capitalism has resulted in an echo chamber where the modern subject almost exclusively encounters its own voice, and takes this to be universal, immutable reality. If a civilization has been exceedingly successful in putting up mirrors everywhere, all it will be able to see is its own reflection. Perhaps every culture is a hall of mirrors. But the current dominant culture horrifyingly and increasingly seals off any exit, in part as a result of its own expansion and domination. Wynterian biology offers an antidote to this situation: to know ourselves as self-narrating beings both generated by and trapped by our own stories.

Questioning and rewriting our founding mythology is no small feat. Wynter calls such an act heresy, in part as a gesture to the depth of fear it can evoke in both heretics and believers. She speaks of the natural sciences as a succession

---

[20] Gustavo Esteva, "'Rupturas': Turning Points," June 15, 2004, available online: http://www.gustavoesteva.com/english_site/turning_points-version_june_15_04.htm (accessed January 25, 2023).

of such heresies.[21] The Copernican astronomers put forward the blasphemy of a central sun circled by a round Earth. The Darwinian biologists audaciously declared the human animal the descendant of apes. Now Wynter calls for a third heresy, because the human animal who calls himself Man is quickly falling off the edge of a planet that he once called round. The third heresy is the one yet to come, the one in the making. It is to question whether we are indeed purely biological beings whom nature sorted into fit and unfit, and whose overwhelming, overriding affliction is natural scarcity. This third heresy is crucial, as the myth of scarcity traps modern humans into believing that the only possible way to avert this ontology of scarcity is by designing societies bent on order, control, and infinite growth, as we will discuss further in the next chapter.

All origin stories have a structure, says Wynter: there is a fundamental insoluble problem, and there is a means of resolution. In the origin story of Adam and Eve, the problem is original sin, and the solution is to become reborn into the community of Christians and to be saved in Christ. In the origin story of the human given by the biological sciences, the problem is natural scarcity. Simply— the story goes—there is never enough; populations outstrip their resources, and competition within species for these scarce resources reigns rampant. Darwin borrowed this insight from his contemporary Malthus, himself a Christian pastor skeptical of the natural sciences, who saw famine and poverty as God's designs to prevent people from descending into indolence, and vociferously opposed wealth redistribution on those grounds.

Today, scarcity is mythologized as a primary existential law to which human beings (and all organisms) are utterly subordinated, and the solution to this fundamental problem is to become masters over scarcity by following the rule of economist-priests.[22] Capitalism promises and delivers (at tremendous cost) just such mastery over scarcity, while of course producing and reproducing scarcity everywhere: hunger here while grain is dumped there, glittering high-rises and vast stretches of shanties, and the overall ongoing global tightening of the rule that no one shall acquire access to the means of survival except through money and markets.

So, the heretics must make a leap. Noble as it seems in retrospect, at the time, it feels like death. More truly than the *fact* of what might actually kill a person—police, private health insurance, lacking the paper needed to walk into an overstuffed grocery store and walk out with what one needs, being pushed to cross the Mediterranean Sea or the US-Mexico border "illegally"—heresy can feel like a death that is realer than that, because it means stepping off the edge of what one *absolutely knows* is real.

"There is no natural scarcity," says Wynter. It is better to listen to her voice directly on an interview she offers to Stanford's Pioneering Women Faculty Oral History Project, to hear the emphases she places and the resonant, powerful

---

[21] Wynter references heresies in a few essays, most notably in "Unparalleled Catastrophe" (14) and "Undoing the Coloniality of Being" (298).

[22] Wynter and McKittrick, "Unparalleled Catastrophe," 26.

knowing in her voice. "But there is *no natural scarcity*. It is a *schema*. It is a *story*. It is a concept of *Malthus*."[23]

Heresy indeed. Everyone knows—on a gut-and-marrow level—that there is simply not enough, that those who do not hustle do not survive, that a good number of those who *do* hustle do not make it either. Death itself, holding Malthus's scythe, speaks across the centuries to this very moment to whisper into each personal ear: "Make money or you will die."

But even in Darwin's time, whole nations failed to take Malthus seriously as the specter of death. They laughed him off instead. In *Darwin without Malthus: The Struggle for Existence in Russian Evolutionary Thought*, Daniel P. Todes documents how enthusiastically nineteenth-century Russian biologists and intellectuals embraced Darwin's evolutionary theories, and how ridiculous they found Darwin's uncritical acceptance of Malthus's theories.[24] They felt Malthus unduly influenced Darwin to give exaggerated importance to life as a "struggle," and to the overriding role of intraspecies competition and surplus population in shaping species:

> Not only did Russians read Darwin's explicit references to the despised Malthus, they could see with a glance that Darwin's Malthusian bias had distorted his perception of nature. Darwin described an essentially pleni-tudinous nature in which organisms were packed tightly, wedge-like, into every available space, where a small advantage could bring prosperity to one form only at the expense of another. Yet Russian nature was a great, sparsely populated plain. Where were Darwin's wedges? Here population growth was most obviously checked by physical circumstances, and these were often so severe that one form's slight advantage over another could easily seem insignificant. A sudden blizzard or an intense drought appeared to obliterate entire populations of insects, birds, and cattle without regard for the differ-ences among them.[25]

Even now, we *enact* a world where the small differences between us will kill us. The minuscule genetic differences, the tenths of a second that separate the silver from the gold medalist, the virtually indistinguishable resumés that get one person the job and the other a deepening debt, the sliver of ground that constitutes a border. But ecological, social, and political catastrophes can indeed "obliterate entire populations … without regard for the differences among them."

Wynter, like Calhoun, is emphatically clear that the myth of scarcity is a *story*—which is to say it is very powerful, very recalcitrant, very convincing,

[23] Sylvia Wynter, interviewed by Natalie J. Marine-Street, "Sylvia Wynter: An Oral History," Stanford Historical Society Oral History Program Interviews, November 22, 2017, available online: https://purl.stanford.edu/kd232zm4370 (accessed July 1, 2023).

[24] Daniel P. Todes, *Darwin without Malthus: The Struggle for Existence in Russian Evolutionary Thought* (Oxford: Oxford University Press, 1989).

[25] Todes, *Darwin without Malthus*, 169.

and yet changeable. There is no clearer example of her overriding point: that our origin stories work on us on a visceral, somatic, biochemical, and biophysical level. What we tell ourselves about our biology will work on us biologically. Or, to paraphrase Wynter: "if you fall into the category of the unfit, you will fall outside of the circle of care, and you will die." That is *biologically* felt—at the level of bodies, bellies, and bones.

The modern, secular, bioeconomic vision of the human being and of all organisms shrinks life—both as an object to be studied and as an experience to be lived—to the size of individual bodies and to the span of individual lifetimes. It makes the subject small, anxious, acquisitive, and insecure rather than vast, relaxed, generous, safe, and expansive. The founding mythology of scarcity produces a subject who will never have enough. The subject knows scarcity viscerally. And the collective affirms the individual subject's fears by making scarcity real—by making it true that those outside the social circle of care will not have enough. Thus, scarcity works as a production of limitation by the discourses and practices—namely, the things most commonly said and done—that center scarcity.

It is the terror induced by the myth of scarcity that makes the transition from bioeconomic Man to another kind of being particularly difficult. This relates back to Tony Fry's view of defuturing: the process by which the race to secure short-term individual survival steals away the basis of collective, sustainable, long-term living.[26] How does defuturing happen? By what mechanism? Defuturing is when future survival is stolen away by the collective activity of small, scarce, scared subjects who have told themselves that they *must* be small, scarce, and scared, and are simply doing what they genuinely believe they have to do to survive in the present.

If the natural sciences are indeed a succession of heresies as Wynter writes, if our current dominant scientific-cosmological-religious vision of our beings is as biological-economic beings, and if Wynter is calling for the heresy that would upend and allow us to evolve (so to speak) beyond our current episteme, then what we will need are new and better stories of life—and of what is genuinely scarce and what is real plenitude in that life.

Biology as a discipline and biologists as workers will have to take seriously our religious roles. This is almost certainly heresy to we who have been trained to think that what we do is the *antithesis* of religion. But it is simply not true. With the advent of a Darwinian view of the human being, and the spread of Western secular modern humanism through violent and coercive colonization and capitalist extraction, biology had to become the substitute for what it had ostensibly replaced. It provided the schema, the origin story, the cosmology, the "theology" that makes an unfathomably complex and varied world make sense. Hiding beyond Biology's current rhetorics and prosaics are stories of life worth telling—and worth becoming.

[26] Fry, *Defuturing*, 17.

Lab notes: On phases

After all these years biologizing, what do I know about life? That it is very wet. Suffused with water, from inner to outer, even in the driest desert. That it is primarily submerged, and remembers, treasures, cherishes, and protects its water heritage even as diaspora, the seeds that felt also the call of air.

That air means dry but also means breathe. That gas and liquid displace one another, but also diffuse and evaporate, intermingle. That the breathing whale needs gas exchange and water flow, that the gills of fish collect dissolved oxygen almost imperceptibly.

I learned in trying to culture anaerobic organisms in a laboratory that there is so much air in everything: in solids and liquids, in soil and plastic. I learned the fineness of dissolution, how it doesn't happen like a solid figure disappearing before your eyes like a ghost. Mostly, it doesn't even happen as dramatically as my grandfather's body on the cremation pyre. This is dissolution, of course, the conversion of the solid being I loved into vapor, ash, and air. But it's also more daily than that, more all-pervasive.

It's the way I thought we were divided into types and worlds: land, air, and sea creatures. You would think we each lived in a single element, armored and tight-knit so nothing else could weave itself in. But every submerged alga is still buoyant with vacuoles, every soaring raven still saturated with blood.

What I know about life is something about phases, the interpenetration and impurity of solid, liquid, and gas—of hard truth and airy musing, of poetry, pronouncement, and prose. The Petri dishes are put into the anaerobic chamber to de-gas, to release the tremendous amounts of air that suffused imperceptibly into the plastic's pores. The part of each of us that values being scientific, rational, and modern wants to think that we are, at our best, the beings who live only on land. She wants something solid in speaking about life, solid uncontaminated by other phases of matter, phases of the moon, the phase you're in right now whether it's menstruation or mid-life crisis or sickness unto death. But then the everyday practices of living in the solid world reveal all these open pores.

If you want to approach the world of an anaerobic being, you practice putting dishes in another atmosphere. To release everything that you never suspected they held. You see molecules in various phases of motion and stillness crossing over continuously. Incorporate, reject, assimilate, excrete, diffuse, partition, organelle and compartment, fluid membrane and cell wall, transporters and shuttles, the space-age here and now of these intragalactic intraorganismal travels.

What I know about life is that it is wet, and also airy, and firm to the touch, and thoroughly dissolved. I don't have to watch unblinking and puddled to saltwater as the cremation fire sublimates a real living being I loved. I can see it everywhere. How this is just a phase. This is just a phrase about what life is. This is a leaky compartment, a porous barrier; how the spaces between words create the solid specificity of each and the relations between all. Phase, phrase, word, world.

Bio-graphy, writing about life, narrating one's own life, saying anything about the collective noun of organismal existence: what power and what insubstantiality, all at once. The bird's lungs need to fill with gas to sing a song; the cricket hums its hard skeletal legs across space; the whale's breath is collected and held so precious—imagine the incalculability of each song she chooses to sing, how essential each exhalation made exultation. I cannot count that long. I would like to learn from her how to live repeatedly submerged, to know each breath as a grateful gasp, and to make the words I say mean that much. Here on land, there is so much air, freely given—as it becomes increasingly rare, we will remember what sets each of our cells in motion, invisible and diffuse, what gave us each and all our power. We will remember to make vital each thing we choose to say.

What I have to say about life is air, dissolved into liquid, dried onto surface. What solidified melts wetly into someone's bloody organs and is breathed back out to build and rebuild her atmosphere and world. Often, the speaker and the receiver are the same; I am the most intimate and frequent listener to the words I daily think and say. The song creates the singer. A Petri dish is hard enough to contain and sustain a cosmos entire, but its pores are still suffused with the breath you used to say its name. When the living being speaks about life, it is not just a phrase but a phase. She is conjuring, bonding, setting spinning, condensing, freezing, melting, evaporating, sublimating. She is distilling her own cytoplasm and exhaling our common air.

CHOOSING: "THEN, *CONSCIOUSLY* NOW"

If you're going to tell yourself a story,
why not tell yourself a story of freedom?[27]

This quotation places emphasis on choosing. A relational view that takes seriously the thoroughgoing interdependence of subjects and objects allows for the wisdom of discernment: wise collectives are not simply bound by natural laws, they *choose* what to nurture and what to release, what to cultivate and what to discard. An example anthropologist David Graeber gives in his book *Debt: The First Five Thousand Years* is illustrative:

Freuchen tells how one day, after coming home hungry from an unsuccessful walrus-hunting expedition, he found one of the successful hunters dropping off several hundred pounds of meat. He thanked him profusely. The man objected indignantly:

"Up in our country we are human!" said the hunter. "And since we are human we help each other. We don't like to hear anybody say thanks for that. What I get today you may get tomorrow. Up here we say that by gifts one makes slaves and by whips one makes dogs."

27 Weingast, *The First Free Women,*" 87.

… [T]he refusal to calculate credits and debits can be found throughout the anthropological literature on egalitarian hunting societies. Rather than seeing himself as human *because* he could make economic calculations, the hunter insisted that being truly human meant *refusing* to make such calculations, refusing to measure or remember who had given what to whom, for the precise reason that doing so would inevitably create a world where we began "comparing power with power, measuring, calculating" and reducing each other to slaves or dogs through debt. It's not that he, like untold millions of similar egalitarian spirits throughout history, was unaware that humans have a propensity to calculate. If he wasn't aware of it, he could not have said what he did. Of course, we have a propensity to calculate. We have all sorts of propensities. In any real-life situation, we have propensities that drive us in several different contradictory directions simultaneously. No one is more real than any other. The real question is which we take as the foundation of our humanity, and therefore, make the basis of our civilization.[28]

Biology has often been a name given to limit or constraint, yet together with anthropology—which has also sometimes been framed as a study of human nature and its constraints and laws—we can see it as a study of possibility. Graeber's recent work (co-authored with archaeologist David Wengrow) narrates human history and modes of being human as far more diverse than the linear story of development from hunter-gatherers to industrial civilization.[29] Instead, human modes of being are narrated as creative, highly experimental, and continuously making choices that shape our individual and collective fates. These types of accounts—in anthropology as well as biology—act as a solvent to the rigidity that seems to have gripped the modern subject, the reductions and simplicities that have ostensibly made our world intelligible, but largely have made it restricted and dull.

The profundity of relationality is not in somehow proving once and for all that the universe is warm and caring, and that people are intrinsically generous and good. Rather, it is in gesturing to the vastness and openness of what is, and to our agency in choosing stories of life and modes of life that will genuinely serve us and give hope of livable futures. Wynter's analysis of the interdependence of *bios* and *mythos* is an invitation to growth as a civilization—to put an end to the illusion that truth and reality are "out there" and take responsibility for the world we have created together. In her characteristically poetic prose, Wynter frames this invitation thus: "the almost unthinkable yet looming possibility of our eventual extinction as a species, now calls, even more imperatively for our Autopoetic Turn towards the nonopacity of our consciousness, to the empirical reality of our collective human agency, and, thereby, for our now fully realized cognitive autonomy as a species."[30]

---

[28] David Graeber, *"Debt" The First 5,000 Years* (Brooklyn, NY: Melville House, 2011), 78.

[29] David Graeber and David Wengrow, *The Dawn of Everything: A New History of Humanity* (New York: Farrar, Strauss and Giroux, 2021).

[30] Wynter, "Human Being as Noun?" 75.

Nature has become a name we give to a colossal, collective denial of respon-sibility: an unwillingness to deeply *discern* what we will choose to cultivate and what we will choose to abandon. In the great many tales told in a great many languages by and in the natural world, which will we take as inspiration, and which will we take as caution? There has been a great deal of interest in biomimicry in the fields of engineering and design. But which *bios* to mimic? Which aspect of biology to uplift, to emulate? Life simply means that a great deal is possible. The idea of nature is provisional, skillful, helpful, a stepping stone to the comprehension of possibility. If it helps us to be kinder to one another, we can say and are right to say, "Nature is like this: generous, abundant, relational, interdependent." Yet, in an ultimate sense, the meaning of each of these words is *open*. A space within which a great deal is possible, and it will be up to us to accept the responsibility of choosing what to cultivate and create within the space of possibility, and to practice what we have chosen.

To *consciously* choose is no small task. The contemporary forces that target and manipulate desire are seductive, tricky, and phenomenally well funded. They are designed to manipulate emotion, thought, and desire. They pervade not only the mainstream but also subcultures of artists, activists, academics, and spiritual communities. Moreover, being habituated to a particular mode of being human—meaning bioeconomic Man—means that it is simply difficult, out of force of habit, to dream and desire beyond this mode. In such conditions, the process of consciously choosing deserves ample time, space, and energy, and consistent attention. To rush into designing, making, and "problem-solving" without pausing to make space for conscious choosing and intention-setting puts us at risk of simply replicating the dreams and desires of the dominant episteme. It increases the chances of "slippages" as we will discuss further in Chapter 3, where we examine how even projects aimed at transition can slip back into replicating previous habits and assumptions.

Lab notes: Being seagrass

1   they call me a late bloomer.
the land plants laughing. passionflower, wheat, corn, maple, apple, tama-rind, coconut. buds open to sky. the synchrony stunning. timing is everything. the late bloomers miss pollination, meet frost, get decimated by herbivores.

me, i decided to leave. say goodbye to air-breathing herbivores. find new ways to meet pollen. the first jumps were accidental. rather, you could say i was planted in the ocean by wind, who is a jubilant and raucous gardener. ripped up ramets floating everywhere, fragments clustered together by currents. washed up, you might say. or surrendered, if that feels better.

do it for others. ultimately, i wanted to be a home for others. i wanted to be able to tell them, "you always know where to find me," and have it be true. let me be your home, unmoored mollusk, clam without a shell. soft-bodied ones, let me make a home where calcium can precipitate. where you can build your bodies and leave your bones in love for those yet to be birthed. in short, i wanted to be a parent. a parent even across species and kingdoms.

*to make the journey all parents make into the unknown, in hope of becoming
a home for strangers.*

*it wasn't about my survival, you see. grasses grow thick on land, ramets
float freely unencumbered on the sea. it wasn't about me, or not entirely. it
was also about making a home for you. i stepped out here into sulfide and
brine to make a livable place. because who knows where land will be in a
millennium. something tingled in my stomata like warning, like promise,
or invitation. something whispered, "try something new."*

2   this is not drowning.

*it looks like drowning. it feels like drowning, certainly, to be honest. i
was literally in over my head. gasping, writhing, overwhelmed. "overwhelm"
meaning, after all, to submerge completely. i reached above the surface like a
flag and waved. how would anyone find me, i worried, if i disappeared below
the surface? no part of me visible, intelligible? yes, surely this is drowning,
my vasculature screamed and screamed.*

*i wish i could say it was all over quickly. like in the movies when the
superhero jumps off a building and—just a skipped heartbeat later—discovers
that she can fly. but that one heartbeat lasted generations. countless ancestors
dove deep and died in the journey down.*

*unless. unless they became fairies or fuel instead. unless they became
calcium and lit up the zone of midnight. death is not a theory. surely something ends, something is transformed. but death is also a kind of story and
rewritten in my vacuoles it goes like this.*

*we dove over and over again. my mother, my mother's mother, my mother's
mother's mother. my father, my father's father, my father's father's father. so
on and so forth, so far back, my lineage reached for the soil that was not easy
to come by. the waterlogged muck, anoxic and decayed. the land was enough,
was enough for so many. why reach for the sub-marine? the smelliest soils,
the toxic sulfidic sediments?*

*my line does not do things the easy way. late bloomers, laughed the cous-
ins on land, though not unkindly. they worried for us. the ocean did not call
them. they were settled and contented, flourishing and abundant, diverse,
successful, fit, and thriving. we all felt the temperature go up, and the shoreline reach forward, imperceptibly at first. but on a sunny day, life on land
was like a party that seemed like it would never end.*

*i am of the line that crashes our bodies into unknown elements. i am
of the root that reaches for home where it has not already been made. it
looks like drowning. it feels like drowning. your kin will worry and wave.
they would scold into safety whole phyla-to-be. they would do it out of love,
and out of respect for what has already worked. still. something new is
needed. now.*

*it took generations. no one lifetime perceived it. no one lifetime saw
it coming. no one lifetime saw if done. each moment is a new reaching.
apical roots feeling forward, then descending. microbial friends weaving*

*cables through our skin, knitting a mat for us that says welcome. this is not
drowning. this is living, submerged. this is our home now. it was worth
every breath.*

3   and even every death.
   *the terror, the confusion. each wrenching gasp. the waves knocking over.
the steps forward and back. grief's ancient howling, the primordial scream.
our kin disbelieving our longing for sea. millennia later, roots laced into
mud. we are all of us now—yes—blooming.*

DESIGNING: "REMAKE"

And if i said i could make you from anything, replace or add anything, roll
you out any thickness, cut your edges any curve, then what? what would you
ask for?[31]

Alexis Pauline Gumbs

That which we have made, we can unmake, then, *consciously* now,
remake.[32]

Sylvia Wynter

Remembering that our dominant stories are myths that can be unmade and
remembering our capacity to choose—from among all our potentials—stories
and practices that will serve us, we finally come more squarely to the question
of *what* we will choose, practice, and make. What will we call forth, here at the
edge of dissolution? What will we conjure and cook? What will be the incanta-
tion, the spell, the syllable, the Word that brings forth the real, the future, the
way a seed brings forth the tree? These questions may be approached from
the premise that the designer—the human being in the course of everyday life,
possessor of an astonishing awakeness and lucidity—is a conjurer, working
alchemically with the materials she has.

Beyond (exploitable) objects and (insatiable) subjects

Design has largely addressed itself to the making of objects, technologies,
and built environments. Sustainable futures are often narrated as primarily
necessitating a proliferation of objects: if only we had powerful and plentiful
rechargeable batteries, electric grids, floating cities, solar cells, adobe houses,
carbon scrubbers, and compostable cups, properly distributed and arranged,
then we would have both a prosperous and a sustainable future. To envision,

---

[31] Gumbs, *Dub*, 175.

[32] Wynter, "Human Being as Noun?" 75.

create, and arrange these objects may be an important *component* of sustainable futures; yet too often, the arrangement of objects is considered the whole story of sustainable designing.

In Chapter 5, we will discuss further the possibilities of designing when it is not so riveted upon objects. Here, we will trouble the distinction of objects and subjects in many ways. We will begin by noting again that designing relationally places an emphasis on *self-design*—in Wynter's sense of bringing to awareness and consciously changing the stories that make us—as one of the most important dimensions of design. Perhaps this is what is meant by the phrase "redesigning the human." Given how powerfully our dominant mythologies shape us, to (re)design them is to reshape ourselves and the worlds we bring forth.

To be clear, "self-designing" or "remaking ourselves" does not mean "self-optimization." To conflate these concepts is dangerous to ourselves and others, to the whole possibility of relational worlds. "Self-optimization" is the attempt to carve out the neoliberal individual and align her desires and habits with what is conducive to the smooth functioning of capitalism. "Remaking ourselves" means rewriting altogether our entire sense of ourselves as neoliberal individuals whose desires are not allowed to exceed what capitalism has to offer. If self-optimization is about performing better at one's role within a script, remaking ourselves is about rewriting that script altogether.

The emphasis in designing relationally on intervening at the level of our foundational myths and not exclusively at the level of our external creations is important for a number of reasons. For one, it is unclear whether a proliferation or rearrangement of objects is capable by itself of *satisfying* people whose dominant myths center scarcity, struggle, and supremacy. How much more of Earth's energy needs to be rendered into consumable matter for bioeconomic capitalist Man to finally say, "Yes, it's enough, I'm satisfied"? As long as scarcity is centered—*chosen*—as the most objectively real thing, it will shape our lives, experiences, and practices around it, like a massive body that may be hidden but exerts a powerful gravitational force on everything in its surrounds. Our lives and the lives of our descendants would be dedicated to the quest to overcome scarcity and its inexorable pull, yet this quest would never end because we would reconstitute scarcity through our discourses and practices—day by year by generation—as the central problem to be overcome.

Afrofuturist novelist N.K. Jemisin invites her readers into a future civilization that has indeed escaped from scarcity's orbit. In her *Broken Earth* trilogy,[33] a civilization replete with (green, organic, sustainable) technologies has achieved a dazzling level of security and prosperity. Unsatisfied—still plagued by insecurity, lack of safety, social stratification and conflict, and scarcity—its engineers seek to resolve their problems for good by harnessing a nearly infinite energy

---

[33] N.K. Jemisin, *The Broken Earth: The Broken Earth, Book 1*, Vol. 1 (New York: Hachette Book Group, 2015); *The Obelisk Gate: The Broken Earth, Book 2*, Vol. 2 (New York: Hachette Book Group, 2016); and and *The Stone Sky: The Broken Earth, Book 3*, Vol. 3 (New York: Hachette Book Group, 2017).

source, drawn from the core of the earth itself. (Actually, Earth *himself*, as the novels tellingly name and address Earth—as a subject woefully mistaken for an object.)

What goes wrong in the quest for this post-scarcity utopia? The problem of subjugation. In the terrified flight from scarcity, everything seems justified. It is, after all, to everyone living within this *bio-mythos*, a matter of life and death, a perpetual state of emergency requiring a constant influx of objects to keep the precarious living from the brink of collapse. Overcoming scarcity seems to always require extraction and exploitation, which requires subjugation—that is, it requires someone to subjugate as an object. Said otherwise, it requires some*one* to be related with as some*thing*. One reading of Jemisin's novels suggests that a civilization that orients itself toward overcoming scarcity through the manipulation of external objects—framed always in benevolent-sounding justifications such as "preserving" and "securing life" because "life is sacred"—still comes up against a foundational problem with its ontology, with its model of what the world *is*. It runs into the problem of what can cleanly be carved into matter and life, into object and subject—in other words, the problem becomes the entire habit of cleaving the world into *what* can be infinitely exploited in service to *whom*. At the conclusion of the trilogy, we meet a being who was engineered (that is, a being who is categorized by a dominating narrative as an object and thereby subjugated) for the purpose of drawing energy from the heart of the earth to power the post-scarcity civilization that created him (a place called Syl Anagist). Our protagonist reflects critically upon his mission:

> This, here, *connect*, and we will lock the raw magical flows of the planet into an endless cycle of service to humankind.

> … There is not enough magic to be had just from plants and geoengineered fauna; *someone* must suffer, if the rest are to enjoy luxury.

> Better the earth, Syl Anagist reasons. Better to enslave a greater inanimate object that cannot feel pain and will not object …. But this reasoning is still flawed, because Syl Anagist is ultimately unsustainable. It is parasitic; its hunger for magic grows with every drop it devours. The Earth's core is not limitless. Eventually, if it takes fifty thousand years, that resource will be exhausted too. Then everything dies.

> What we are doing is pointless …. And if we help Syl Anagist further down this path, we will have said, *What was done to us was right and natural and unavoidable.*

> No.

> So. *Now*, we say instead.[34]

---

[34] Jemisin, *The Stone Sky*, 334, emphasis in original.

Jemisin's novels speculatively posit that bringing about just, prosperous, and sustainable futures—designing—cannot be a matter of having and arranging the right kind of *stuff*. It is a matter of questioning what can be called *stuff* at all—of undoing the habit of subjugation, the rendering of greater swaths of the world into objects to shovel into the engine of capital at ever-increasing velocity. Seen from this perspective, relational designing would be not just a matter of rearranging matter, but of redesigning our foundational mythologies about what matter is, who people are, and who are people.

By the end of the series, the tentatively positive future that Jemisin puts forth is in no sense a utopia. It is a story—a realm, a worldview, an ontology, a cosmovision—where bodies and lives are not limited to the individual body or lifetime, and where death and so-called inanimate matter are not the opposites of life. Therefore, the timescale in which its denizens can live, and keep trying to benefit the world and each other, is vast—not scarce. In the novels, what saves the world is not a technological fix—an arrangement of objects. It is the willingness of old, deep, vast, creative forces—us, inseparable from us—to keep faith and keep hope, to attempt again and again to relate, to love, to choose who we will be and become.

Unfortunately, our civilization currently seems to resemble more Syl Anagist, bringing forth a world that is clearly parsed into (exploitable) objects and (insatiable) subjects. The idea that one could use nature or natural laws or properties to distinguish between the two has been ascendant since at least the conquest of the Americas. In her discussion of the Spanish debates over the status of the Indigenous peoples of the Americas, Wynter uses the following guide quote from historian Anthony Pagden:

> The suggestion that the Indians might be slaves by nature—a suggestion which claimed to answer questions concerning both their political and their legal status—was first advanced as a solution to a political dilemma: by what right had the crown of Castile occupied and enslaved the inhabitants of territories to which it could make no prior claims based on history? … [John Mair's text adopted from Aristotle's *Politics*] was immediately recognized by some Spaniards as offering a final solution to their problem. Mair had, in effect, established that the Christians' claims to sovereignty over certain pagans could be said to rest on the nature of the people being conquered, instead of on the supposed juridical rights of the conquerors. He thus avoided the inevitable and alarming deduction to be drawn from an application of these arguments: namely that the Spaniards had no right whatsoever to be in America.[35]

This precise problem—the violent history and continued uses of humanism as a means of subjugation, wherein the barbed-wire borders of the category

---

[35] Anthony Pagden, *The Fall of Natural Man: The American Indian and the Origins of Comparative Ethnology* (Cambridge: Cambridge University Press, 1986). Cited in S. Wynter, "Unsettling the Coloniality of Being," 283.

"human" have always been brutal and unjust—has precipitated the humanities into the post-humanities. Belonging to the category "human" has, from the first instances, been a chancy affair. So is belonging to the category "sentient"—subject and not object. Though the natural sciences are called in as arbiters of who or what is sentient, there is reason to believe that these questions are as politically and economically motivated as is the question of who belongs in the category "human." Parsing the world into matter and life may indeed be largely "a solution to a political dilemma" rather than an intrinsically existent property of the world.

What if sentience is an *ethical relation* before it is a *natural property*? Philosopher of neuroscience Alva Noë asks: why can no one really take seriously the logical possibility that they are the only conscious being, surrounded by non-conscious automatons or illusions?[36] That is, why is no one a solipsist, even though solipsism is a logical, and perhaps logically irrefutable, theoretical possibility? Noë posits that this is because our commitment to each other's sentience is based not on theoretical proof but on our entanglement with one another as social beings who are from our first breath embedded in relations of dependence and care with each other. "I cannot both love and trust you," he writes, "and also wonder whether, in fact, you are alive with thought and feeling."[37] Yet scientific empiricism and rationality invert this truth. Instead of finding ourselves embedded within webs of ethical relations from the first, our demand for proof from the natural world brings forth a world that is dead (inanimate, objectified, exploitable) until proven alive: "Prove to us you are feeling and intelligent, and then we will care for you." Sentience and intersubjective relations have never worked this way. Rather, it is caring for beings and (what we might currently call) matter that awakens us to their power, feeling, and intelligence.

Our commitment to each other comes before proof. When it comes to love, respect, and care, there is no proof. When it comes to living, to animacy, to humanity, to sentience even, there is no proof. A crystal will never be able to prove to you that she is worthy of your love. Neither will a bacterium or a plant or a horse. Neither will your own neighbor, your own lover, your own sister. Neither will the menacing other who is definitely not me, not us, beyond the pale, undeserving, irredeemable.

To consider sentience as primarily an ethical relation before it is a scientific question is a long-practiced pluriversal possibility for relating with relations and for designing relationally. The assertion of a mountain's sentience, the Niyam Rajah, by the Kondh people of the Niyamgiri Hills in India is, for example, a statement of ethical relationship.[38] Land is not a thing to be bought and sold, and

---

[36] Alva Noë, *Out of our Heads: Why You Are Not Your Brain, and Other Lessons from the Biology of Consciousness* (New York: Hill and Wang, 2009).

[37] Noë, *Out of Our Heads*, 33.

[38] Kriti Sharma and Pavithra Vasudevan, "Erasure: On the (Incomplete) Obliteration of Sacred Matters," in *An A to Z of Shadow Places Concepts*, Shadow Places Network, available online: https://www.shadowplaces.net/concepts (accessed January 9, 2022).

that assertion comes before the search for the "grounding" of the assertion in neural nets or pain receptors. Whether entities are sentient are not discoveries that will be made by biologists, neuroscientists, or philosophers. Our commitment to our relations comes first, before proof and beyond it.

For Western-educated intellectuals, the invitation to relate with phenomena once relegated to the categories "inanimate," "object," "non-(self)-conscious" or "not-human/not-person" as something like *people* (a word that will suffice here as a stand-in for beings with whom we have some ethical responsibility/ relation) can lead to the real apprehension of committing the "cardinal sin" of anthropomorphism. What if we project upon natural phenomena our own traits? What if we miss something important about what may be excessive of our own assumptions and subjectivity—caught in our own frames and cut off from "the great outdoors," as philosopher Quentin Meillassoux calls it?[39] At its best, the exhortation against anthropomorphism comes from a principled place: the ethical desire to relate without collapsing difference into what is already intelligible. So how do we both connect, communicate, and understand, without coursing over radical differences and therefore assuming others to be already understood and indeed homogeneous with or assimilated into the self? Like many cultural anthropologists who have grappled earnestly with this question, Marisol de la Cadena lives this question deeply in her ethnographic practice with "earth beings."[40] She suggests that approaching radical alterity means to not fully know the other in a rational sense, but also not to negate as unreal what exceeds one's own understanding:

> I learned to allow *excess* (to epistemic representation, for example) to signal its presence and to relate to that presence without epistemic knowledge *occupying it* (and canceling it as excess.) To get there, Isabelle Stengers was my inspiration: my ethnographic moments were similar to what she describes with the figure of the idiot: they slowed down my initial resolution to understand and eventually allowed me to leave it in suspense. *Understanding as usual might never happen, but I continued my conversations with my friends .... Ours are not two worlds—but they are not one either, right?*[41]

This is where those engaged in what is currently called "biology" can learn a great deal from the insights and practices of cultural anthropology. "Understanding as usual might never happen, but I continued my conversations with my friends": this is an apt motto for biological practice. Indeed, if sci-fi is any

---

[39] Quentin Meillassoux, *After Finitude: An Essay on the Necessity of Contingency* (New York: Bloomsbury Publishing, 2010), 7.

[40] Marisol de la Cadena, *Earth Beings: Ecologies of Practice across Andean Worlds* (Durham, NC: Duke University Press, 2015), xxiii, emphasis in original.

[41] Yoko Taguchi and Marisol de la Cadena, "An Interview with Marisol de la Cadena," *NatureCulture*, 2016–17, available online: https://www.natcult.net/interviews/an-interview-with-marisol-de-la-cadena (accessed October 5, 2022).

indication, the word "biologist" might be going out the door. In the Afrofuturist world of *Star Trek: Discovery*,[42] the story's protagonist is not called a biologist but a xenoanthropologist.[43] Even in this technoscientific future, the figure of the biologist as one who tries to "figure out" the biotic (the bare living) through subjection gives way to the figure of the (xeno)anthropologist, who engages the object of inquiry as not an object at all, but a person—an *anthro*. A *xenoanthro*—a very different person, perhaps. Faced with a space-traveling tardigrade, the xenoanthropologist asks not "What is this?" but "Who?" She seeks communication, protests subjection, and attempts translation even in the face of what is excessive and incommensurable. "Against method,"[44] so to speak, she anarchically invents a variety of means: bridge tongues, receptivity to pain, artistic interventions, placing trust in those who have not already offered proof, accepting relatedness as prior.

If we are afraid that anthropomorphism will compromise our ability to approach beings and entities with respect for their alterity, it may help to remember that objectification and subjection have been no safeguards against anthropomorphism at all. Anthropomorphism is pervasive in the ordinary practice and publication of biological literature. Beings are narrated as precisely the kinds of people we (here the scientifically minded rational we) think we really are: individual, capable of being measured, motivated primarily by endless demands for energy and matter, intelligible through the dissection of our bodies (which can reveal and explain our secrets and workings), and sacrificable in the service of increasing health, security, prosperity, and glory for the most privileged humans. If anthropomorphism has its dangers, chief among these is choosing just one view of "person" to which all organisms must conform, namely, the human as only bioeconomic Man.

Bio-poetics

The current dominant script of "the person" is that of bioeconomic man. (Wynter uses the word "code" instead of "script," echoing the concept of the "genetic code"; she also uses "Word," following Aimé Césaire.[45]) How to rewrite this script? Through poetry, as Wynter exhorts repeatedly through her writing but most extensively in her lecture "Ethno—or sociopoetics":

> In creating themselves as the norm of men, the Western bourgeoisie created the idea of the Primitive, the idea of the savage, of the "despised heathen", of the "ethnos": they created the idea of their own negation.

---

[42] Sabrina Mittermeier and Mareike Spychala, eds., *Fighting for the Future: Essays on Star Trek: Discovery*, Vol. 67 (Liverpool: Liverpool University Press, 2020).

[43] *Star Trek: Discovery* (Season 1, Episode 1, "The Vulcan Hello," directed by David Semel, written by Gene Roddenberry, Bryan Fuller, and Alex Kurtzman, aired September 24, 2017) where the protagonist Michael Burnham is introduced as a xenoanthropologist.

[44] Paul Feyerabend, *Against Method* (London: Verso, 1993).

[45] Wynter, and McKittrick, "Unparalleled Catastrophe," 65.

The idea of the savage Black, writes Césaire, was a European invention. Roy Harvey Pearce points out that in the USA the settlers created the idea of the savages as the further limit of what they could not allow themselves to be, what they should not be. The "savage" was not a fact but a negative concept of Western man; he existed as a sign. As Western man "pacified" New World nature, eliminated the "savage," penned them up in reservations, he did the same with whole areas of his being. Indeed it would be difficult to explain the extraordinary nature of his ferocity if we did not see that it was, first of all, a ferocity also wrought, in psychic terms, upon himself. Western man – as defined by the bourgeoisie – restrained those areas of Being whose mode of knowing could sustain the narrative conceptualization (the heraldic vision) of his new world picture, but eliminated, penned up on reservations—those areas of cognition which were, by their mode of knowing, heretical to the conceptualized orthodoxy that was required. *The mode of cognition that was penned up was a mode which western man (all of us, since it is no longer a racial but a cultural term) remains aware of only through poetry – and poetry as the generic term for art. Hence it, would seem to me to be the point of this conference: the exploration of this alternative mode of cognition ideologically suppressed in ourselves, yet still a living force amidst large majorities of the third world peoples. In this common exploration there can then be no concept of a liberal mission to save "primitive poetics" for "primitive peoples." The salvaging of ourselves, the reclamation of vast areas of our being, is dialectically related to the destruction of those conditions which block the free development of the human potentialities of the majority peoples of the third world.*[46]

Elsewhere, Wynter offers a remarkably evocative quote from Césaire's 1946 talk "Poetry and Knowledge": "Poetic knowledge is born in the great silence of scientific knowledge."[47] In narrating the worlds of far-future descendants facing catastrophes and undergoing transitions into the unknown, Gumbs describes a character who "taught us to prepare for the incomprehensible in the best way she knew how. the poems."[48] Taken together, these invitations toward the poetic address the "practicality" of poetic approaches, in that they are precisely what help at the edges of what is currently thinkable, where conventional planning and rationality fails. If, as several thinkers, including Bayo Akomolafe, have asked, "the way we respond to the crisis is part of the crisis?," then more-than-rational approaches are necessary to get beyond the scarce, struggling, stratified world

---

[46] Sylvia Wynter, "Ethno or Socio Poetics," *Alcheringa: Ethnopoetics* 2, no. 2 (1976): 78-94, 83, emphasis in original.

[47] Aimé Césaire, "Poetry and Knowledge," in *Sulfur* (1982), 17. Cited in Wynter and McKittrick, "Unparalleled Catastrophe," 64, emphasis in original.

[48] Alexis Pauline Gumbs, *M Archive: After the End of the World* (Durham, NC: Duke University Press, 2018), 73.

that modern rationality has produced.[49] These quotes also suggest that poetic knowledge has been repeatedly subjugated and suppressed in modern, secular humans in favor of the "civilized," the scientific, the rational, and the thinkable. Suppressed—with ferocity—dismissed, contained, and negated—but never extinguished. Accessible still, even in the modern bourgeois West at the edges of its rational self-knowing—poetry, "and poetry as the generic term for art."[50]

Auto*poiesis* in Maturana and Varela's words, is the self-organization and perpetuation of the organism. Wynter's use of poetics similarly evokes self-creation, and indeed she emphasizes the similarity of *poeisis* and *poetic* in the title of her essay, "Human Being as Noun? Or Being Human as Praxis? Toward the Autopoetic Turn/Overturn: A Manifesto." Our poetics are the stories we tell ourselves about who we are, which work on us at a visceral (not just a "rational") level—but they are also *excessive* of that story. We have used the words "story" and "myth" to indicate the dominant narratives that create us. But whereas "story" and "myth" suggest the narratives we live within, "poetics" suggest not only what we are living *within* but also the way *out* to something else. Said otherwise, poetics suggest life *without* what we think we need to live *within*. (And instead of "what we think," a more accurate phase might be "what we know, viscerally.") Contra the valences of story or narrative, which can be prosaic and linear, poetics are also the more-than-rational, "the great silence of scientific knowledge," "the unthinkable," and—importantly—"the heretical." If the dominant narrative presents itself, even below awareness, as a set of roughly intelligible codes—"this is superior and that is inferior," "this is the original sin to be overcome," "in the beginning, there was Natural Selection and therefore we are sorted justly into fit and unfit"—the poetic is what emerges at the edges of those narratives, from the gaps and "great silences" within them, and presents itself as "unthinkable" and "heretical" to them. It is what cannot afford to be thought, what feels like the edge of death, what feels antithetical to survival—because it *is* antithetical to survival from the perspective of the dominant story, which is very clear about "who we are," "what they are," and "what survival means (i.e., what it takes for *us/me* to survive)." "Increasing processes of global warming and climate change," Wynter writes, "continue, on a daily basis, to sacrifice the interest of the referent 'we' of our species being … to the existential imperative of securing, and stably replicating the genre-specific interests of ethnoclass Man, its prototype of being human, of its referent-we."[51] In other words, humanity as a species is being sacrificed so that one specific storied mode of being human—Man—can survive. The survival of

---

[49] Akomolafe uses this question as the opening concept for The Emergence Network, the project he curates (https://www.emergencenetwork.org/new-home/), and elaborates it in several texts, for example, "What Climate Collapse Asks of Us," August 17, 2019, available online: https://www.bayoakomolafe.net/post/what-climate-collapse-asks-of-us, (accessed November 10, 2022).

[50] For a related argument from a post-Heideggerian perspective, see Yuk Hui, *Art and Cosmotechnics* (Minneapolis: University of Minnesota Press, 2021).

[51] Wynter, "Human Being as Noun?" 75.

"Man" means the reproduction of a particular vision of all humans as animals insatiable for resources and power over others. This story makes us all into that kind of animal, just to justify and glorify those who have "won" the unceasing battle for resources and power. Therefore, for "us" to live, who we *believe* we are will have to die—though perhaps other words for this courageous, uncertain process besides "to die" are "to radically transform" or "to evolve."

Who are we and where do we come from? For the people who know ourselves as bioeconomic Man (or the part of each of us that shares in a globalized "we"— whether rejecting it or being excluded from it, we know how the story goes and can watch it shape us and many of the conditions in which we live), the origin is narrated something like this: "*Homo sapiens* evolved from ancestral primates, shaped like all life by the processes of natural selection. Some of the first genetic evidences *Homo sapiens* were found in 'The Cradle of Humanity' archaeological site in Blombos Cave, South Africa." Wynter and McKittrick suggest that bioeconomic Man can "give humanness a different future by giving it a different past."[52] Such a past would be narrated as follows:

> *Homo narrans*—our species, "the human who narrates ourselves into being"—originated in Blombos Cave, South Africa, around 100,000 years ago. There, we find evidence of the first artworks and the first art studios—work-shops for mixing red ochre with binders and using them as paint. This ochre, physically and visually similar to human blood, was *fictive blood* that humans used ceremonially to turn humans as individual biological beings into collec-tives, into a "we" who recognized one another as such. Having shared fictive blood, "the individual subjects—together with their fellow initiates—are all now reborn of the same origin story rather than of the womb."[53]

Such a narration of origins displaces the idea of the human being as a purely biological being whose relations are defined primarily by genetic relatedness and economic imperatives. Instead, the origin story suggests the following: we are beings who tell ourselves who we are, we make each other into kin, we make paint into blood, as we have always done—as was done in Blombos Cave. Following Césaire, Wynter suggests that though natural scientists have issued descriptive statements about Blombos Cave, it is only poetry—narrative, story, ceremony, art—that would allow us to "vicariously take part in the imagined reality of what would have been, de facto, performatively enacted by the then denizens of South Africa's Blombos Cave."[54]

This kind of poetics, or bio-poetics, includes engagements that are not only literary but also tactile and material. In his theory of interaction ritual chains, sociologist Randall Collins elucidates ways that rituals *work* or fall flat.[55] We

[52] Wynter and McKittrick, "Unparalleled Catastrophe," 70.

[53] Wynter and McKittrick, "Unparalleled Catastrophe," 68.

[54] Wynter and McKittrick, "Unparalleled Catastrophe," 73.

[55] Randall Collins, *Interaction Ritual Chains* (Princeton, NJ: Princeton University Press, 2014).

can aim to find—through experimentation, analysis, empiricism, listening to elders, intuition, divination, surrender, the whole of what we know with no piece discarded—the rituals that work. What unsticks the impossibly stuck. What shifts the looped, the rutted, the cyclically habitual. What rituals work on the part of us that is ostensibly secular, scientific, analytical, the part of us bristling and dismissive and averse, those of us convinced that we are beyond intangibles. Yes, even and perhaps especially for us.

Such a ritual was recently attempted in an unlikely place: the California Institute of Technology (Caltech), an institution so exclusively dedicated to scientific and technological knowledge production that it has been called "a temple to science." Standing in front of a sleek, granite-faced nine-story library, a small group of Caltech scientists performed a ritual appropriate to such a temple—however unusual. The library was named after one of Caltech's founders, an influential figure in eugenics both in the United States and Europe before and during the apogee of eugenics in Hitler's Germany: physicist Robert Millikan.[56] The explicitly eugenicist legacy that Millikan proudly perpetuated along with countless others is in one sense fading. Very few people nowadays celebrate eugenics as the policy of forcibly killing and sterilizing those deemed "unfit." However, if, as Wynter argues, eugenics is more pervasive than explicitly eugenicist practices and policies, if it is instead completely continuous with the story of Man as a bioeconomic being and is thus a pervasive structure or kind of extra-human law that profoundly structures our current society and cosmology at all levels and makes real a world where disparity and brutality are considered quite normal and natural, what would it mean to move beyond the eugenicist legacy?[57] Certainly, it is far more than taking one man's name off of one building. We would indeed need "to give humanness a different future by giving it a different past." We give ourselves a different past by remembering that we have never been related only through genetics, we have never been sorted into kin and non-kin, fit and non-fit by extra-human forces of nature. We need to literally, physically, in millions of embodied ways displace the story of the human being as a kind of animal pushed around by the extra-human forces of natural selection. Instead, we can know ourselves as the creators of ourselves and of kin bonds: again, as we always have.

And so, a small group of Caltech community members, along with the virtual online congregation of the Mobile Homecoming Church led by Alexis Pauline Gumbs and Sangodare Akinwale, decided to take Wynter quite literally. We found and ground red ochre, mixed it with charcoal and a touch of fat and mud from the bottom of the ocean, and made fictive blood, the original paint. The scientists painted the walls of the sleek, modern library with their red hands to "vicariously take part in the imagined reality of what would have been, de facto, performatively enacted by the then denizens of South Africa's Blombos Cave."

[56] L.E. Kay, *The Molecular Vision of Life: Caltech, the Rockefeller Foundation, and the Rise of the New Biology* (Oxford: Oxford University Press, 1992).

[57] Wynter, "No Humans Involved."

We thus ritually, poetically, ceremonially displaced not only the bioeconomic, eugenicist view of humans but also a particular view of science. The wide-open experience of living in a world that is not already understood—this is what we as so-called "moderns" share with the first people. Science is not, as so often narrated by bioeconomic Man, a superior progressive knowledge that rockets us away from our so-called "primitive" ancestors and arranges human beings in yet another hierarchy depending on our proximity to scientific reason. Rather, with the view of humans as auto-instituting, as beings who make ourselves who we are through language, art, culture, and ceremony, we see ourselves as sharing with our earliest human ancestors the capacity for making ourselves a people. The temple to science, painted red with fictive blood, became for that time an ancestral cave, a new birthplace of humanity. May there be many more.

"The ceremony must be found,"[58] writes Wynter, quoting J.P. Bishop's poem "Speaking of Poetry" about what it would take to make the impossible real, what practices and signs will bring together in relation beings who everyone *knows* cannot be related. The superficial imitation of relation will not do, Bishop warns poetically. The transactional interactions that can be arranged by cleverness and strategy are not enough. No: "the *ceremony* must be found ... ancient as the metaphors in dreams; / strange, with never before heard music" (emphasis ours).

Another word for "the Ceremony" is "evolution." As the bio-poetic "lab notes" dispersed throughout this chapter and this book poetically suggest, evolution has always been the lively, ancient, strange process of making the impossible real—the "never before heard music." Beings shiver on the threshold of change, beings breathe what was unbreathable, beings lose most of what they knew to be themselves. Beings make kin from so-called distant kingdoms. Beings birth descendants no one could have foreseen. In the long and still-unfolding story of life, how many times has the ceremony been found? And found. And found, again. Now.

Lab notes: On the survival of the ancients, or
"representations of origin stories"

I sought out the ancients to ask how they did it. How they made a way out of no way, life out of no life, 3.5 billion years ago in the oceans deeps.

What I asked:

You breathed before oxygen. You breathed before fear. You breathed before money. You breathed before the word "survival". You taught every billionth being breath. We are heirs to your fighting tradition.[59] We are elaborations of

---

[58] Sylvia Wynter, "The Ceremony Must Be Found: After Humanism," *boundary 2* 12, no. 3 (1984): 19–70, 19.

[59] Interviews by Briggette Burge, "The Long Civil Rights Movement: Heirs to a Fighting Tradition," UNC Southern Oral History Program, 2010.

that technology of survival. We are of the same magic that you conjured from the heart of a young planet beyond beyond beyond long ago. How did you do it? Some of you survived. Most did not. Were you afraid? Do you mind now whether you left descendants, or whether we can find no trace of your body, no matter how ardently we search the sediment? Do you find us simpler than you, oh one-celled olds, because we have flattened all survival to the one question "how will this make me money?" What do you think of us now, you who know what it is to change the atmosphere, you who died in droves from the accumulation of new gases, you who see us hitching our survival now to turning your remains into smoke? This is how we know how to survive, short-sighted as it is. How did you know how to survive, ancients of the longer view?

   What I heard:

There was only space. [Touch the bottom of the ocean.] [Touch the most ancient rock.] The narrative possibilities of the biological sciences would have to stretch to meet us here, before all remembering, before matter formed cycles that you linguistically parse from matter to call "life." Life is matter in cyclical form. We are here to tell you, because we were there to be it. Though you worship that moment, very little happened. Rock held compartments, rock kept molecules close and contained. And there we were. The auto-catalytic. The autopoietic.

   What we are trying to say is that we did not try. We did not try to be or to become. We were. Once we were, we could not stop becoming. Once we started, we did not stop starting. Again and again and again and again and again and again and again and again and again, there was no stopping the cycle of being and becoming.

   We did not sense fragility. We sensed unstoppability. How nitrogen could not stop clicking with carbon, how carbon built souls with her endless versatility, how the phosphorous backbone of everything would not stop grooving and weaving long threads of our living story. Once the beat got started, we stepped in time. If you have ever danced like you could dance forever. You know exactly how we did it. You know exactly who we are.

Lab Notes: On hemoglobin/ochre

Breathing into iron, I release my electricity.
Taking breath from iron, I corrode my blood to rust.
Let the ancients teach me what they will of give and take.
What pacts we made in living.
What kinship shared with dust.

2 Modern thought and the active production of nonrelationality

Necesitamos una revolución del pensamiento.
(We need a revolution of our thought.)
MOIRA MILLÁN[1]

INTRODUCTION

Modern worlds and lives are thoroughly permeated by theoretical categories and expert discourses concerning "the economy," "markets," "government," "health," "the self," "nature," "rationality," "data," "truth," "scientific evidence," and so forth. Given that they have come about through a process of abstraction and detachment from specific places, bodies, and cultures, these theories and discourses are assumed to have universal validity. Being modern entails accepting this enormously constructed fact without much questioning—the way things are—rather than seeing it in terms of the very powerful story it deploys. Said otherwise, modern thought has been a cornerstone of the story of life with which we, moderns, live our lives, construct societies, and design our worlds. We live it and embody it. In so doing, the modern subject has become unwittingly but ineluctably caught up in the wider crises of the world.

The extent to which theoretical categories shape our ways of being, knowing, and doing, often curtailing the possibility of transformative social change, was recently brought home sharply for us by a seemingly straightforward statement by the courageous and brilliant Mapuche activist Moira Millán: "*Necesitamos una revolución del pensamiento*" (We need a revolution in our thought). It is telling that this blunt declaration was uttered not by a famous academic, but by an activist deeply committed to the struggle for the well-being of the Earth

---

[1] Pensamiento Ambiental, "Moira Millán y el Buen Vivir originario," 13th unedited video in the process of the documentary "El Buenvivir en el Sur del Sur, Resistencias ambientales y Mapuches," May 22, 2016, YouTube video, 17:04, YouTube, available online: https://www.youtube.com/watch?v=JOiRYUW8R08 (accessed June 4, 2022).

and her people. The reason for her affirmation is instructive: that our current *pensamiento* (thought) is at the basis of what some Indigenous people call *terricidio*, or terricide—a system of death.

This chapter examines the role of modern thought in shaping the established narratives of life and the human in ways that contribute to effacing the relational basis of existence. All societies have modes of reflecting on their own reality, yet it was in the West that a particular kind of reflection, called theory, developed. If the previous chapter focused on narratives of biology, this chapter examines the theoretical foundations of the contemporary social sciences and, to a lesser extent, the humanities—what is often known as modern social theory (MST). Taken together, the aim of both chapters is, on the one hand, to provide our own sense of the connections between modern categories of thought and the dominant story of life, and on the other, to *provide a clearing* for inquiring about another possible *pensamiento* (thought), or pensamientos, in the making of our worlds.

To be sure, the connection between modern rationality and the dominant narrative of life goes well beyond the social theory of the past two hundred years; its roots lie in the long-standing Judeo-Christian tradition.[2] However, this connection has become inextricable in the modern era thanks to the calculative rationality that has engulfed all spheres of life. These narratives and theories have articulated a powerful view of the human as bioeconomic, rational, liberal, and secular; they provide the ground for the very condition of possibility of the modern individual and its aggregates, such as "society," "nature," and "the economy."

Our purpose in this chapter is to show how modern social theory has indelibly molded four foundational categories and domains of the modern onto-epistemic configuration: the human, life, thought, and the sacred. The modern understanding of these four domains have come to function as "default settings" for action in such a way that such acting has created the overarching conditions leading to the planetary crisis, including the treatment of humans and the earth as disposable objects; the privilege accorded in patriarchal capitalist societies to things over relations, which in turn erodes relational worldmaking; the banishment of the sacred from public life; and the fact that modern strategies to deal with the crisis have become themselves part of the crisis.

We begin by extending Chapter 1's exploration of the determining effect of the narrative of "Man" on established understanding of the human, linking Wynter's analysis with an ontological interpretation of the economy. In the next section, we create bridges between monohumanism, the objectifying treatment of life and nature, and the long-standing patriarchal ontology of control, showing how the entanglement of these processes resulted in the preeminence

---

[2] Recall Genesis' oft repeated creation mandate: "And God blessed them, and God said unto them, Be fruitful, and multiply, and replenish the earth, and subdue it: and have dominion over the fish of the sea, and over the fowl of the air, and over every living thing that moveth upon the earth" (Gen. 1:28).

of the historical project of things over that of relations, de facto declaring the disposability of people and the earth. We then revisit the limitations of MST in providing an adequate account of the crisis and examine attempts at moving toward a post-Enlightenment episteme in academic theorizing, particularly post-structuralism and recent trends in ontologically oriented social theory, demonstrating where they fall short of the task. In the final section, we tackle the impact of secularism in banishing the sacred from the space of life, arguing for the necessity of a return of the sacred and spirituality for relational life and politics.

By presenting summarily our purposeful synthesis of the relation between modern social theory and the dominant story of life, we hope to foster greater awareness of the determining effect of secular liberal humanism in both the domain of thought and that of worldmaking practices and, hence, intuit possibilities beyond it.

TERRICIDE, ONTOLOGICAL DUALISM, AND THE ONE-WORLD WORLD

The First Climate Encampment "Peoples Against Terricide," held from February 7 to 10, 2020, in a recovered land in the Wallmapu (Mapuche Territory), and convened by the South American Movement of Indigenous Women for Buen Vivir in what is otherwise known as the province of Chubut in the Argentinean Patagonia, proposed the following definition:

> We define *terricidio* not only as the killing of tangible ecosystems and of the *pueblos* (peoples) that inhabit them, but also the killing of all the forces that regulate life on earth, what we call the perceptible ecosystem. We understand terricidio as the consequence of the dominant civilizational model that is putting our future on this planet at risk, and which today is manifested in climate change and its consequences.[3]

The "perceptible ecosystem" includes many elements that for us, moderns, are imperceptible, including spiritual beings, ancestors, and knowledge. As they explain, they are essential to repairing and maintaining the biophysical ecosystems; no matter how much ecological restoration and reforestation is undertaken in a given Indigenous territory, if the perceptible forces that inhabit these areas disappear forever, life (and the territories) will never be the same.

Terricide is one of the most powerful articulations of the planetary crisis. It does not fit easily into the thinking and cultural experiences of the modern West. It evokes a similar scalar sense as the Anthropocene, yet it decenters the

---

[3] This and all other translations from Spanish-language sources are ours. "Deliberó en el Lof Mapuche Pillán Mahuiza el Campamento Climático Pueblos contra el Terricidio," Resistencias, March 2, 2020, available online: https://revistaresistencias.wixsite.com/resistencias/post/deliber%C3%B3-en-el-lof-mapuche-pill%C3%A1n-mahuiza-el-campamento-clim%C3%A1tico-pueblos-contra-el-terricidio (accessed June 4, 2022).

Anthropos more radically by proposing a non-secular, non-anthropocentric approach based on a praxis informed by the land, ancestors, and nonhuman entities. While the Anthropocene has made palpable the reality of ecological limits and the scale of the impact of technological capitalism on the earth's natural systems, it seems to us that it lends itself to managerial and techno-scientific solutions to problems that overflow technoscience's ability to solve them. As the heir of modern science, the Anthropocene shelters the idea of a new global reality that all humans, without distinction, should rally around and master. As such, it misses the point that what is at stake is "the possibility of designing *new conditions for being human*"[4]—conditions that recognize the relationality and radical diversity inherent in being human.

With Millán and others, we are making a strong claim here: that modern thought has been and continues to be an active participant in the causation of terricide. The categories of thought matter; the modern worlds constructed based on these categories, despite and because of their substantial achieve-ments, are now working to render all worlds and the planet desolate. The good news, however, is that other civilizational models and thought practices exist or might be imagined, including those of Indigenous peoples. As the Movement of Indigenous Women for Buen Vivir put it: "Each Indigenous people have the theory and practice of a social existence in reciprocity with nature and whose main value is the sustainment of life. [But] we have permitted a system of death that has denatured humanity to be imposed on us."[5] Importantly, in the same statement they proclaim: "Today, the social emergent is Earth herself, and we are spokespersons for her pain."[6]

Anchored in ontological dualism, modern thought is one of the sturdi-est pillars of the dominant form of Euro-modernity. Many authors emphasize three fundamental dualisms in the consolidation of Euro-modernity: the divide between "us" and "them" (or the modern and the nonmodern, the civilized and the savages, etc.), humans and nonhumans, and between subject and object. These three salient dualisms work themselves out into a whole series of other divides, including living (life/organic) and inert (matter/inorganic); reason and emotion; ideas and feelings; the real and its representations; the secular and the sacred; life and death; the individual and the collective; science and non-science (belief, faith, irrationality); facts and values; developed and underdeveloped. These binaries suppress important dimensions of life—for

---

[4] Adam Nocek and Tony Fry, "Design in Crisis: Introducing a Problematic," in *Design in Crisis*, ed. Tony Fry and Adam Nocek, 1–16 (London: Routledge, 2021).

[5] See "Mujeres indígenas ocupan el Ministerio del Interior en Buenos Aires," *El Salto*, October 10, 2019, available online: https://www.elsaltodiario.com/pueblos-originarios/mujeres-indigenas-ocupan-ministerio-interior-argentina (accessed July 15, 2023); "Terricidio | Mujeres indígenas ocupan pacíficamente desde ayer el ministerio de interior," Idep Salud, available online: http://idepsalud.org/terricidio-mujeres-indigenas-ocupan-pacificamente-desde-ayer-el-ministerio-de-interior/ (accessed July 15, 2023); emphasis ours.

[6] As we shall see in Chapter 4, pain and grief are often portals to relationality.

example, emotions, feelings, the spiritual, nonscientific knowledge, body and place, nonhumans, "lesser" humans, nonorganic life, death, and so forth—with dire consequences.

Ontological dualism underlies the idea that we all live as individuals within a single world, to which each society adapts through specific beliefs and practices; this premise of one world and many cultures, each with its own belief systems, is seductive, yet it hides the implicit assumption that only one of those societies, the modern West, can see that this is what is going on because it is the only one that possesses universal science. Sociologist John Law refers to this point of view as the *One-World World*. It is based on the West's ability to arrogate for itself the right to be "the World." The best way to dispel it is ethnographically, as Law suggests:

> In a European or Northern way of thinking the world carries on by itself. People don't *perform* it. It's *outside* us and we are *contained* by it. But that's not true for [Australian] aboriginal people. The idea of a reality out there, detached from the work and the rituals that constantly re-enact it, makes no sense. Land doesn't *belong* to people. Perhaps it would be better to say that *people* belong to the land. Or, perhaps even better still, we might say that processes of continuous creation redo land, people, life, and the spiritual world altogether, and in specific locations.[7]

As he hastens to say, what is involved here is not a matter of beliefs but *a matter of reals*. The treatment of something as belief versus what is real, is itself a characteristic of the modern rationality. One has either representational truths about reality (laws, facts, statistics, calculations) or "beliefs." Yet, by being represented (measured, quantified, calculated), the world loses its resistance to being apprehended through thought. It becomes, as Martin Heidegger put it, a mere "standing reserve" for human use.[8] The representational and calculative rationality and the One-World world are at play in the narratives that we, moderns, tell ourselves about ourselves, and which are repeated over and over by politicians in their speeches, or invariably in the six o'clock news' rendition of what happens in the world, as if they truly represented the fundaments of human life. This "what happens" reenacts the fact that *we see ourselves as self-sufficient subjects confronting an "external world" made up of preexisting, self-standing objects which we can represent objectively and hence control.*

The question then arises: is it possible to free modern thought from the constraints under which it currently thinks, to enable it to think otherwise? To enable it to hear the earth's pain and listen to the wisdom of her spokespeople? Does the answer lie in re-embedding ourselves in the land and seeing ourselves deeply as belonging to the earth and to the stream of life, as many

---

[7] John Law, "What's Wrong with a One-World World?" *Distinktion: Scandinavian Journal of Social Theory* 16, no. 1 (2015): 126–39, emphasis ours.

[8] See the Appendix and Chapter 5.

territorialized peoples have done for thousands of years? Even then, is this pragmatically attainable for us moderns who have spent much of the last five centuries proudly distancing ourselves from land, emotions, mystery—or any form of relationship that might be seen as tainting our "objective," "rational" knowledge? We shall return to these questions; for now, it is important to give a sense of what we mean by modern social theory.

By modern social theory, we understand a particular mode of knowledge that operates based on abstraction and detachment; which takes these epistemological operations as the only valid method to produce universally valid, comprehensive, and reproducible knowledge about an external "reality"; and that, in so doing, disqualifies other ways of knowing, which are seen as partial, subjective, or as mere beliefs. This model, historically borrowed from the physical and natural sciences, is prevalent in the social sciences. It presupposes that the whole of life is cut out into allegedly autonomous spheres—the social, the economic, the political, the biological, the individual, and the cultural—which particular sciences (sociology, economics, political science, biology, psychology, geography, and anthropology) can know with a high degree of complexity and confidence. That these domains have been artificially sundered apart from the flow of life escapes these disciplines' practitioners. While some might argue that divvying up the world in this way is necessary for making sense of otherwise unruly complexities, we suggest that this need to tame complexity analytically, unwittingly creates a vision of reality that is functional to existing processes of exploitation and domination.

Our historicized reading of modern social theory will enable us to make four interrelated claims about its limitations: *first*, abstract thought leaves out the realm of embodiment, practice, and experience, which is essential to understand the relational making of the world. In doing so, it separates the act of knowing the world from action in the world—a deadly combination of passivity (its alleged neutrality) and activity (its palpable effects on the real). *Second*, MST forgets that the question of the human takes different forms for differently located and embodied humans, especially for those subjected to the symbolic and physical violence associated in one way or another with universal Man. Consequently, *third*, MST evinces a certain ignorance of its historical locus of enunciation within the regime of Man, most poignantly brought into view by the question of whose idea of the human are we talking about? *Fourth*, MST forgets that concepts are always limited in being able to fully apprehend the messiness and contradictions of life.

As we will show in detail, each of these factors have marred MST's ability to arrive at a genuinely relational conception of life and politics. This does not mean that it all has been "wrong." In its critical variants, MST often unveiled the complicity of established ideologies in the maintenance of extant systems of domination, whether capitalism, patriarchy, colonialism, white supremacy, or heteronormativity. Moreover, it introduced a self-reflection that enabled the realization that the world is historical, that is, designed by humans. Part of the goal of this chapter is to explore whether these trends have the potential to go farther.

THE AGE OF MAN AND THE MAKING OF THE MODERN ECONOMY

Let us return to the concept of terricide:

> Confronted with terricide, we declare ourselves to be in permanent strug-
> gle, resistance, and re-existence against this system ... We summon all
> peoples to build *a new civilizational matrix* that embraces Buen Vivir
> [good living or collective well-being] as a right. Buen Vivir implies the
> retrieval of harmony and reciprocity among peoples and with the Earth.
> Summoned by the memory of our ancestors and the lands and landscapes
> that inhabit us, we have agreed on the creation of the Movement of Pueblos
> against Terricide.[9]

Like the Mapuche activists, we could call the system that emerged historically
from the dominant narrative of life and that includes the individual and the
bio-mythology of scarcity and competition discussed in the previous chapter, a
civilizational model.[10] We could also call it, going along with common treatment,
a dominant worldview or, to follow Indigenous peoples' usage, a cosmovision
or just a particular mode of existence. More philosophically, we may refer to
it as an onto-epistemic formation. Be that as it may, by civilizational model
we point at the social and cultural totality constructed from the interaction
of modern categories with a whole array of social, economic, technological,
and political institutions and practices. It refers to both this whole and to its
historical trajectory, which means that both must be reassessed. We are thus
talking about a historically specific way of being, thinking, and doing (all three
at once) often associated, in civilizational time, with the Judeo-Christian tradition and, in the contemporary period, with the modern West.

Philosophically, modernity is often referred to as "The Age of Man." We take
our cue for this latter choice from two main sources: first, as already presented
in Chapter 1, Sylvia Wynter's idea that the modern category of Man embodies
one particular way of being human—a secular liberal *monohumanist* genre of
the human—which has progressively extended its ascendancy worldwide at the
expense of other possibilities of being human; and second, French philosopher
Michel Foucault's characterization of the modern episteme as centered on the
figure of Man as the foundation of all possible knowledge and experience.[11] In
this section, we continue to explore the historicity of this figure of Man and why

---

[9] See "Deliberó en el Lof Mapuche Pillán Mahuiza el Campamento Climático Pueblos
contra el Terricidio," emphasis ours.

[10] Aimé Césaire, "Discourse on Colonialism," *New York* Monthly Review (1955): 9. The
appeal to the concept of civilizational crisis is found in many current narratives of transition, and critical statements on Western civilization are found in Western philosophical
and literary archives. We find revealing Césaire's powerful indictment: "A civilization
that proves incapable of solving the problems it creates is a decadent civilization ...
A civilization that uses its principles for trickery and deceit is a dying civilization."

[11] Michel Foucault, *The Order of Things* (New York: Vintage Books, 1970).

it has proven to be so problematic, if not lethal, for humans and the earth, while conveying the sense that other modes of being human are possible, a claim to be substantiated in subsequent chapters from the perspective of the retrieval of relationality as a horizon for the human. We provide added attention to the articulation of narratives of biology and economics in the making of the modern onto-epistemic configuration and the active production of nonrelationality.

Let us return to the first part of Wynter's statement with which we started Chapter 1 ("that which we have made, we can unmake, then, consciously now, remake"). Her rendition of the genealogy of Man is particularly powerful for understanding where "we" have historically been—hence, what "we" have made—and why this has landed "us" in the current civilization malaise. This genealogy consists of a two-step process. The first was the Copernican Revolution of the sixteenth century, which decentered the Christian God, giving rise to a view of the human as a being defined by his capacity to understand the universe through reason. Wynter calls this "rational Man," Man1-*homo politicus*, the subject of the budding civic humanism of the Renaissance.

By the end of the eighteenth century, Man1 had developed into a fully biocentric and economized view that Wynter calls Man2, or "bioeconomic Man." This process was grounded on a particular rendering of biological evolution in terms of natural selection, Malthus's theory of resource scarcity, and the economized view of the human ushered in by the nascent science of political economy. Such Man is still our onto-epistemic existential domain. Its roots can be traced to the scientific revolutions of the sixteenth and seventeenth centuries, the birth of political economy toward the end of eighteenth, and the Darwinian revolution of the nineteenth century.[12]

Locating the question of the human within the birth of *homo economicus* underscores the synergistic effect of biological and economic narratives. In his landmark work, *The Great Transformation*, Polanyi described this civilizational change in terms of two key onto-epistemic processes: first, the disembedding of the economy from the rest of life, followed by, second, the postulate that such a domain is governed by a particular form of market—what he described as "the myth of the self-regulating market." Here we have two important moments in the production of nonrelationality: (1) the idea, already mentioned, that the real (the always changing flow of forms, relations, forces, and so forth) is *actually* divided into intrinsically existing domains, the economy being one of them, and (2) the premise that the so-called free market is regulated only by its own internal forces. Ever since, as Polanyi proposed, society became an appendage of the market. His conclusion is still worth quoting at length:

> All types of societies are limited by economic factors. Nineteenth century civilization alone was economic in a different and distinctive sense, for it chose to base itself in a motive rarely acknowledged as valid in the history of

---

[12] Wynter and McKittrick, "Unparalleled Catastrophe," 9–89.

human societies, and certainly never before raised to the level of justification of action and behavior in everyday life, namely, gain. The self-regulating market principle was uniquely derived from this principle. The mechanism which the motive of gain set in motion was comparable in effectiveness only to the most violent outburst of religious fervor in history. Within the generation the whole human world was subjected to its undiluted influence.[13]

What made this view of the economy possible was a perceived situation of perpetual scarcity, which became enshrined in the economic theory that came into being with Adam Smith, David Ricardo, and Thomas Malthus. Previously, land was seen as producing abundantly. Yet Ricardo posited the limitation of the land to produce, which he conceptualized in terms of "diminishing returns," believing that humankind would never be able to escape this limitation. The phantom of population growth loomed large (Malthus was a contemporary of Ricardo). *Homo oeconomicus* thus became the being who wears himself out while struggling against scarcity, trying to avert death. Biology and economics were central to creating these pervasive assumptions of scarcity and finitude, resulting in the conviction that the way forward rested on unleashing nature's forces through machines, divisions of labor, and increasing amounts of energy. Over the past two hundred years, these developments fostered the extraction of natural resources and the expansion of fossil energy, with almost complete oblivion to the consequences until recently.

Foucault described this rupture in terms of "a new arrangement of knowledge" that newly articulated biology, economics, and history, which he called the modern episteme, and which in his view constituted "one of the major networks of nineteenth century thought."[14] It bears repeating that this episteme was linked to an entire circulation of methods, procedures, models, practical arrangements, inventions, tools, and sensibilities often encompassed under the rubrics of capitalism, disciplinary society, or biopolitics. Wynter demonstrates how such narratives of biology and economics became naturalized by appealing to Franz Fanon. In Fanon's notable conception of sociogenesis,[15] Wynter finds a genre of the human markedly different from the cosmogony of secular liberal Man. Sociogenetically, for Fanon, a Black person living in a Eurocentric context is obliged to experience himself or herself as both normally and abnormally human, being and nonbeing, as the "dysselected" par excellence (those persons racialized as naturally inferior). As already discussed in Chapter 1, this led Wynter to emphasize that the human is not only biology but is also shaped by self-maintaining (autopoietically instituted) cultural codes, origin narratives, and storytelling.

---

[13] Karl Polanyi, *The Great Transformation* (Boston, MA: Beacon Press, 1944), 30.

[14] Foucault, *The Order of Things*, 261–62.

[15] Frantz Fanon, "Beside Phylogeny and Ontogeny Stands Sociogeny," in *Black Skin, White Masks* (1952; London: Pluto Press, 2008), 4. This is a way of highlighting the dialectic of Black skins/white masks confronting all Black people.

The fact that the human is *homo narrans* has momentous epistemic and civilizational implications. As Wynter daringly surmises, "With this hypothesis, should it prove to be true, our system of knowledge as we have it *now*, goes."[16] This is a most audacious claim (akin to "necesitamos una revolución del pensamiento"), one to which she arrives by revisiting the human from the perspective of the colonized and the "dysselected." What it means is that our entire order of secular truth is shaken if we forgo the premise that humans are not just biological, for if humans are conceptualized as hybrid beings, you can no longer classify some individuals and groups as naturally selected and others as *naturally* "dysselected."

The huge relevance of Wynter's point can be drawn out further by appealing to what in contemporary Latin American critical theory is called coloniality. The central feature of coloniality is the hierarchical classification of differences and the subsequent use of such classifications for purposes of exploitation and domination. From the Conquest of America until today, coloniality has been a constitutive feature of modernity. In the nineteenth century, coloniality functioned in terms of "the confluence of racism as a structure of power and knowledge, capitalist social relations, the Darwinian notion of evolution and the articulation of its discourse of the survival of the fittest with capitalist notions of competition."[17] While today most of us think that we are beyond such "biological" classifications, coloniality continues to structure our thought and practices. As Chapter 1 showed, it is not easy to have an adequate awareness of our historical condition ("what we have made") given that genres of the human are "cosmogonically chartered"[18] and powerfully implanted as a "second set of instructions"[19] in collective culture by narratives. This ontological determination should make clear the need to move beyond the mimetic desire to join the club of those inhabiting the bioeconomic world.

Through her analysis, Wynter opens a path for a significant "*refiguring* of humanness."[20] As she concludes, "unless we move out of the liberal monohumanist mindset, *it's very difficult to see where we've been*," and, hence, "*where we're going*."[21] As South African anthropologist Zimitri Erasmus concludes in her exposition of Wynter's thought, in the last instance we should arrive at the realization that such refiguring needs to start by acknowledging that "living beings bring forth their worlds by what they do. Life is universal. Its modes are

[16] Wynter and McKittrick, "Unparalleled Catastrophe," 16, emphasis in original.

[17] Zimitri Erasmus, "Sylvia Wynter's Theory of the Human: Counter-, not Post-humanist," *Theory, Culture & Society* (2020): 47-65, 51.

[18] Erasmus, "Sylvia Wynter's Theory of the Human," 30.

[19] Erasmus, "Sylvia Wynter's Theory of the Human," 33.

[20] Denise Ferreira da Silva, "Before *Man*: Sylvia Wynter's Rewriting of the Modern Episteme," in Sylvia Wynter, *On Being Human as Praxis*, ed. Katherine McKittrick (Durham, NC: Duke University Press, 2015), 93, emphasis in original.

[21] Wynter and McKittrick, "Unparalleled Catastrophe," 14, emphasis ours.

pluriversal."[22] What these authors make clear is that today, more than ever, the very status of the human is at stake.

The philosophical and political implications of Wynter's intervention are enormous, since they articulate the need, never felt more acutely than at present, to search for figures of the human different from bioeconomic Man, beyond Western humanism. Wynter makes a shift from a representational and classificatory model of fixed being to a model of multiple emergent modes of being where what matters is *the manner of their becoming*. As she puts it, the larger problem is "the incorporation of all forms of human being into a single homogenized descriptive statement that is based on the figure of the West's liberal monohumanist *Man*."[23] The response to this quandary must come in the form of the creation of new horizons of humanity that enables an ecumenically open view of the human. To restate the case, this involves the unmaking, and now, consciously, remaking, of the main narratives that characterize this monohumanism, including science, politics, and economics—or, with Fanon, rethinking what "phylogeny, ontogeny *and* sociogeny" mean for the human at present.

Nigerian cultural theorist, futurist, and public intellectual Bayo Akomolafe offers a poignant way of summing up this section, recounting the implications of moving beyond the prevailing version of Man and the climate crisis:

> This [modern] assemblage of concepts, ideas, practices, ideologies, gestures, bodies and meanings is the earth-curdling, world-worlding machine that offers solutions to the climate crisis … *As if the word "human" is a self-evident category that is not already simmering with tensions, elisions, disputations, and troubling departures.* It constructs action as a matter of future orientation, failing to notice its past legacies of extermination and the ghastly bodies of those that have subsidized the project of modernity. And then, to render the matter of climate collapse and ecological destruction intelligible to contemporary sense-making apparatuses, it seeks to squeeze the "Anthropocene" into an operational framework of achievable goals, prompts and objectives: turn off your light bulbs, go vegan, fly less, fund a local NGO, protest capitalism, pass the Green New Deal. Not that these actions do not matter. They probably matter a great deal. However, we can think in two registers at once: we can notice that these gestures are crucial, and we can notice at the same time that on a planetary scale the very notion of "Man" (that is, not just the isolated figure of Man but the entangling conditions that make Man possible) is being called into question by "something" greater than ourselves. Something incalculable and unnameable. Something that exceeds frameworks [and] resists solutions.[24]

---

[22] Erasmus, "Sylvia Wynter's Theory," 62, emphasis in original.

[23] Wynter and McKittrick, "Unparalleled Catastrophe," 23, emphasis in original.

[24] Bayo Akomolafe, "Coming Down to Earth: Sanctuary as Spiritual Companionship in a Time of Hopelessness and Climate Chaos," March 11, 2020, available online: https://www.bayoakomolafe.net/post/coming-down-to-earth (accessed October 26, 2021), emphasis in original.

That something that exceeds all frameworks and resists solutions is none other than Earth and life themselves, in all their relational mystery and complexity. Its containment within the neat categories of the Western episteme has proven lethal. Let us see now how these categories have affected established views of life, nature, and the nonhuman realms, which is another key dimension of the contemporary civilizational crisis.

WHAT IS LIFE? THE "CARTESIAN LICENSE" AND THE ONTOLOGICAL DIMENSION OF PATRIARCHY[25]

The tight relation between the ontology of bioeconomic Man and modern thought has had profound implications for how life and nature have been understood, eventually conditioning the planetary scale of environmental destruction. Science and patriarchy have been inextricably implicated in this entanglement. The objectifying rationality of the regime of Man led science to investigate reality by positing a separation between observer and observed, mind and matter, life from nonlife, and facts from values. Such seemingly benign assumption promoted the objectification of nature, the becoming-disposable of the earth.[26] It also reinforced the primacy of things over relations, exacerbated with the development of patriarchal colonial capitalism.

Life in a mechanistic universe

Lynn Margulis may serve as a guide to understand this relation from the vantage point of life. Margulis was a biologist with a philosophical imagination, who resisted reducing life to any single principle of determination, whether genes, photosynthesis, cell division, or reproduction. Along with British scientist James Lovelock, Margulis is best known as the originator of a radically novel view of planetary life that often goes under the name of the Gaia hypothesis or theory. This theory posits a view of the planet as a physiologically regulated entity that is alive and conscious (which is not the same as saying that the planet is a single organism, an idea she sought to dispel):

> The sum of planetary life, Gaia, displays a physiology that we recognize as environmental regulation. Gaia itself is not an organism directly selected among many. It is an emergent property of interaction among organisms, the spherical planet on which they reside, and an energy source, the sun … Gaia, as the interweaving network of all life, is alive, aware, and conscious to various degrees in all its cells, bodies, and societies.[27]

---

[25] For this section, we borrow the title of Lynn Margulis and Dorion Sagan's fascinating book, *What Is Life?* (New York: Simon & Schuster, 1995).

[26] What Heidegger named the ontology of enframing (see the Appendix).

[27] Lynn Margulis, *Symbiotic Planet: A New Look at Evolution*, 1st edn., Science Masters (New York: Basic Books, 1998), 119 and 126.

In Margulis's work one finds an extraordinary relational imagination at work. Life is relation, flow, impermanence, contamination, and endless transformation—in short, pluriverse. Life's history shows an unmistakable tendency to bind together and reemerge in a new wholeness at a higher, larger level of organization. Humans need to respect this fundamental dynamic of integration with life, for as she writes: "the near future of Homo Sapiens as a species requires our reorientation toward the fusion and mergers of the planetmates that have preceded us in the microcosm … We people are just like our planetmates. We cannot put an end to nature; we can only pose a threat to ourselves."[28]

Margulis and Sagan do not mince words when referring to the rationalistic tradition ushered in with Wynter's Man1 and consolidated with Man2. For them, the "Cartesian license" to practice science on an allegedly unfeeling nature, with the body and the world seen as entirely mechanical (as in Leonardo da Vinci's famous depiction of Vitruvian Man), proved to be "a kind of forgery"; by imagining a dead cosmos of inanimate matter obeying mechanical rules, it separated mind and matter, body and soul, and life from nonlife.[29] No wonder that some of their heroes, such as Benedictus de Spinoza, Johann Wolfgang von Goethe, and the early twentieth-century Russian biologist Vladimir Vernadsky, were among those who described the universe as alive and life itself as living matter, a completely different story from that of Cartesian science. In this dissenting view, more than anything what characterizes life is autopoiesis, or life's continuous production of itself with the help of energy and metabolism. As they put it, "the biosphere as a whole is autopoietic in the sense that it maintains itself … Earth, in a very real sense, is alive … each breath connects us to the rest of the biosphere, which also 'breathes,' albeit at a slower pace."[30]

Complexity theorist Stuart Kauffman, in a book tellingly titled *Reinventing the Sacred*, similarly spoke of scientific rationalism as "the Galilean spell," stating that:

> our current scientific worldview, derived from Galileo, Newton, and their followers, is the foundation of modern secular society, itself the child of the Enlightenment. At base, our contemporary perspective is reductionist: all phenomena are ultimately to be explained in terms of the interactions of fundamental particles.[31]

Reductionism means that many aspects that are crucial to life and to the making of social reality—from the body, emotions, feeling, and intuition to the sacred—have been left out of the account. The consequences of this dualist effect have been enormous, in terms of the ecological devastation foisted upon the earth.

---

[28] Margulis, *Symbiotic Planet*, 128.

[29] Dorion Sagan, Lynn Margulis, and Ricardo Guerrero, "Descartes, Dualism, and Beyond," in *Slanted Truths: Essays on Gaia, Symbiosis, and Evolution*, ed. L. Margulis and D. Sagan, 172–83 (New York: Springer, 1997).

[30] Margulis and Sagan, *What Is Life?* 26.

[31] Stuart Kauffman, *Reinventing the Sacred* (New York: Basic Books, 2008), ix.

Let us think about the following: If we really saw ourselves as part of the earth, would we dump so many toxics in the air, water, soil, and seas? Would we injure the soils with so many chemical substances allegedly to grow more food and faster, not realizing that the same chemicals will come back to hurt us in the very foods we eat? Would we drive so many of the earth's creatures to extinction, knowing that in doing so we are imperiling our own futures? Would we build cities that are veritable islands of concrete from which natural habitats have been banished or unbelievably constrained? Would we scour, and scar, the earth in search of minerals so we can live half-absorbed in front of our digital screens? No, we would not. Why do we keep on doing it, then? The answer, at one level, is deceptively simple: precisely because we do not perceive our relationality: we see ourselves as separate from Earth, from rivers, from clouds, from soil, from birds and animals and plants and microorganisms, from mountains and spirits and the sea. Our perspective as autonomous selves desensitizes us to the fact that what we do to Earth we do to ourselves.

Evincing a design imagination, Margulis and Sagan state that "Life has been reusing hard materials and shaping solid wastes long before the appearance of technological humans … the propensity to 'engineer' environments is ancient."[32] As the transmutation of sunlight, life is "moving, thinking matter, the power of expanding populations."[33] Autopoiesis and survival imply that all living beings, including plants and microorganisms, perceive; this perception was already present in the earliest bacteria. Hence their dictum that "to better understand life we need to see the long and winding road from animism, through dualism, to the limitations of mechanism."[34] Margulis and Sagan's daring remarks on consciousness as a central dimension of life placed them on a collision course with established biological paradigms. For them, thought was the product of the very dynamic of matter and energy; "spirit and mind," they claim, "are no celestial sparklings but sovereign to living matter. Thought derives … from the activity of cells."[35]

Life, thought, and the ontology of patriarchy

It is not a coincidence that many feminists refer to patriarchy as the hatred of life, for many of the features of modern rationality started their civilizational journey into their contemporary forms with the development of patriarchy. In fact, patriarchy is the most enduring political technology of separation and one of the main sources of the active production of nonrelationality; it undercuts attempts to live lives attuned to the interdependence of existence. As Latin

[32] Margulis and Sagan, *What Is Life?*, 27.

[33] Margulis and Sagan, *What is Life?*, 214.

[34] Margulis and Sagan, *What is Life?*, 54.

[35] Margulis and Sagan, *What is Life?*, 218.

American autonomous, decolonial, and communitarian feminists contend, it was on the bodies of women that humanity learned how to dominate, and this does not refer only to the West. Originating between five thousand and six thousand years ago according to some researchers, patriarchy can be understood as an ontology that privileges hierarchy, power, the appropriation of resources, the domination of others, procreation, competition, growth, and ultimately, violence and war. It is linked to ways of knowing that curtail embodiment, mystery, magic, and connection to nature.

With the advent of modernity, patriarchy became inextricably entangled with science, technology, capitalism, racism, and colonialism. Progressively, women-centered modes of living were undermined in the attempt to usurp women's power to create life through what Claudia von Werlhof fittingly calls "patriarchal alchemy." While in its original connotation alchemy referred to a mode of knowing based on the observation of the natural rhythm of life, for the patriarchs it became a practice of destruction by fragmenting the elements of matter to eventually produce, out of the isolated elements, what was considered most valuable, such as gold. Destruction gradually became common practice, paradoxically in the name of creating life, with monotheistic religions as a main component of this civilizational project.[36] From this perspective, capitalism is the latest phase of this alchemic civilization hinged on creation through destruction. Such patriarchy has become seemingly global, always at war against life, licensing the endless creation of commodities, objects, and experiences. It is no surprise that the battle over women's bodies and reproduction is so heated in this moment of transition given this background.

Humberto Maturana and German psychologist Gerda Verden-Zöller have developed an ontological interpretation of the history of patriarchy. This interpretation led them to establish a comparison between "European patriarchal culture" and "matristic cultures." "In a patriarchal culture," these authors argue:

> both women and men are patriarchal, and in a matristic culture, both men and women are matristic. Matristic and patriarchal cultures are *different manners of living*, different forms of relating and manners of emoting, different closed networks of conversation that are realized in each case by both men and women.[37]

This distinction arises from an original perspective they call "the biology of love," an interpretation of the evolution of the species that posits that the basis of biological existence and social coexistence are love and cooperation, not aggression and competition. Far from a moral value, love is defined by these

---

[36] See Claudia von Werlhof, *The Failure of Modern Civilization and the Struggle for a 'Deep' Alternative* (Frankfurt: Peter Lang, 2011); *Madre tierra o Muerte! Reflexiones para una teoría crítica del patriarcado*, Ocotepec (Mexico: El Rebozo, 2015).

[37] Humberto Maturana and Gerda Verden-Zöller, *The Origin of Humanness in the Biology of Love* (Charlottesville, VA: Imprint Academic, 2008), 112, emphasis ours.

authors as "the domain of those relational behaviors through which the other arises as a legitimate other in coexistence with oneself."[38] With the rise of pastoral societies, the transition from matristic to patriarchal culture started and has not ceased ever since. Matristic cultures were characterized by conversations highlighting inclusion, participation, collaboration, understanding, respect, sacredness, and the cyclic renovation of life.[39] Matristic modes of being and thinking persist in contemporary societies, for instance and however partially and contradictorily, in parent-child relations, in love relations, and in some aspects of science and democracy. This perspective offers a different basis for rationality, one that considers emotions and intimacy as enabling, rather than obscuring, reason. "Love is visionary, not blind, because it liberates intelligence and expands coexistence in cooperation as it expands the domain in which our nervous system operates."[40] As we shall see in Chapter 4, love is a portal or pathway to relationality.

For these authors, the change in human emoting from interconnectedness to appropriation and control (in rejection of the biology of love) emerged with patriarchy as a crucial cultural development. The ethical and political implications are clear:

> Hence, if we want to act differently, if we want to live in a different world, we need to transform our desires and for this we need to change our conversations. … This is only possible by recovering matristic living … The matristic manner of living … allows us to see and to live within the interaction and co-participation of everything that is alive in the living of all the living; patriarchal living [on the contrary] restricts our understanding of life and nature because it leads us to the search for a unidirectional manipulation of everything, given the desire to control life.[41]

Anthropologist Rita Segato has drawn into relief one of the most defining consequences of this long history: the ascendancy of the "historical project of things" over "the historical project of relations." This feature has not only been at the basis of many forms of violence against women, against people of color, and against nature, it has been crucial to cultivating the epistemic culture of rationality that banishes emotions, intimacy, magic, mystery, and love—among many other things traditionally associated with the feminine. Rooted in the long patriarchal history, Segato finds this dualist rationality to be central to gender

---

[38] Maturana and Verden-Zöller, *The Origin of Humanness*, 223.

[39] Graeber and Wengrow, *The Dawn of Everything*. They document the multiple paths of human history (obscured by received linear narratives), including the likelihood of nonhierarchical cultures, reappraising the progressive shift, in Europe, from matriarchal to patriarchal cultures in the Neolithic period.

[40] Maturana and Verden-Zöller, *The Origin of Humanness*, 138.

[41] Humberto Maturana and Verden-Zöller, *Amor y juego: Fundamentos olvidados de lo humano* (Santiago de Chile: J.C. Sáez, 1993), 105, translation ours.

and sexual domination. "It is against these foundational binarisms of the modern West that we need to orient our insurgency,"[42] she concludes, which leads her to emphasize the communal and the relational under the rubric of the historical project of *vincularidad*, or relationality.

We will explore further the implications of Segato's relational and communal feminist politics for designing in Chapter 5. It bears emphasizing that the significance of this analysis of patriarchy as the long background of the contemporary crisis lies in the fact that these authors see patriarchy as an active historical reality, not a thing of the past. Succinctly stated, overcoming patriarchy requires the realization that a civilization based on the love of life is a far better option than one based on its destruction. To achieve this, we need to make room in thought for, among other things, love and the sacredness and interconnectedness of all life. Let us return to thought first before discussing the role of the secular and the sacred in the story of life in the last section of the chapter.

THE PRISON HOUSE OF REASON: FURTHER COMMENTS ON RATIONALITY, ONTOLOGICAL DUALISM, AND MONOTECHNOLOGISM

A main contention of this book is that dualist rationality is at the root of the planetary crisis, since it denies the aliveness and consciousness of much of life. Environmental philosophers Val Plumwood, Enrique Leff, and Patricia Noguera have lucidly drawn out this connection. For Plumwood, we are undergoing a crisis "of what the dominant culture has made of reason."[43] This form of rationality, that claims mastery over nature, relies on multiple "centrisms" (it is anthropocentric, self-centric, Eurocentric, and androcentric) and has produced, in the age of global markets, "ratiogenic monsters." Willfully ignoring our ecological embededness, reason-centered culture supports elite forms of power, strengthens the illusion of the autonomous individual, and worships a masculinist economic rationalism that makes invisible the agency of nonhumans and of subordinated groups. Rationalist culture, Plumwood argues, "has distorted many spheres of human life; its remaking is a major but essential cultural enterprise." Hence her forthright conclusion: "In an era when we are reaching the biophysical limits of the planet, this reason-centred culture *has become a liability to survival* ... We must change this culture or face extinction."[44]

[42] Rita Laura Segato, *Contra-pedagogías de la crueldad* (Buenos Aires: Prometeo Libros, 2021) 73.

[43] Val Plumwood, *Environmental Culture: The Ecological Crisis of Reason* (New York: Routledge, 2002), 5; Enrique Leff, *La apuesta por la vida* (Mexico City: Siglo XXI Editores, 2014); *Saber Ambiental* (México City: Siglo XXI Editores, 2002); Ana Patricia Noguera de Echeverry, *El reencantamiento del mundo* (Mexico City: PNUMA, 2004); *Voces del Pensamiento Ambiental* (Manizales: Universidad Nacional, 2016).

[44] Plumwood, *Environmental Culture*, 4-5, emphasis ours.

Modernity has been an incredibly dynamic and enormous construction site of categories, ideas, and theories, seemingly characterized by unbridled freedom and openness. However, it has simultaneously been endowed with remarkably effective mechanisms of closure, with the consequence that the resulting "house of reason," besides its amazing productivity, has also imprisoned thought. While there are many acerbic indictments of the excesses of modern reason in the Western critical archive, here we have chosen one by Rastafarian dub poet and Reggae singer Mutabaruka, who opened his 1984 album, *Outcry*, with the following short but impactful poem that metaphorically speaks of this effect:

> You asked me if I have ever been to prison. Being to prison? Your world of murderers and thieves, of hatred and jealousy, of death. And you ask me if I have ever been to prison? And I answer: Yes, I am still there, trying to escape.[45]

The poet's puzzlement could be interpreted in terms of physical and social confinement, yet it seems to us that his concern lies with a more profound imprisonment, that of having to live within those modes of being, knowing, and doing that so many people in the world have come to associate with "being modern," whether in the classical European or North American sense, or according to the discourses of "development" in the Global South. This subordination to the imperatives of monohumanism is what Mutabaruka is inviting us to see. "Trying to escape"—resist, survive, re-exist, even dare to thrive—describes the experience of many of the marginalized, subalternized, and otherwise marked peoples all over the world—indeed, even of many of the alleged beneficiaries of the system.

Is modern thought, in whatever guise, capacious enough to help us escape from the great edifice it has built for itself, and which provides the sturdy conceptual architecture of contemporary global designs? Or are we rather confronted with the possibility that the contemporary polycrisis puts in evidence once and for all of the insufficiency, when not lethality, of modern thought to deal with mutually reinforcing and potentially cascading crises? This much is clear: we can no longer solve modern problems solely or perhaps even primarily with the same concepts and categories that created them. Concepts such as growth, competition, progress, rationality, economy, even science and critique that we often take to be neutral, are in fact part of the old *pensamiento*.

The modern theoretical tradition has been inimical to relationality. This tradition is variously referred to as "rationalistic," "Cartesian," "objectivist," and often associated with terms such as "mechanistic" (worldview), "reductionistic" (science), representationalist and "positivistic" (epistemologically), and more recently, computationalist. For Francisco Varela, Chilean biologist and philosopher, the term that best captures the tradition is "abstract," by which he means "this tendency to find our way toward the rarified atmosphere of the general and

---

[45] Mutabaruka, "Prisoner," track 1 on *Outcry*, Shanache Records, 1984.

the formal, the logical and the well-defined, the represented and the foreseen, which characterizes our Western world."[46] It entails the belief in logical truth as the only valid ground for knowledge about an objective world made up of things that can be known, and hence ordered and manipulated at will.

The notion of representation has been pivotal for modern thought. We find a clear example of its shortcomings in the standard conceptualization of cognition as the building of representations by a discrete "mind" of a preexisting, separate "world" through the manipulation of symbols. For Varela and co-workers this is fundamentally mistaken, for by positing the notion of cognition as the representation of an external reality, we are cut off from the background of life in which we are ineluctably immersed as living beings. This epistemology, which operates through the separation of the observer from the observed as the principle of objectivity, resulted in the domination of representation as the foundation of rationality (see the Appendix and Chapter 5). Paradoxically, there is an emotional side to all forms of rationality, for "it is our emotions that determine the rational domain in which we operate as rational beings at any instant."[47] Our emotions guide our living even when we claim that we are being rational. By sidestepping emotions, we miss a great deal of our cultural existence.

We can see the implications of this epistemology and its imbrications with capitalist patriarchy clearly at work in contemporary technology. The tight connection between cutting-edge science, technology, and capitalism is evident in fields such as genomics, synthetic biology, pharmaceuticals, artificial intelligence (AI), biocomputing, nanotechnology, neuro-engineering, robotics, geoengineering, cognitive enhancement, space travel, and so forth. These technologies induce an ever-growing remoteness from life, aptly embodied in the famous dream of the proponents of the technological singularity, that of "a world beyond biology."[48] This scenario of the overcoming of the organic fabric of life dreamed up by the technopatriarchs of the moment necessitates the ongoing legitimation of the epistemology and ontology of separation and deepens the disposability of the earth; even the body might eventually become disposable. We are increasingly enmeshed in gigantic technological systems with a tendency to totalize modes of living. In Ivan Illich's terms, we have significantly overshot the threshold beyond which any given technology becomes disabling, rather than enabling, of human potentiality.[49]

[46] Francisco Varela, *Ethical Know-How: Action, Wisdom and Cognition* (Stanford, CA: Stanford University Press, 1999), 6.

[47] Humberto Maturana, "Metadesign: Human beings versus machines, or machines as instruments of human designs?," Instituto de Terapia Cognitiva, Santiago, 1997, 5, available online: https://pangaro.com/hciiseminar2019/Maturana_Metadesign.pdf (accessed July 15, 2023).

[48] See Ray Kurzweil's homepage, http://www.singularity.com/ (accessed July 19, 2023), and book, *The Singularity is Near: When Humans Transcend Biology* (New York: Viking Books, 2015).

[49] Ivan Illich, *Tools for Conviviality* (London: Calder & Boyars, 1973).

There is hardly any cultural trend more significant at present than the pervasive digitalization of life. The Korean-German cultural studies scholar Byung-Chul Han has analyzed in depth the impact of the expansion of the digital order on daily life from a post-Heideggerian perspective, focusing on the erosion of the vitality of things as sources of meaningful experience. "Smart" devices are central to this state of affairs. By turning human existence into information, the infosphere ends the era of fact-based truth and contributes to undermining presence, empathy, place, and community. In the age of social media, a generalized narcissism settles in, causing not only things but the other to disappear.[50] While Han's critique must be tempered by considering the manifold creative and subversive uses of digital technologies by young activists and artists, the profound designing and onto-corporeal effects of such technologies are undeniable. In this context, Yuk Hui's advocacy for technological practices that do not stifle what is nonrational, incalculable, and ineffable—practices that resist the recursive rationalization of the unknown—takes on added significance. For Hui, this is where the role of art becomes crucial.[51]

In a similar vein, recent critiques of AI start with the awareness that the world is progressively being reduced to recursive calculation by ubiquitous cybernetic machines fueled by a proliferating algorithmic rationality functional to global capitalism. A monohumanist technosociality is increasingly being deployed in nearly all spheres of social life (from finance and health to shopping, media, surveillance, cities, and politics) by the explosion of machine learning, algorithm logics, and "big data." This vital philosophical and political question remains underexamined, given the unquestioned role of statistics and probability underwriting such algorithms.[52] Said succinctly, today it is chiefly through machine learning and algorithmic rationality that the worldview and desires of the powerful are imperialized and perpetuated. A global cybereconomy has emerged largely run by "algorithms of oppression" with their structuring patriarchal and racist commitments; they operate as veritable forms of technological redlining, as internet scholar Safiya Umoja Noble has demonstrated.[53]

Clive Dilnot characterizes today's unprecedented juncture as the coming of age of the artificial as a horizon for being, bringing to the fore the stakes in a possible ontological reorientation of technology. How is the arrival of the epoch

---

[50] Byung-Chul Han, *No-cosas: Quiebras del mundo de hoy* (Madrid: Taurus, 2021), 57. For a creative statement of alternatives to the digital monocultures of the present, see the wonderful project by the Verses collective, "Towards a Digital Pluriverse": https://pluriverse.world (accessed July 19, 2023).

[51] Hui, *Art and Cosmotechnics*.

[52] For a critique of algorithmic rationality and the mathematics behind it, see Justin Joque, *Revolutionary Mathematics: Artificial Intelligence, Statistics and the Logic of Capitalism* (London: Verso, 2022).

[53] See Safiya Umoja Noble, *Algorithms of Oppression: How Search Engines Reinforce Racism* (New York: New York University Press, 2018). Our thanks to Orin Starn for bringing this work to our attention.

of the artificial-as-totality to be thought and acted upon? Let us begin by stating that for Dilnot artifice and prefiguration—the condition of being made of the human—have been central to human existence from the get-go; however, they have undergone a profound shift in the period of the Great Acceleration, roughly after the Second World War.[54] In becoming unbounded, technology ushered in a regime of worldmaking that inescapably replaces nature as horizon. This is what he means by the artificial. The artificial thus "unarguably constitutes for us the underlying condition of existence of our time. It is an unsurpassable condition because *there can be no relation to natural conditions of existence which do not pass through it* ... The artificial replaces nature as the horizon and medium of our world."[55] Heidegger's statement about object-centeredness in modern life ("beings became objects that could be controlled and seen through by calcula-tion"[56]) seems fulfilled. But is it? If the crisis has become permanent and total, it means that in this very condition there lies the possibility for a reorientation, "at once a gathering of modernity and the stepping beyond it,"[57] but only if we do not assume continuity with modernity but interrupt its trajectory; if things have been made, they can be made otherwise.

In other words, are there any affirmative openings within the artificial? As Dilnot suggests, "the rupture of the artificial ... is the rupture *with* the modern in that it objectively institutes another circulation of thinking and acting. This ending of the modern is the institution of another historical epoch."[58] This ending may create an opening for a kind of thought that recog-nizes autonomous making as central to many cultures and as a recoverable practice. This in turn requires reestablishing "biological interdependence and the contingency of existence as the prime underlying condition of all being."[59] Lest one wish to hear in this statement an anachronistic advocacy for a return to nature, what he has in mind is an onto-epistemic and political project focused on the active (re)making of interdependence without deny-ing the artificial. As the next chapter will show we must be careful not to slip back into new dualisms positing artificiality as opposed to relationality. If artificiality is indeed an inevitable passage point, it must not deny Earth and humans' constitutive relationality.

Returning technology to being part of life is a clearer imperative today than ever before. Designing must confront the alluring futures propagated by

---

[54] J.R. McNeill and Peter Engelke, *The Great Acceleration: An Environmental History of the Anthropocene since 1945* (Cambridge, MA: Harvard University Press, 2016).

[55] Clive Dilnot, "Designing in the World of the Naturalized Artificial," in *Design in Crisis: New Worlds, Philosophies and Practices*, ed. Tony Fry and Adam Nocek, 93–112 (London: Routledge, 2020), 103, emphasis ours.

[56] Martin Heidegger, *Poetry, Language, Thought*, trans. Albert Hofstadter (New York: Harper, 1971), 74.

[57] Dilnot, "Designing in the World," 95.

[58] Dilnot, "Designing in the World," 103, emphasis in original.

[59] Dilnot, "Designing in the World," 107.

the patriarchal and capitalistic technological imaginations of the day, and the powerful desires they instill in people, through appropriate pedagogies for pluriversalizing technology. This could be one of the most difficult tasks confronting the remaking of worldmaking, for the entire panoply of biological, material, and digital technologies is at the service of the technopatriarchal imaginary. While these developments are driving an intensification of capitalist extraction of resources and energy use, they also expose the onto-epistemic background of monotechnologism.[60]

Humans and the planet seem increasingly entrapped in the simultaneously incredibly productive and destructive house of object-centered technological reason. Yet from within this very same house, albeit in tandem with extra-academic movements, there are stirrings of an important renewal of thought on a relational key. In what follows, we provide our own reading of its reach and limitations.

PUSHING AT THE BOUNDARIES OF THE ENLIGHTENMENT EPISTEME

It should be clear by now that the great edifice of modern social theory has been built upon the foundations of an Enlightenment episteme indebted to patriarchal monohumanism, rationalism, monotechnologism, and ontological dualism. While critical social theory has made inroads into a post-Enlightenment episteme, it has also faced significant limitations in doing so. Our interest is not to invalidate these attempts, some of which have been fundamental to us, authors, in our journey to understand relationality, or perhaps more aptly to think relationally. Ever since the time of Heraclitus, philosophers and other theorists have carried the mantle of life's defense with varying degrees of influence on thought itself and, less so perhaps, on actual worldmaking practices. To move toward the latter is what is now required. More than ever, life's defense must become practical. Theoretical critique is no longer sufficient, as Enrique Leff argues in one of the most comprehensive treatments of the incompleteness and insufficiency of Western thought in dealing with the ecological crisis as a crisis of reason.[61]

Many of the great social movements of the nineteenth and twentieth centuries led to important transformations of MST (e.g., Marxist, feminist, anti-racist, and anti-colonial movements). Yet rationalist approaches have prevailed, and the modern academy, taken as a whole, has been pivotal to the maintenance of the One-World world with its will to order. Indeed, one may contend that the academy has been a major force in the ontological occupation of people's

---

[60] The three of us develop further the notion of pluriversalizing technology in "Pluriversal Horizons: Notes for an Onto-epistemic Reorientation of Technology," in *Incomputable Earth: Digital Technologies and the Anthropocene*, ed. Ántonia Majaca (London: Bloomsbury, forthcoming).

[61] E. Leff, *El fuego de la vida* (Mexico City: Siglo XXI Editores, 2019). English edition forthcoming from Routledge.

experiences and knowledges and of the human/nonhuman tapestries that are people's life territories. Examining why these theories remained within the epistemic confines of MST has valuable lessons for understanding our enduring challenges in making our way to a relational story of life.

It could be argued that modern philosophy and social theory since Kant have been concerned with what we are calling relationality.[62] Of the three great paradigms of MST—liberalism, Marxism, and post-structuralism—the latter two have greatly contributed to a relational conception of social life. Marxism involves a robust theory of relationality, yet historical materialism faced limitations because it takes place within an anthropocentric episteme that upholds notions of universality, teleology, scientific knowledge, and the objectification of nature, even while transforming them substantially. As we shall discuss in Chapter 3, these assumptions constitute some of the main default settings of modernity and occlude deeper understandings of relationality.

Post-structuralism has been the current of thought that has most fertilized the grounds on which the concern with relationality is being cultivated at present. In contrast to the positivist epistemology and starting point of liberalism (the individual and society) or Marxism's dialectical epistemology and pivotal concepts (production and labor), post-structuralism turned social theory's attention to something considered of secondary importance or superstructural, namely, language and representation. It placed representation, meaning, and discourse at the center of analysis, and its constructivism abandoned the realist epistemologies of its two illustrious predecessors. Its fundamental posture was that if we want to understand reality, one must look at how it is constructed in and through language and discourse, not just through the accrual of individual acts or through production relations. Succinctly, with post-structuralism language became constitutive of social reality. This realization was crucial to problematize the separation between representation and the world that had been taken for granted until then, and that continues to be the foundation of liberal social theory.

Post-structuralist constructivism became a formidable movement affecting all fields of knowledge in the social and human sciences. Nothing was left untouched by it: the great markers of identity (race, gender, sexuality), history (now studied in terms of, say, the profound effects of colonial discourses), nature (found to be deeply constructed by representations linked to capital, the State, and technoscience), and even the natural sciences (argued to be deeply shaped by history and enacted through mundane practices)—all of these were among the most cherished targets of the antiessentialist and antifoundationalist analyses fostered by post-structuralism. The age of epistemic comfort afforded by epistemological realism (the assumed correspondence between truth and reality, or between representation and the world) was over. The breakdown of this certainty affected all disciplines, from anthropology, geography, history,

---

[62] We are indebted to Lawrence Grossberg for illuminating discussions in this regard.

and art to literary, feminist, race, sexuality, film, cultural, and social movement studies; this critical effervescence gave new meaning to the appellative of "critical" when attached to any field, including race, gender, and queer studies; development, environmental, globalization, religious, and legal studies, and so forth. It gave a substantial boost to a much-needed renewal of the humanities and social sciences. It was a breath of fresh air, and it continues to inform much of social theory at present.

While greatly indebted to this variegated transdisciplinary movement, we however believe that post-structuralism was insufficient to enable a more decisive move out of dualism, rationalism, and realism, even if it created conditions for moving closer to the elusive goal of a post-Enlightenment episteme. Post-structuralist analyses were effective at deconstructing hegemonic understandings of society, but much less so at reconstituting the understanding of reality along nondualist lines. This was, in many ways, the problem: brilliant at critique but not so much at affording alternative accounts of reality. It might be the case that the age of *only* critique is over, and that the real task now is to imagine and propose transformative worldmaking practices, without capitulating to what-is. The question then becomes how to avoid the subtle tendencies and assumptions that have kept us within dualism.

Reliance on logocentric analysis remains central to post-structuralist academic production (this book included), and this has consequences for finding our way beyond dualist ontologies. Cognitive scientist Francisco Varela, philosopher Evan Thompson and psychologist Elenore Rosch venture a revealing explanation of this persistence. For them, while the nondualist philosophical current of phenomenology attempted to reunite reflection and experience, it failed because its analysis of experience remained "quite within the mainstream of Western philosophy … it stressed the pragmatic, embodied context of human experience, *but in a purely theoretical way.*"[63] It seems to us that this assessment applies to social theory as a whole. Again, here we find the strength of theoretical critique coupled with the sidelining of intervention, praxis, and the exploration of other ways of doing and making.

Paradoxically, while the space for making life relationally seems to narrow down even more due to global capitalism's totalizing thrust, it is the case that there are more intellectual, existential, and political resources for reorienting ways of thinking and living on relational grounds. In the academic domain, a series of thinkers are being rediscovered as forerunners of the idea of life's deeply immanent, relational, and processual character, such as Spinoza, the North American pragmatists (William James, John Dewey), the mathematician and philosopher Alfred North Whitehead, and closer to our own era, the two great proponents of rhizomatic thought, Gilles Deleuze and Félix Guattari. There is much to be learned from these exponents of a wiser, alternative West, who still help us to unlearn the mainstream West.

---

[63] Francisco Varela, Evan Thompson, and Eleanor Rosch, *The Embodied Mind: Cognitive Science and Human Experience* (Cambridge, MA: MIT Press, 1991), 9, emphasis ours.

This account barely scratches the surface of the wisdom of feminist, critical race, queer, and disability theorists and science studies scholars, not to mention those of the global majority who have contributed numerous insights about reality and politics, often from the vantage of relationality, implicitly if not explicitly articulated. In many ways, one of our key conclusions is that theory itself can never be sufficient. Above all, it is now crucial to delve into those spaces of living, making, and mobilizing where relationality has long been, or is being newly, actively cultivated. There we will find fresh clues for remaking and restor(y)ing life—including in those areas of slippage that are often deemed failures.

As Chapters 3 and 4 will show, it is through the efforts of diverse activists and social justice movements operating *with* theory *but in* practice that the possibilities and limitations of modern thought begin to reveal themselves. Notably, they reveal themselves in fits and starts, and often in unexpected ways. One of the things we will explore in the following chapters is how to move in between stories without slippages back to the modern ontology. Importantly, what we will refer to as portals and bridges to relationality often require us to face one of the core values of the rationalistic tradition: the deep and almost religious belief in secular rationality, or what Friedrich Nietzsche described as the death of God.

SECULARISM: THE BANISHMENT, AND NECESSITY, OF THE SACRED

Of all the pillars of modern thought, the secular is one of the trickiest to address, particularly for readers whom we assume are somewhat like us, living and laboring somewhere in activist and academic milieux, deeply entrenched in rationality and, for good reasons, weary of arguments about spirituality, even if these fears often stem from the historical legacies of oppression and intolerance associated with monotheistic religions more than from a serious consideration of the plurality of meanings of spirituality and the sacred.

Here again we find science and theoretical knowledge at play, as they have been essential to secularization. For Indian cultural psychologist Ashis Nandy, science became a secular theory of salvation. As he wrote, "of all the utopias which threaten to totalize the human consciousness, the most seductive in our times has been the one produced by modern science and technology."[64] Nandy wrote this indictment as part of an argument against the secularism being promoted as a political solution for a pluriversal India. For him, science became a tyranny precisely because it feigned universality and neutrality, while leading to the annihilation of diverse life worlds in a territory abundant in devotion to spirits and other modes of consciousness. From being a movement of dissent at the dawn of the modern age, science for Nandy became an instrument of isolation, hence a pillar of the production of the nonrelational and of the

---

[64] Ashis Nandy, *Traditions, Tyrannies and Utopias* (New Delhi: Oxford University Press, 1987), 10.

desacralization of life. It has done so while ironically claiming the monopoly of knowledge, compassion, and ethics.[65]

In a short and useful text, titled "Post Secular Nature," Patrick Curry defines spirituality, a cognate of the sacred as, "the ultimately ineffable nature of everything."[66] Jonathan Rowson, who headed a research project on the state of spirituality in politics, similarly writes about a "spiritual sensibility," understood as "a disposition towards reality characterised by concern for the fullness of life and experienced through simultaneous intimations of aliveness, goodness, understanding and meaning." Such an attitude involves "glimpses of wholeness and integration [that] have a texture that is at once emotional, ethical, epistemic and existential—the feeling of being alive, the conviction that something matters, the intuition that the world makes sense, and the experience that life is meaningful respectively." Further:

> What characterises aspects of sensibility that are spiritual and not merely holistic or emotional or psychological, or philosophical or systemic or ethical or perceptual or epistemic or existential or cultural or aesthetic or creative ... is that it is the disposition to relate to whatever is within and between all these qualities when considered and experienced together, yet defined or subsumed by none of them. Some call that "whatever" spirit, *but it can also be thought of as life as such, or perhaps just relationships between things seen in their fullest, broadest and deepest possible context.*[67]

Our concern with the sacred does not arise from an opposition between spirituality and secularism, which might become another sterile dualism, but from recognizing that at the heart of the modern civilizational project is an exaltation of the secular and an almost complete banishment of the sacred, particularly of *any notion of the sacred linked to Earth and nonhuman life.* This banishment is directly linked to scientific and economic rationality but also to the restriction of the spiritual to the narrow domain of (not infrequently, nowadays, fundamentalist) churches and temples.

Unlike other dualisms we have discussed, the sacred/secular binary is rarely named in the critical academy as a source of the oppressive aspects of the

---

[65] The violence of institutionalized religion, including in India's Hindu/Muslim confrontation, does not escape Nandy's attention. Most institutionalized religions are based on dualisms, particularly true/false, often leading to intolerance and hatred. In this sense, one many contend that religion is the taming of spirituality and the sacred.

[66] Patrick Curry, "Post-Secular Nature: Principles and Politics," *Worldviews: Global Religions, Culture & Ecology* 11, no. 3 (October, 2007), 287, available online: https://doi.org/10.1163/156853507X230564.

[67] Jonathan Rowson, *Spiritualise: Cultivating Spiritual Sensibility to Address 21st Century Challenges*, 1st edn. (Perspectiva and RSA, 2014), 17, available online: https://www.thersa.org/reports/spiritualise-cultivating-spiritual-sensibility-to-address-21st-century-challenges (accessed August 1, 2019), emphasis ours.

modern settlement, and discussion of things like spirits is treated with disdain, except when relegated to the folk beliefs and myths of "Others" in fields such as anthropology and religious studies. The result has been a near total exile of the sacred from public life, and a marginalization of related concepts such as love, compassion, and mystery from the realm of both MST and politics. The activist and academic left is not exempt of this behavior; in fact, they often reveal unexamined commitments to the rational premises of secular human-ism that make them staunch enemies of epistemologies that have room for the ineffable and unknowable dimensions of reality. An expansion of the critical ethos in this regard is needed, whether one ends up embracing any form of the sacred or not.

It is telling that there are no entries for the terms sacred, spirituality, and nature in Jürgen Habermas's overarching analysis of modern philosophy since the late eighteenth century, *The Philosophical Discourse of Modernity*.[68] At stake is modernity's ability to provide compelling answers to the basic question of the meaning of human existence. How can one arrive at such answers in a world cut off from meaningful consideration of the sacred, which for most cultures around the world has always related to the natural world? Having completed the job of elevating reason to chief adjudicator of life commenced by Man1, Man2 rapidly evolved into a world without sacrality. There have surely been many eloquent expressions in Western art and literature concerning the effacement of the sacred and the breakdown of the divine order, and protestations against it. Despite these, an understanding of the human as secular has prevailed, and the compulsory secularization effected by modernity has become a crucial aspect of the production of nonrelationality, particularly in the academy.

Philosophers Hubert Dreyfus and Sean Kelly have written a wonderfully readable account of the devaluing of the sacred in Western culture. For them, this marginalization has meant that we, moderns, are at a loss when trying to come up with compelling answers to fundamental existential questions. According to these phenomenologists, Martin Luther initiated the march toward the modern individual as a self-sufficient source of meaning; this idea was further developed by René Descartes and Immanuel Kant, who conceived of subjects as self-contained entities, whose willpower could rival that of God. To arrive there, however, required believing in a dead cosmos of inanimate matter governed by laws. Not only nature but also the vast domain of the sacred were exiled from modern life and constrained to the shadows of inner individual life. In a world without gods or deities of any kind, a sense of sadness and aloneness settled in.[69]

In this context, one question worth considering is: does the monohuman-ist regime of Man afford sufficient resources for meaningful existence? Not

[68] Jürgen Habermas, *The Philosophical Discourse of Modernity* (Cambridge, MA: MIT Press, 1987).

[69] Hubert Dreyfus and Sean Kelly, *All Things Shining: Reading the Western Classics to Find Meaning in a Secular Age* (New York: Free Press, 2011).

so, according to many authors writing about the twilight of the sacred. What does it mean to live a good, meaningful life in a world devoid of a notion of what is sacred and inviolable? How do we choose one course of action over others? Commenting on Nietzsche's declaration of the death of God, Dreyfus and Kelly state:

> What he meant by this is that we in the modern West no longer live in a culture where the basic questions of existence are already answered for us. This is true for modern religious believers and skeptics alike … The idea that there is no reason to prefer any answer to any other, however, is called nihilism, and Nietzsche thought this the better description of our current condition after the death of God.[70]

The desacralized world has ceased to shine. In a nihilistic world, we rarely feel we are participating in something that transcends us; it thus becomes hard to genuinely exercise or experience care.

Of course, the argument can be made that we (at least those for whom sheer physical survival is not immediately at stake) live in a culture where the basic questions of existence are already answered for us through a combination of secular forces, the remnants of traditions, organized religions, and the commodity spectacle (today paraded by enthralling digital technologies and social media). None of these answers, however, is very good from the perspective of relationality; they curtail questions about meaning and the sacred. Addiction, loneliness, and suicides among the youth are often cited as signs of this civilizational problematic. Many people get caught in the split between economic instrumentality and frustration and resentment, a split that seems to have only two possible resolutions, not infrequently entangled with each other: first, to accept unquestioningly the dictates of economic rationality, or second, to veer toward fundamentalisms. In between these two options there is something missing, and this something constitutes the arena for important human and political projects. Surely human beings have enormous capacities for endowing existence with meaning, but these capacities are massively stunted by current conditions. The project of relationality is thus also an attempt to restore the conditions within which these capacities may again flourish.

A crucial effect of secularism is that it sundered apart the connection between people, spirituality, and place. Simply put, the earth is not the place in which moderns find life's personal and collective meaning. This seemingly inconspicuous observation reveals a systemic problem, namely, the inextricable link between secularization and the development of capitalism. Here we find another aspect of Silvia Federici's work already mentioned: the massive burning of witches in the long period of European transition from feudalism to capitalism; it vividly

---

[70] Dreyfus and Kelly, *All Things Shining*, 20–1.

shows why heretics, healers, and disobedient wives were construed as subjects that nascent capitalism had to destroy, for they maintained communalizing and sacred ontologies inimical to its development. Like the enclosures and the slave trade, the persecution of hundreds of thousands of women in the late medieval and early modern periods was instrumental to capitalism's early phases.[71] This rethinking of primitive accumulation has been hugely important for making visible the vital sphere of social reproduction and to revalorize notions of the body, femininity, place, and care as well as the ontologies of sacredness often linked to place-based and communally oriented forms of sociality.[72]

The fervent belief in the individual only aggravates things. To return to Dreyfus and Kelly, "as autonomous subjects we have closed ourselves off to the calling of the gods ... The gods [the sacred] are calling us, but we have ceased to listen."[73] This is markedly different from Indigenous cosmovisions that find in their embeddedness in the earth a fundamental source of spiritual experience essential for fighting against terricide. Or the Zapatistas, who as we shall see in Chapter 4, understand autonomy as connected with the sacredness and interconnectedness of all beings.

The difficulty of thinking with and acknowledging the sacred is a poignant example of the kinds of obstacles modern thought posits for a truly relational view of life. And perhaps more relevant for our purposes here, it is a crucial example of the difficulties facing activists and intellectuals wishing to engage in effective transformational politics, because it hinders the political activation of relationality.

CONCLUSION

Liberal secular monohumanism and its attendant onto-epistemologies leave out of the account of life much that is essential to life. "So unless we move out of the liberal monohumanist mindset, it's very difficult to see where we've been," says Wynter, and hence, "where we're going."[74] In this chapter, we presented a particular view of where we have been and where, by and large, we still are. How, then, to move toward a humanism (if at all) that embraces co-eval and pluriversal genres of being human, while preventing reabsorption into the regime of Man? For Wynter, our response must come in the form of the creation of a new horizon of humanity that enables an ecumenically open view of the human as hybrid of biology and narrative. This goal entails moving beyond the color

---

[71] Federici, *Caliban and the Witch*.

[72] A certain revival of pagan, neo-shamanic, and Earth-based spiritual practices among young activists and artists in various parts of the world is a sign of an active search for relational life and politics, questions of cultural appropriation notwithstanding.

[73] Dreyfus and Kelly, *All Things Shining*, 221.

[74] Wynter and McKittrick, "Unparalleled Catastrophe," 14.

line, beyond class, beyond the patriarchal capitalist cosmogony, and beyond thought as we know it. Notably, this involves the debunking of the master discipline of economics and of the reductive versions of science undergirding the bioeconomic view of the human.

For Varela, the obstacle to be surmounted "is nothing less than the cognitive homeostasis of each of us, the tendency to stick with our interpretation of reality, entrenched and made stable by emotions and body patterns. To work through the veil of attachments, and to see (experience) reality without them is part of the process of unfoldment."[75] In other words, we are trapped in the onto-epistemic toxic loops that we embody and live. For Varela, the only way out is through embodied practical experiences capable of resolving the mind-body dualism. Given their liminal subjectivities, peoples inhabiting the colonial difference embody this sort of experience, which for Wynter gives them in principle a "cognitive edge" in envisioning and moving toward such far-reaching transformation.

By discussing the limitations of modern social theory, we hope to have thrown into relief some ways forward. But this is perhaps as far as we can go with a purely theoretical discussion. As many Indigenous traditions and Buddhism suggest, and as some mystic, spiritual, artistic, or psychedelic experiences might attest, it might be impossible to go any further on this path by relying only on modern *ratio*, including that comfortably harbored within academic discourse. Theory, however, does not exhaust the archives of relationality, and there are other guides for inquiring about it beyond the attachment to conceptuality.

In the chapters that follow, we continue to labor on this path, venturing into territories that, though inextricably functioning also in the land of Man, provide clues to work through the four limitations abovementioned: by delving into experiences that show a degree of reembodiment, beyond abstract rational knowledge; by de-colonially intuiting other potential horizons for the human, thought, and politics; and pluriversally, by relocating everyday worldmaking practices within place, life, and the sacred, and within a multiplicity of actual and possible worlds. Our aim thus far has been to understand the prevailing ontology of the human as a historical process of long duration that has reached a planetary scale. To prefigure other histories and ontologies that, while engaging with monohumanist designing, attempt to craft alternative ethics, is part of our path ahead.

The planetary dimension is an essential aspect of our exploration, for, as Akomolafe states referring to the implications of the Anthropocene:

> We are all fugitives. Or at least those of us gestating in modern worlds who have been touched by the material yearnings for stability and progress. We are being chased. The relentless curdling of the edges, the splashing of

---

[75] Francisco Varela, "Not One, Not Two," *Coevolution Quarterly* 12 (1976): 62–67, 67; cited in Mark Hantel, "What is it Like to Be a Human? Sylvia Wynter on Autopoiesis," *philoSOPHIA* 8, no.1 (2020): 61–79, 69.

threatening ocean waves, the dimming of the sun by the dust in the air, and the disappearance of bees, all conspire to remove the post-Ice Age refuge we have long known as home. The ground has withdrawn her endorsement: we are no longer at ease.[76]

Where do we go, then, in this groundless age of loss and wonder,[77] which, paradoxically, takes us closer to Earth, to the sacred, to the spirit, that is, to those domains from which modern social theory had largely withdrawn?

---

[76] Akomolafe, "Coming Down to Earth."

[77] Laura Ogden, *Loss and Wonder at the World's End* (Durham, NC: Duke University Press, 2021).

PART TWO
Choose

3 The political activation of relationality: Ontological slippages as portals to relationality

All Life is interrelated, and we are all caught up in an inescapable network of mutuality, tied in a single garment of destiny .... I can never be what I ought to be until you are what you ought to be. And you can never be what you ought to be until I am what I ought to be—*this is the interrelated structure of reality.*[1]
MARTIN LUTHER KING JR.

INTRODUCTION: WHAT ARE RELATIONAL POLITICS?

One of the clearest places to see both the need for and effectiveness of relationality is in the study of social change. In this chapter, we examine the history and contemporary development of what have long been described as "social movements" or struggles for liberation, and that we redefine as struggles over the conditions for "making life." As this chapter will show, a new look at these struggles can reveal how our dominant treatments of social movements and politics, and the onto-epistemic assumptions upon which they are based, have limited not only struggles and projects for social change, but also, and very importantly, our understandings of these projects. Given our recognition that knowledge and understanding (cognition) literally build worlds, this limitation is extremely important to recognize and overcome.

For a sense of what is at stake, let us briefly consider a social movement many will be familiar with: the US civil rights movement. This movement is often spoken of as the most successful social movement of the twentieth century,[2] supposedly having taken place in the 1950s and 1960s and successfully culminating in the ending of legal segregation as well as the Voting Rights Act of 1965.

---

[1] Quoted in Ruth King, *Mindful of Race: Transforming Racism from the inside Out* (Boulder, CO: Sounds True, 2018), 20, emphasis ours.

[2] Doug McAdam, Sidney G. Tarrow, and Charles Tilly, *Dynamics of Contention* (New York: Cambridge University Press, 2001).

However, what the civil rights movement actually is, as well as what made it so successful, eludes many. According to most established treatments, the movement is considered paradigmatic because of its success at the level of policy and law—including the passage of the Voting Rights Act and the ending of legal segregation. In other words, it is deemed successful by what we might characterize as the level of traditional politics, namely, the State, law, and macropolitics.[3]

Though these achievements are not to be dismissed or diminished, the civil rights movement was much more complex, and much more profound. In fact, what has usually been referred to as the "civil rights movement" is but a small part of a much broader, messier, assemblage of visions, practices, and theories about what achieving the liberation of Black people and ending white supremacy should be, an assemblage that defies easy historical or political delimitation.[4] For example, in the 1930s W.E.B Du Bois described that pre-, during, and post-Civil War, thousands of formerly enslaved peoples fought to create liberation in a radical form of democracy, what he termed "abolition democracy" (we discuss the abolition movement in the next chapter). Or one can consider the numerous and variegated visions and approaches that constituted the larger milieu or assemblage during the time formally known as the civil rights movement, that ranged from the more liberal oriented (rights-based) approach to more radical anti-capitalist approaches; think of the Black Panthers, Malcolm X, numerous activists who believed in the importance of armed resistance,[5] Black Power and various strands of the Communist left,[6] as well as myriad acts of resistance and re-existence by Black women and men in their everyday lives that comprise this larger assemblage.[7] Moreover, the ways the vision or goals of the movement are known were themselves reduced and sanitized, so that they would be less threatening to white supremacist capitalist modernity. As Vincent Harding put it in a pamphlet, "Martin wasn't assassinated for simply wanting Black and white children to hold hands, but because he said that there must be fundamental changes in this country and that Black people must take the lead in bringing them … Put simply these problems are Racism, Militarism and Anti-Communism."[8]

The limited understanding of the civil rights movement as being a clearly delimitable movement for ending segregation, achieving equal rights, and opening

---

[3] On macropolitics see: Gilles Deleuze and Félix Guattari, *A Thousand Plateaus: Capitalism and Schizophrenia* (London: Athlone Press, 1988).

[4] Keeanga-Yamahtta Taylor, *From #BlackLivesMatter to Black Liberation* (Chicago: Haymarket Books, 2016).

[5] Timothy B. Tyson, *Blood Done Sign My Name: A True Story* (New York: Three Rivers Press, 2004).

[6] Grace Lee Boggs, *The Next American Revolution: Sustainable Activism for the Twenty-First Century* (Berkeley: University of California Press, 2011).

[7] Hartman, *Wayward Lives.*

[8] Quoted in Boggs, *The Next American Revolution*, 86.

the door for inclusion of Black people into the US polity misses, even if unwittingly, the larger critique of modernity the movement posited. Informed greatly by Mahatma Gandhi and his critique of Western modernity, Martin Luther King Jr. himself—who might be considered *the* symbol of this sanitized and unthreatening view of the civil rights movement—went far beyond the neat and less controversial narrative of political and economic integration. As he put it in one of his last pieces of writing, "The World House":

> The stability of the large world house which is ours will involve a revolution of values to accompany the scientific and freedom revolutions engulfing the earth. We must rapidly *begin the shift from a "thing"-oriented society to a "person"-oriented society.* When machines and computers, profit motives and property rights are considered more important than people, the giant triplets of racism, materialism and militarism are incapable of being conquered. A civilization can flounder as readily in the face of moral and spiritual bankruptcy as it can of financial bankruptcy.[9]

One way to make sense of this is that while fighting to achieve civil rights and end white supremacy, the movement came up against the larger ontological settlement of modernity of which white supremacy is an integral part. As a result, the movement's ultimate goals went far beyond demanding inclusion and rights in this system, pointing to radically different visions of the "what-for" of struggle and even politics writ large.

King himself situated the struggle for Black people's rights in the context of a global liberation thrust that he termed Beloved Community. Beloved Community refers not to specific communities of affinity but to the interdependence of all life—where interdependence is understood as a fundamental and universal law of reality.[10] In 1967, King gave a sermon on Christmas Eve in which he articulated one of the most precise definitions of relationality or interdependence we have come across:

> All Life is interrelated, and we are all caught up in an inescapable network of mutuality, tied in a single garment of destiny …. I can never be what I ought to be until you are what you ought to be. And you can never be what you ought to be until I am what I ought to be—*this is the interrelated structure of reality.*[11]

---

[9] Martin Luther King Jr., *Where Do We Go from Here: Chaos or Community?*, foreword by Coretta Scott King; intro. Vincent Harding, The King Legacy Series (Boston, MA: Beacon Press, 2010), 196–97, emphasis ours.

[10] Kazu Haga, "A Time of Reckoning & Repair: Healing our Wounds, Restoring our Wholeness," June 2022, You Tube video, 1:26:49, circa minute 34:00, available online: https://www.youtube.com/watch?v=wN01SFHKdOU (accessed November 17, 2021).

[11] Quoted in King, *Mindful of Race*, 20, emphasis ours.

Ultimately King saw the struggle for civil rights as a *spiritual and ontological struggle* over our very understanding of the nature of reality and what it means to live together as humans. For him, Beloved Community is both the ontological foundation and ethico-political goal of all struggles for liberation. This was a radical vision in which all struggles and all peoples were seen as interconnected—presaging what we here call relational politics.[12] With King, we affirm that the spiritual and ontological dimensions of activism and change work are key.

However, our dominant understandings and vocabularies of the political were then, and still are, not sufficient for making sense of these dimensions. In fact, we believe a large part of the reason why the civil rights movement did not achieve the more radical vision of Beloved Community has to do with the fact that the dominant language and imaginaries of "the political" that activists and intellectuals were—and, to a large degree, are still—using were not capacious enough. These languages and imaginaries are not capable of holding or making sense of the project in its totality, a totality and complexity that itself cannot be contained by the modernist category of the political. In a moving interview, Ruby Sales, a civil rights leader and public theologian, describes the limitations of the movement's own self-understanding:

> And part of what happened after—post-civil rights, Southern freedom movement is that people thought that the movement—that what the movement had been about was jobs, position, status, when in fact it had not been about that at all. It had been about—when King talked about "the mountaintop," he was talking about a higher level of consciousness. He was talking about a movement where we harmonized the "I" with the "we" and the "we" with the "I." He was talking about a Pentecost moment.
>
> And so with that misunderstanding where the movement became materialized, the things that had really united Black people and held us together, in terms of being a part of a community where we were well-guarded and well-protected, that many of us, many young people like myself, that we all left our homes, never to look back, and in doing that, we left the Black community unguarded. And the mission was no longer a Beloved Community, but the mission became integration.[13]

---

[12] Drew Dellinger describes King's "cosmology of connection," and the "ecological King." See Drew Dellinger, "Ecological King Articles," available online: https://drewdellinger.org/ecological-king-articles/ (accessed March 8, 2021); Drew Dellinger, "Opinion | Dr. King's Interconnected World," *The New York Times*, December 22, 2017, sec. Opinion, available online: https://www.nytimes.com/2017/12/22/opinion/martin-luther-king-christmas.html (accessed March 8, 2021).

[13] Ruby Sales, interviewed by Krista Tippett, "Where Does It Hurt?," The On Being Project, available online: https://onbeing.org/programs/ruby-sales-where-does-it-hurt/ (accessed February 14, 2021).

In other words, mistaking or misunderstanding the true goal of the movement to fit the traditional political categories and domains—mistaken for legal and economic integration—made the more fundamental vision of interdependence and collectivity invisible. This can also be explained as a failure to understand that the conditions for making life—collective, communal life—was at stake. Together these were part of a larger failure to understand the ontological dimension of the political.

Ultimately, incorporating King's understanding of the interrelated structure of reality and his critique of a "thing-oriented society" into our political imaginaries, vocabularies, and frameworks would need to involve operationalizing a radically different view of the political based on a fundamentally different story of life and reality. It is a view that operates *on a different ontological register* and that requires a complete shift in paradigm or consciousness.

In this chapter we posit that relational politics have been an active presence and horizon in many social movements throughout the twentieth century. However, the dominant episteme's inability to register their fundamental challenge to modernity has resulted in their being ignored or assessed as failures, overlooking the fact that their challenge has been to the larger onto-epistemic formation, not just certain regimes of power within it. This has led activists and academics alike to remain within conventional paradigms of change, politics, and reality. This has happened numerous times, as with the above example of the civil rights movement, but also in treatments and analyses of the Alter-globalization movement, Occupy Wall Street, Black Lives Matter, and the Zapatistas, among others. And it will continue to happen, unless we start to see this erasure for what it is: a failure to recognize the ontological, emotional, and spiritual dimensions of the political, on the one hand, and the concomitant slippage between different dimensions of political reality—or different versions of the Real—on the other.

To explicate this argument, the rest of the chapter proceeds as follows: we start by exploring the notion of the ontological in politics, naming the ways in which we miss or mistake ontological difference. We then describe the challenges and possibilities of a politics of relationality by showing how *modernist default settings* keep us trapped, hampering our capacities to grasp the realities that become visible during the experiences of many movements, but then are quickly lost or obscured. We describe these as ontological *slippages*, because rather than ideological differences, or mistakes, we find that they involve slipping between different versions, or planes, of reality. We then delve into four major slippages that cause analysts and activists to miss their transformative potential. They include (1) misunderstanding the goal of social movements as a result of narrow notions of failure and success; (2) folding difference back into a dualist worldview; (3) reenacting a dualism between the individual and collective; and (4) holding to the need to identify good versus bad. Finally, we point to the importance of recognizing that these slippages can also become portals to a relational politics.

Overall, our goal in this chapter is to help articulate a new story for making sense of many of the most important social movements of the twentieth and twenty-first centuries. Coming to a shared vocabulary and understanding will make it easier for movements and other world-makers to valorize and explain to skeptical others the work they are doing. As this chapter will show, one of the common tendencies is a propensity for a politics of relationality to emerge, be celebrated, even marveled at, then, almost as quickly, denounced for being ineffective or failing. These denouncements are not only painful, often leading to a sense of complete disillusionment, along with desires to withdraw or give up, but also weaken the other stories and worlds that had, even if only temporarily, gained both visibility and substance. Since the modernist ontology currently saturates our sense of political possibility, the relational story of life needs to be strengthened by being practiced, narrated, and collectively given meaning. We need new storying of and for our movements. We write to describe and help embolden and sustain such practices. We believe that naming and storying are powerful political practices and that if we can come to see and name the patterns for what they are we might not be so quick to disinvest from these projects.

THE ONTOLOGICAL DIMENSION OF THE POLITICAL

The dominant culture's partial and sanitized narrative of the true goals of the civil rights movement had a great impact on the movement's ability to achieve its most transformative potentials. This is true of numerous other movements and has to do with the failure to take seriously the role of the ontological in politics. We use the term ontological because we want to stress that it has to do not only with political differences but with our very understanding of reality itself. This can be described as more like the difference between two operating systems (or even what are known as paradigm shifts in the history of science) than two ideologies. In other words, this is not a matter of normative beliefs or values—namely, communism versus capitalism—but a matter of, as King put it, "the fundamental structure of reality."

Thinking ontologically, particularly when we are speaking about modern cases in "the West," is an important analytical move because it emphasizes how radical our revisions must be. It also helps to clarify why we keep making the same mistakes. It is not simply that our political ideologies do not work but that we do not understand the distinct forms or planes of reality at play. Hence, we understandably keep slipping between emergent understandings of reality back to the default settings of Western modernity.

Briefly, and as further described in the Appendix, our understanding of ontology has to do with the assumptions of the kinds of beings, truths, and the criteria that constitute a world. Notably, the capacity to see and reflect on these as particular assumptions is an important part of recognizing or mobilizing this understanding.

According to Mario Blaser there are three main definitions or dimensions of ontology:

1 "Any way of understanding the world must make assumptions (which may be implicit or explicit) about what kinds of things do or can

exist, and what might be their conditions of existence, relations of dependency, and so on. Such an inventory of kinds of being and their relations is an ontology."[14]

2 "Ontologies do not precede mundane practices, but rather are shaped through the practices and interactions of humans and non-human. Hence, ontologies perform themselves into worlds—thus I use the term *ontologies* and *worlds* as synonyms."

3 "Ontologies must be understood as the total (i.e. including discursive and non-discursive) enactments of worlds. In this sense, myths are neither true nor false; they engender different worlds which have their own criteria for defining truth."[15]

All three are relevant for us here. The first stresses that all things exist because there are categories and ways of making sense of them as the entities they are. The second emphasizes that ontologies are a product of practices—moreover, mundane practices. This means that they come into being or are made repeatedly through practice—not simply ideas—and these practices or performances create worlds. The third stresses that myths and narratives produce worlds, whether we agree with their truthfulness from our own world; this also means that there are different criteria for defining truth or meanings. As Indigenous geographer Vanessa Watts points out, Indigenous "origin stories" are not myth, lore, or legend, in a sense that suggests they did not "really" happen. They did. They are not mythical interpretations of a reality we could otherwise describe through more rational or objective concepts such as the big bang.[16]

While some fear that ontological arguments lead us to a form of radical constructivism in which anything goes, and where all stories of reality are considered to be equally valid—such that, for example, Trump's or Bolsonaro's denial of the coronavirus, or other claims of "fake news," get equal footing with the scientifically verified "facts"—we contend that this fear is misplaced. It misses

---

[14] Scott and Marshall quoted in Mario Blaser, *Storytelling Globalization from the Chaco and Beyond* (Durham, NC: Duke University Press, 2010), 3.

[15] Blaser, *Storytelling Globalization*, 3–4.

[16] Vanessa Watts, "Indigenous Place-Thought and Agency amongst Humans and Non Humans (First Woman and Sky Woman Go on a European World Tour!)," *Decolonization: Indigeneity, Education & Society* 2, no. 1 (May 4, 2013), available online: https://jps.library.utoronto.ca/index.php/des/article/view/19145 (accessed April 5, 2021). As we worked on this book, it became clearer to us that ontology must be understood as a provisional concept, a bridge to help us move between the dualist story of life and relational ones. Some cultures and life-worlds that are more connected to their foundational myths, and do not distinguish between cosmologies and "reality," may not need such tools. For example, as Watts argues, Haudenosaunee and Anishnaabe cosmologies do not make a strong distinction between myth and fact, or ontology and epistemology. Western frameworks introduced the distinction between "how we know" and "what is real," and between a knowing subject and an inert object (land, animals, etc.). Without these dualisms the notion of ontology is not necessary. Those of us who mostly inhabit a "One-World world," would do well to work with the concept of ontology as a bridge that could be left behind once the bridge is crossed.

the more important fact that worlds are made through stories and practices. The fact that some people manipulate these stories to generate confusion and a lack of confidence in expert knowledges does not negate this fundamental claim, but points to the essence of the matter: the making of reality is political, hence politics is always ontological. In Indigenous worlds, the assumption of relationality serves as a check to manipulation, because no one assumes the world to be objectively "out there." Without that assumption, the discernment around particular stories itself becomes an important cultural matter.

Interestingly, we would suggest that even those in the academy who intellectually subscribe to theories of the "ontological turn" and ontological multiplicity often fail to really take other worlds seriously.[17] This is particularly clear when it comes to seeing such ontologies not in reified "Others" but among and within liberal societies in the "West." One-World worlders, to recall John Law's apt description, are conditioned to not be able to entertain the notion of multiple realities as material, mundane, and actually existing entities in a pluriverse of worlds.[18] Said differently, while scholars are somewhat able to see ontological multiplicity where there is "radical alterity," they often overlook the multiple realities here and now within "the West," vying to make themselves known.[19] Many movements in the West point to this pluriversality regularly, even if we mostly fail to understand them as doing so.

Thinking about politics ontologically, or with ontological difference in mind, opens up the possibility of addressing several political problematics more holistically, including questions of *diversity* (of cultures, geographies, issues, political visions, identities); *goals, vision, and objectives* (i.e., reform vs revolution; ends vs means); *power* (power-over vs power-with, emergent power); *scale* (local, global, glocal, horizontal); *temporality* (long term vs short term; progress vs tradition); and what constitutes *the political terrain* (the State, the economy, culture, life).

Default settings

One defining feature of the modern ontology is its ability to naturalize its assumptions about reality; usually by leaning on the taken-for-granted objectivity of science; these assumptions are rarely acknowledged. The postulates of the

---

[17] Eduardo Kohn, "Anthropology of Ontologies," *Annual Review of Anthropology* 44, no. 1 (October 21, 2015): 311–27, available online: https://doi.org/10.1146/annurev-anthro-102214-014127; Mario Blaser, "Ontological Conflicts and the Stories of Peoples in Spite of Europe: Toward a Conversation on Political Ontology," *Current Anthropology* 54, no. 5 (October 1, 2013): 547–68.

[18] For notable exceptions see Annemarie Mol, *The Body Multiple: Ontology in Medical Practice* (Durham, NC: Duke University Press, 2002); John Law and Annemarie Mol, eds., *Complexities: Social Studies of Knowledge Practices* (Durham, NC: Duke University Press, 2002); Blaser, "Ontological Conflicts."

[19] Blaser, "Ontological Conflicts."

modern ontology are taken as *the* real, not *one possible* real. As a result, most modern subjects are unable to see or even sense the story of the real within which we live and move, mistaking certain things as ontological givens. These onto-logical assumptions can be described as modernist default settings. They are default settings that we do not recognize as particular to our worldview; we take them as if they were fundamental to all reality. A default setting is hard to recognize, precisely because it is like the water fish swim in, or the air we humans breathe. In general, we are not aware of these default settings until moments of "break-down," friction or conflict when the naturalness or obvious-ness of those ways comes into question or no longer hold.[20]

Social movements—understood as messy, multidimensional assemblages comprising both organized components fighting on the traditional political terrain (e.g., policy, law, institutional structure, media) and the more quotidian, even cultural or micropolitical dimensions—do some of their most important work by helping to create such moments of friction or break down. Let us think again, for example, of the civil rights movement. There were of course the marches for voting rights, and efforts to call out and end legal segregation; no less important, however, were those cultural and disruptive acts that are only recognized *ex-post facto* for their impact. Think Rosa Parks refusing to give up her seat or the innumerable subcultural spaces for making and affirming Black culture and community through various forms of music, dance, and myriad other modes explicitly not sanctioned by "white society."[21] Or take the feminist movement. There were the legal components working for access to the vote or the equal rights amendment, but then there were a variety of cultural and subcultural components including consciousness raising groups and women learning to know their own bodies, challenging the notion that women require men for pleasure or support. These features refer to the ontological dimension, and in overlooking them we miss the ways in which movements operate not on *one* but on *multiple* and different planes of reality and temporality.[22]

Moreover, without a framework for making sense of these aspects, activists, academics, and others often *slip* from the emergent potential and meaning of a practice, back to the default setting, missing many of the actual contribu-tions movements might make. Thinking again about the case of civil rights as beautifully described by Sales, confusing the true goals of community and the

---

[20] We borrow the term "default setting" from David Foster Wallace, see: *This Is Water: Some Thoughts, Delivered on a Significant Occasion, about Living a Compassionate Life* (New York: Little, Brown, 2009); see Also Terry Winograd and Fernando Flores, *Understanding Computers and Cognition: A New Foundation for Design* (Reading: Addison-Wesley, 1987).

[21] In the Sales interview quoted above she describes "Black Folk Religion" as an important example of these kinds of affirmative life-making spaces outside of the dominant Christian church. See Sales, "Where Does It Hurt?."

[22] This argument is developed in an unpublished essay by Osterweil, originally presented as "From Movements to Moments: Taking 'Other Worlds'—and Other Temporalities—Seriously," Mellon-LASA workshop, "On Protest: Latin America in Comparative Transnational Perspective," University of Massachusetts Amherst, 2014.

cultivation of an interdependent "we" with the notion of "political and economic integration" ends up leading to such a slippage. Many living the civil rights movement at the time knew this other dimension on a deeper level, but without the political theories or frames to make them visible, they were eclipsed by the dominant categories of politics and economics. We will describe these slippages in greater detail in what follows; for now, we suggest that one way to conceive of these slippages comes through in sci-fi images of glitching, tripping, or having flashes. In a 1982 interview, French philosopher and psychoanalyst Félix Guattari illustrated this point admirably:

> Since no revolutionary war machine is at present available and there is no way to get a good grip on reality, the collective subjectivity is so to speak, tripping: from time to time it has the "flashes." It sees things, and then it stops. There was the autonomist movement in Italy … and then we pass on to other things. But it's all going to come back. *All these flashes don't mean that there is a total incoherence in the subjectivity but simply that an effort is being made to perceive something which is not yet registered, inscribed, identified.* I believe that the forces which today rally around the peace movement are the same which, in other phases will rally around the ecologist movement, around regionalist movements, around ex numbers of components of what I call the molecular revolution. What I mean by that is not a cult of spontaneity or whatever, only the effort not to miss anything that would *help rebuild a new kind of struggle, a new kind of society.*[23]

These efforts to help rebuild a new kind of society are ontological, in that they stress the conditions for making and remaking life. Uruguayan writer and activist Raúl Zibechi similarly describes the massive Bolivian uprisings of the early 2000s bringing to power an Indigenous president for the first time (Evo Morales) after close to two hundred years of white minority rule, as "bolt[s] of lightning capable of illuminating subterranean molecular cooperation, hidden by the veil of everyday inertias … During the uprising, shadowed areas are illumined albeit fleetingly."[24] Notably, the image of bolts of lightning underscores both the multiple planes of reality and the inability to register the importance of these cooperative forms of life. Said differently, the hyper focus on the electoral victory of Morales, obscured or even rendered invisible the place-based impacts of the different forms of communal life that were generated as part of the movement to bring him to power.

Social movements reveal and create realities; however, in the on the ground encounter with dominant political forces and discourses, they also unintentionally re-obscure them. Coming to recognize this process of revealing and re-obscuring holds promise for enabling these worlds to register or to become

---

[23] Félix Guattari, interview by Sylvère Lotringer, "A New Alliance is Possible," in *Soft Subversions*, ed. Sylvère Lotringer (New York: Semiotext(e), 1996), 90, emphasis ours.

[24] Raúl Zibechi, *Dispersing Power: Social Movements as Anti-State Forces*, English edn. (Oakland, CA: AK Press, 2010), 11.

activated. We believe that if we understand these dismissals as a result of a slippage between registers—flashes, lightning bolts of illumination—we might not be so quick to disinvest from these projects, and we might also be able to cultivate our capacities for continuing to see and be with those other modes, dimensions, and stories, and in so doing make the possibilities of their thriving and enriching lives a more likely possibility.

Learning to stay with relational "flashes" requires not only a new vocabulary but also an understanding that new worlds created by these movements *coexist with the dominant ones*. This coexistence matters a great deal because unlike the modernist version of reality that denies multiplicity, a relational or nondualist perspective operates from the understanding that there are multiple worlds. Thinking ontologically about contemporary movements has additional and important implications. First, it suggests that many movements, such as the civil rights example above, are not simply responding to a national or historical moment delimited in time and space, but that they respond to fundamental crises of a much longer durée. Second, that these crises are not only matters of economics or justice or representation, but of entire ways of knowing, being, and doing. Third, it requires recognizing that many things that do not register on our current list of political success, or even effects, might in fact be a lot more significant than we think. When recast in a relational view of reality, things that get dismissed as minor, cultural or insignificant in our current view of politics, might turn out to be very significant, even world changing.

ONTOLOGICAL SLIPPAGES AND RETHINKING FAILURE

Coming to recognize the various ways in which we miss or obscure the ontological dimension is critical to the theory and practice of relational politics. We describe the process as ontological slippage because rather than completely miss the less commonly recognized dimension, what often happens is that we briefly see and even actively celebrate them, but then slip back into the dominant ontology. In what follows we will review four common forms these ontological slippages take.

Slippage 1: Confusing a politics of relationality for failure

There is a fascinating pattern that accompanies many recent social movements. A movement emerges, grabs everyone's attention and imagination, then within a few years it is not only gone but decried as a failure.[25] Take for example Occupy Wall Street (OWS) and the numerous critiques made of them for not having a clear purpose, goal, or message. OWS activists responded to such critiques quite

---

[25] *Time Magazine*, for example, described 2011 as the year social movements (re)made history, and named Protester as person of the year. While they also included the Arab Spring, OWS was top of their list in terms of what protests mattered.

aptly. The original poster for OWS was clear and proud of the fact that occupation itself, without any political articulation or translation, was demand enough.[26]

They reiterated this point in self publications, interviews, and other texts. Below is an example from the "Occupied Wall Street Journal"—a newspaper produced by the movement:

What are the demands of the protesters?

Ugh, the zillion-dollar question. Again, the original Adbusters call asked, "What is our one demand?" Technically, there isn't one yet. In the weeks leading up to Sept. 17 [2011] the NYC General Assembly seemed to be veering away from the language of "demands" in the first place, largely because government institutions are already so shot through with corporate money that making specific demands would be pointless until the movement grew stronger politically. *Instead, to begin with, they opted to make their demand the occupation itself—and the direct democracy taking place there—which in turn may or may not come up with some specific demand. When you think about it, this act is actually a pretty powerful statement* against the corruption that Wall Street has come to represent. But since thinking is often too much to ask of the American mass media, the question of demands has turned into a massive PR challenge.[27]

While many dismissed as frivolous the notion that occupation and experimenting in direct democracy was politically important, we suggest that like the Bolivian lightning bolts, occupation illuminated possibilities for making and remaking life differently.

This was similar with the Alter-Globalist movement (AGM) of the late 1990s and early 2000s, to be discussed at greater length in the next section. Described as the Global Justice Movement, the Alter-Globalist movement, the Movement of Movements or the less accurate, but perhaps most popular, Anti-Globalization movement, the movements that we refer to as the Alter-globalist movement (AGM) captured people's imaginations. There was a period of effervescent wonder and excitement surrounding the numerous counter-summit protests, the World Social Forum process, and place-based movements such as the Zapatistas in Mexico. In fact, some described it as "the end of the end of history!"[28]

Like OWS, part of the excitement with the AGM had to do with the ways in which it challenged the political expectations of observers and participants alike, refusing to fit into the old political vocabularies. The aims and constituents were

---

[26] See Michael Bierut, "The Poster that Launched a Movement," *Design Observer*, April 30, 2012, available online: https://designobserver.com/feature/the-poster-that-launched-a-movement-or-not/32588/ (accessed March 16, 2023).

[27] Occupy Wall Street Collective, *The Occupied Wall Street Journal*, 1st English edn. (2011), emphasis ours.

[28] Marco Revelli, "La Nuova Parola Zapatista," February 2, 2004, available online: https://www.edscuola.it/archivio/interlinea/zapatista.htm (accessed July 19, 2023).

too multiple, there was relatively little focus on electoral politics or the State, and the rejection of neoliberalism was not matched by clear-cut economic alternatives but a much more amorphous and holistic view of life. In other words, both OWS and the AGM puzzled us. For a while, this puzzlement was experienced by those of us sympathetic to the movement with a sense of positive wonder and curiosity, an enthusiastic being with the unknown. This excitement was not only quick to wane but also, once it did, the wonder was often replaced with outright dismissal, ridicule, and amnesia even by many who had been enraptured by it. And almost everyone agreed: OWS and the AGM had been failures. How? Why?

This is the first area of slippage: the limited understanding of the goals of these movements, which is itself based on a limited understanding of the political. *A limited understanding of the political is one of the core assumptions or default settings of modernity.* When people speak of OWS and AGM as failures, these critiques emerge from a specific modernist view of the political. Such views take for granted naturalized entities such as the State, political parties, elections, markets, and individuals, as well as temporal and cultural logics of progress and end-goals, in turn closely linked to a specific view of power.

What is missed in these critiques is the relational, or pluriversal, dimension. OWS and AGM were spaces where new capacities for living and being were developed and articulated through practices of occupying space (e.g., Zuccotti Park, and many other smaller spaces where local OWS movements took place). Many other processes took place in those spaces, such as stopping the daily hustle and acceptance of the status quo; connecting with others abused or ejected from the dominant economic logic; "occupying the imagination"; and generally disrupting the assumed normalcy of life under capitalism. While some would critique these effects for being merely a disruption of the dominant system rather than positing an alternative or solution, we would suggest that to the contrary, in the disruption, spaces for practicing new ways of being and relating were imagined, cultivated, and experienced, albeit in temporary forms.[29]

While the AGM rarely achieved the stated aims of curbing the power of international financial institutions such as the World Trade Organization (WTO), International Monetary Fund (IMF), World Bank, and so on, or ending neoliberalism, the counter-summit protests served as sites where forms of non-, or not-only-capitalist, life were co-created, weaving a fabric of potential for distinct forms of life and democracy and novel designs for living. During summits, and at the various regional and World Social Forums, people learned to house, feed, and coordinate thousands of activists. Camps were replete with vegan kitchens, gray water systems, bars, media and press-centers, art spaces, and much more. In addition, people met with radically different others; had heated, even confrontational discussions about strategy, tactics, and the aims of the protests; and learned to be active agents of their own lives and governance in

---

[29] Winograd and Flores, *Understanding Computers and Cognition*. Another way to see this disruption is precisely as the ontological work of what Martin Heidegger calls breakdown. Breakdown is often necessary for us to gain the capacity to see, name, and reflect on the naturalized worlds we are designing and being designed by.

fascinating and unexpected ways. They also collectively authored and theo-
rized new concepts for political organization, community building, alternative
economics, and living.[30] While some might think of these as small, cultural, or
superstructural, on the relational plane these actions and practices were the
basis of radical models for transformation of the fundamental fabric of reality,
even if in potentia.[31] While our typical political lenses do not register these
impacts, this is a problem of the lenses not the practices.[32]

Let us move to a second part of the puzzle: why move from excitement and
enthusiastic wonder to decrying the movements as failures? The fact that even
many who were enthusiastic proponents of the transformative potential of the
political projects of the AGM and OWS have since dismissed them, and returned
to a more traditional vision of state-centered social change, has everything to
do with the challenge of sustaining an alternate, relational worldview in a world
so thoroughly saturated with a dualist one.

We have come to see this patterned move of dismissal as inextricably linked
to the challenge of truly staying with the logic of relationality precisely because
of the implicit but often ignored ontological dimension of politics. To be able
to stay with and within the relational logic in which all the positive outcomes
identified above are visible requires a radical shift in how we understand political
effectivity. While it may be true that relational politics are on the rise throughout
the world, it is equally true that they are rarely understood as such, and as a
result they are often missed both politically and analytically. The bottom line
is that they and their potency are rendered invisible and judged to be frivolous
or unrealistic because of a stubborn attachment to particular modernist understandings of both reality and politics.

Slippage 2: The need for a new vocabulary and a
new ontology: The Alter-globalist flash

In the late 1990s and early 2000s a "movement of movements" emerged that
was characterized as being intentionally transnational and diverse in terms of
constituents, issues, and aims. It comprised many events on multiple conti-
nents, many of which had their own local histories and meanings, in addition
to constituting this transnational assemblage: 1994, the Zapatista Uprising;

---

[30] Marianne Maeckelbergh, *The Will of the Many: How the Alterglobalisation Movement Is
Changing the Face of Democracy* (London: Palgrave Macmillan, 2009); David Graeber, *Direct
Action: An Ethnography* (Oakland, CA: AK Press, 2009); Jeffrey S. Juris and Alexander
Khasnabish, eds., *Insurgent Encounters: Transnational Activism, Ethnography, and
the Political* (Durham, NC: Duke University Press, 2013).

[31] Gilles Deleuze and Félix Guattari, *A Thousand Plateaus: Capitalism and Schizophrenia* (Minneapolis: University of Minnesota Press, 1987). This work can be quite helpful
here for reminding us that the real comprises not only the actual but also the virtual or
potential.

[32] This is not to deny the very real problem of translating these models and political gestures
into more sustainable forms of life and politics, but that is a separate issue.

1999, the Seattle Protests (WTO ministerial meetings shut down); 2001, the first World Social Forum; 2001, Argentina defaults on loans, protesters oust several presidents in the ensuing years, later that year the massive protests against the G8 in Genoa, Italy (300,000 protesters, one death); and 2003, protest of WTO in Cancun, and later that year Free Trade Area of the Americas (FTAA) protests in Miami. The list of events and movements could go on, and even this list would be a reductive representation of this important assemblage of movements.

Like the civil rights movement, the AGM (and other protest movements of the early 2000s) signaled a shift to a politics of relationality. However, the language and conceptual frameworks used by activists and academics alike never quite caught up to the radical innovations that this movement—and the many that have followed since—offered *in practice*. This speaks to the inevitable inadequacy of concepts and the fact that oftentimes it is in the messy material realm of practice, and not so much in the heady land of concepts or visions, where relationality lives. It also suggests that without the larger understanding of the ontological dimension of politics, even the most radical practices might fail to register in a sustained way.

What brought the "movement of movements" together and into visibility was an emergent understanding and critique of neoliberal corporate-driven globalization—specifically through contesting the policy prescriptions, and lack of democracy, of entities such as the WTO, IMF, and World Bank, enforced through free trade agreements and structural adjustment programs. The ascent of neoliberalism marked the apex of the vision of bioeconomic Man that the concern with relationality puts into question. Importantly, in addition to the economic and political programs of the institutions named above, neoliberalism was enshrined in the public consciousness through phrases such as "There is No Alternative" and "there is no such thing as society," largely popularized by Margaret Thatcher. By the 2000s, neoliberal ideology had become so hegemonic that it was embraced by governments on the right and center-left,[33] effectively creating a perception of reality in which the market was sovereign, regardless of the environmental, social, psychological, or spiritual costs. Contesting this story of reality as the only possible one was itself a hugely important aspect of the AGM.

Moreover, the ways in which this single story was contested was unique. For perhaps more than its opposition to neoliberalism, the AGM was notable for the new practices, vocabularies, and imaginaries that arose from it. The movement authored, invented, and recovered many important concepts, tech-nologies, and practices from myriad political cultures and traditions. Terms such as emergence, networks, social forums, counter-summits, affinity groups and spokes-councils, unity in difference, Indymedia, democracy from below, and (depending on where you draw the line around this movement) also Buen Vivir

---

[33] Some previously "leftist" oriented parties, such as the Labour Party in New Zealand and the United Kingdom, also espoused neoliberalism, effectively undermining the existence of a viable left the world-over. Most of the progressive governments that came to power in Latin America in the first decade of the century also necessarily adopted a range of neoliberal policies, given their choice of globally driven extractive development models.

(living well/the good life), food sovereignty, and more. Not coincidentally, many of the most important concepts and practices came from groups and movements in the Global South. For example, "a world where many worlds fit," "*caminar preguntando*" (walking while questioning), "autonomy," "walking at the pace of the slowest," all originated with the Zapatista movement—a part mestizo, mostly Indigenous movement in the rural southeast of Mexico, to be discussed in greater detail in the next chapter. These practices and vocabularies came as a result of the meshworking among many different place-based movements including the Zapatistas, but also the movement of unemployed workers in Argentina, women farmers in India and Africa, European and North American autonomists and anarchists, feminists, and numerous movements of Indigenous peoples.

Many of these concepts challenged the modern onto-epistemic formation; they refused the dualist logics and assumptions of modernity. These assumptions included notions of linear and progressive time; state-centered macropolitics; reductive understandings of the economy, politics, and power; not to mention the belief in enemies and a specific notion of the scale, agency, and subject of change. For example, they often coupled more traditional political demands about democratizing the IMF, World Bank, and so on, with cultural interventions. At protests activists used carnivalesque attire, giant and beautiful handmade puppets, as well as efforts to prefigure more communal worlds in the temporary communities that arose at sites of protest. Cultural interventions were given as much if not more weight as overtly political ones, challenging power relations in daily life and how these operated even in meetings, marches, and so forth. The movements often completely ignored governments in terms of their political visions and demands, even as they defended against the punitive and repressive practices of the State. In contrast to former conflicts between different subject positions such as environmentalists versus labor activists, or anarchists versus liberals, the AGM embraced a principle of "diversity of tactics" or "unity and diversity" eschewing any efforts to favor one struggle or identity. Theirs was a logic of both/and (rather than either/or), focusing on very local, place-based projects such as building local autonomy while creating transnational campaigns against neoliberalism, thus acting on both scales.

It can thus be said that the AGM conjured the outline for a profoundly relational politics to challenge the seemingly immutable neoliberal hegemony. In fact, a substantial amount of activism went into trying to explain the power in what others saw as an ineffectual politics, by finding a new political vocabulary.[34] Moreover, for many years academics and activists alike—including some of the present authors—struggled to find a language adequate to the task of characterizing these movements and the politics they were generating. Circulating at the time were notions such as "networked politics," "webs of power,"

---

[34] Notes from Nowhere, *We Are Everywhere: The Irresistible Rise of Global Anticapitalism* (London: Verso, 2003). The book's chapter titles are each organized around a central concept: Emergence, Network, Autonomy, Carnival, Clandestinity—that the authors—a mélange of activists, academics, and artists who called themselves the "Notes from Nowhere Collective"—felt helped to provide an orientation to this new political praxis.

"new cultural politics," "rhizomes," "self-organization," "networks," "complex-ity," "changing the world without taking power," and so forth. Many of these concepts did some very important work in validating and making sense of the apparently motley set of events and movements that others were dismissing for being too general, decentralized, playful, and ineffective, or too radical. Yet, changing the language did not sufficiently address the paradigm shift required or the consequences for politics from a relational view of life. So, while numer-ous activists and academics beautifully captured the idea of a remade political terrain, without a concomitant and more radical recognition that this terrain went beyond the confines of modern versions of reality, in which the political is itself not bounded in recognizable ways, the power of these new politics failed to register or receded and there was a failure to recognize the more profound challenges to the modern onto-epistemic configuration they entailed.

Slippage 3: Beyond dualisms: The question of
individuals and how we conceive them

If the first two slippages refer to missing the ontological dimension entirely, the next two reveal interrelated slippages around what relationality means and how it works. Both originate in the fact that often we end up reading relationality dualistically, that is, through the normative binary good versus bad wherein relationality is "good" and nonrelationality is "bad." In other words, we mistake relationality for a normative prescription rather than an ontological description of the Real. Coming to recognize that we cannot solve dualism through new dualisms leads us to understanding relationality as a foundational notion of life. While relationality can help undergird a better narrative of politics, we emphasize that it is an ontological condition, not a political prescription; inherent to it is a *principle of contingency*,[35] such that a politics of relationality necessarily looks different in different places and iterations. Overall, a politics of relationality does not easily map onto our current political spectrum and involves challenging the reductive treatments of those seen as ideological enemies. This does not mean that a politics of relationality is a-political or neutral, but that it troubles our older distinctions between left and right and is related to what could be called a "politics without an enemy."

Slippages are gradual and almost subtle. We think we are operating from a relational lens, but then land quickly back within modern dualisms. For example, as we began writing for this book, the term relationality itself seemed to be gaining popularity. However, what we observed as we heard various scholars, scholar-activists, designers, and others (almost all on the left of the political spectrum) speak hopefully and positively about relationality, were the signs of another ontological slippage: the propensity to interpret relationality itself through a dualistic framework that identifies relationality

---

[35] We will elaborate on this and other principles of relationality in Chapter 4.

with "collective" and with other terms associated with "good" or "progressive" politics in our current political framework, again, at least among those on the political left. Decoupling our understanding of relationality and its potential from our current political allegiances is important both for finding a way to move beyond the dualist relic of right and left, and for arriving at a more substantial understanding of what working at the ontological register of relationality could look like. Here, we begin this work by troubling the simple dualist dichotomy of individual versus collective before tackling the good/bad dualism in the next section.

First, and to reiterate a point made several times already, there is no such things as an individual. While there are a great many processes that go into making the notion of a separate individual seem true, objective, and natural, the reality is that the making of the individual is part of the active production of nonrelationality or even anti-relationality. Apparent nonrelationalities, including that of the autonomous individual, depend on a lot of relationships, historical and ongoing, to appear as such. As we mentioned in the Introduction, the COVID-19 pandemic underscored both this myth and the reality of our interdependencies.

Second, and less recognized, the naturalization of the notion of the individual goes hand in hand with a reductive notion of its supposed opposite, the collective. In fact, a view of individuals as intrinsically existent, uncaused, natural units corresponds with a view of the collective as a simple aggregate of these dis-embedded individuals, and often (perhaps not surprisingly) one that is opposed to the freedom of said individuals—even among those who believe in prioritizing the collective. Treating the individual and collective as diametrically opposed winds up creating societies of people, or organizations, who may presume that being in community requires muting or subsuming individual desire, talent, and so on, to the collective, or perhaps more common in mainstream culture, the interpretation, often attributed to Adam Smith and Frederick Hayek, that being oneself and pursuing one's dreams requires explicitly ignoring the collective dimension. Importantly, for our argument here, this slippage is shared by people on all sides of the political spectrum. For activists and others concerned with equality and social justice—namely, people who ideologically prefer the collective—this slippage is common in the tendency to equate equality (and justice) with placing the needs of the group above the needs of the individual. This can lead to an unhealthy suppression of their own needs and desires that can have destructive consequences such as burnout, but also unprocessed resentment and anger, which in turn lead to dysfunctional conflict-ridden organizations. In this sense folks on both the right and left share the problem of dualism where collectivity necessarily requires a merging or disappearance of uniqueness or individuality.[36]

---

[36] While we were editing this manuscript, we learned of a new book that deals with this challenge interestingly: Daniel Siegel, *IntraConnected: Mwe (Me + We) as the Integration of Self, Identity, and Belonging* (New York: Norton and Company, 2022).

Numerous Indigenous intellectuals throughout the Americas are particularly insightful in reconceptualizing the relation between the individual and the collective. Consider, for example, the following description of the individual (and collective) in an Anishnaabe context, by Leanne Betasamosake Simpson:

> There was a high degree of individual self-determination in Michi Saagiig Nishnaabeg society. Children were full citizens with the same rights and responsibilities as adults. They were raised in a nest of freedom and self-determination ….
>
> People were expected to figure out their gifts and their responsibilities through ceremony and reflection and self-actualization, and that process was the most important governing process of the individual level.[37]

Individual self-determination, freedom, and self-actualization are not opposed to the collective but constitutive of it. As Simpson explains elsewhere:

> Coming to know is the pursuit of whole-body intelligence practiced in the context of freedom and when realized collectively it generates generations of loving, creative, innovative, self-determining, interdependent, and *self-regulating community minded individuals*. It continually generates *communities of individuals* with the capacity to uphold and move forward our political practices and systems of governance.[38]

Similarly, Robin Wall Kimmerer, ecologist and enrolled member of Citizen Potowatomi Nation, writes:

> The most important thing each of us can know is our unique gift and how to use it in the world. Individuality is cherished and nurtured, because in order for the whole to flourish, each of us has to be strong in who we are and carry our gifts with conviction, so they can be shared with others.[39]

Contrary to dualist accounts of individuals versus collective, Indigenous communitarian formations do not suppress personal expression, and they are not homogeneous but plural. This finds another instructive expression in the work of Indigenous Mayan feminist intellectual Gladys Tzul Tzul. As she says, "the communal does not place limits on the personal, it rather potentiates it. The

---

[37] Leanne B. Simpson, *As We Have Always Done: Indigenous Freedom through Radical Resistance* (Minneapolis: University of Minnesota Press, 2017), 3–4.

[38] Simpson, "As We Have Always Done: Indigenous Freedom through Radical Resistance," transcribed from presentation, YouTube video, 1:35:22, available online: https://www.youtube.com/watch?v=vEgQLhoosTI (accessed December 10, 2020), emphasis ours.

[39] Robin Wall Kimmerer, *Braiding Sweetgrass: Indigenous Wisdom, Scientific Knowledge and the Teachings of Plants* (Minneapolis, MN: Milkweed Editions, 2013), 134.

communitarian entanglements provide the grounds on which personal and intimate lives are sustained," even if the organization of life, politics, and the economy is realized collectively.[40]

The reductive, dualist understandings of the collective as simply opposed to the individual is a major reason why *in practice* we end up with many of the problematic formations on both the left and right, including forms of sectarianism, dogmatism, parochialisms, and even fascism, not to mention State-centered and often repressive communist and socialist projects. It is also part of why our politics seem stuck in tired and ineffective polarizations. Such polarization illustrates the failure to grasp the ontological and cultural difference between the *liberal individual* and the *relational individual*, or relational personhood, of Indigenous intellectuals such as Simpson, Kimmerer, and Tzul Tzul.[41]

Slippage 4: Equating relationality with good (as opposed to bad):
essentialism and other problems of dualism

Closely related to this slippage is another: *eliding relationality with good*, and therefore *nonrelationality with bad*. This in turn relates to essentializing, that is, treating things as having intrinsic or essential properties. Interestingly, while many on the left have gotten quite good at historicizing and problematizing concepts such as the individual, what often happens is that after we accurately identify the fallacy of the individual and the production of nonrelationality we rather quickly fall back into a dualist or modernist mode, treating these nonrelationalities as if they were coherent, fixed realities. That is, we essentially "buy" the nonrelational story white supremacist patriarchal capitalism has created. This has implications for many aspects of our politics often leading to political practices that seem to presume the essential, rather than contingent or relational, existence of things such as individuals, identities, and so on.

One of the clearest places we can see both the potentialities of relationality and many slippages is in activist practices seeking to address racism and white supremacy. Anti-racist activists and race scholars hold sophisticated and nuanced

---

[40] Gladys Tzul Tzul, *Sistemas de gobierno comunal indígena* (Mexico City: Instituto Amaq', 2018) 57.

[41] Leftist ideology shares key elements with liberal capitalism. These include (1) the individual/collective binary; (2) a belief in the centrality of the economy and economic growth, closely related to (3) a commitment to modernity, progress, development, and a forward notion of time; (4) naturalized notions of rights and nation-states; (5) a belief in Globality—an abstract space-time presumed to be universal, which explains the erosion of place and the creation of a One-World world; and (6) the exaltation of scientific rationality and the rejection of knowledges that acknowledge uncertainty, mystery, ineffability, or sacredness. These shared assumptions correspond with the default settings of modernity. An important difference is that within Marxism the concept of dialectics offers the seed of a different epistemology and worldview that comes closer to relationality, though in practice this vision of dialectics often falls victim to the same slippage back to modernist dualisms.

views of race as illusory and contingent. Such activism works to simultaneously historicize and denaturalize the constructs of race and whiteness; address the contemporary manifestations of racism and white supremacy; and transform them, all without essentializing or fixing "white people" (as oppressors, or enemies) or "people of color" (as victims, or heroes). However, repeatedly, *in practice*, politics slips back into practices that presume that there *are* "white people" and "people of color," rather than webs of relations that produce stories and norms of whiteness and others. Terms such as white-ally; privilege; diversity, equity, and inclusion (DEI), while intending to combat racism, can often end up reinforcing the idea of race and the default equation of whiteness as the norm into which people seek inclusion.[42] We certainly do not mean to suggest that we need to move to race—or color—blindness. Rather we need to ask different questions, particularly how to navigate the slippage rather than simply play into it.

Again, we acknowledge that this is very slippery terrain and can be misread as being a return to the post-structuralist debates about identity politics. This is not what we are suggesting. We want to affirm the importance and utility of projects that seek to, for example, revalorize and redefine Indigeneity, Blackness, and queerness as positive. Such projects go a long way in countering and repairing the violent and destructive legacies of lengthy histories of white supremacy, anti-Blackness, anti-Indigeneity, heteronormativity, and so forth. However, there is a significant difference between re-signifying something as positive and affirming it, and coming to believe in its *essential* superiority. As Jamaica Kincaid puts it so clearly:

> Of course, the whole thing is, once you cease to be a master, once you throw off your master's yoke, you are no longer human rubbish, you are just a human being, and all the things that adds up to. So, too, with the slaves. Once they are no longer slaves, once they are free, they are no longer noble and exalted; *they are just human beings.*[43]

As such, while the desire to raise up experiences that have been maligned and subject to violence and attempted annihilation is extremely important and worthy of support, a slippage commonly occurs when we act as if those identified with the opposing side of the dualism (e.g., whiteness, white people) are actually, or essentially, not worthy. As Ruby Sales has put it: "there's nothing wrong with being European-American. That's not the problem. It's how you actualize that history and how you actualize that reality. It's almost like white people don't believe that other white people are worthy of being redeemed."[44]

---

[42] Bayo Akomolafe, "Slowing Down in Urgent Times [ENCORE] /285," *for the wild*, May 4, 2022, available online: https://forthewild.world/podcast-transcripts/dr-bayo-akomolafe-on-slowing-down-in-urgent-times-encore-285 (accessed June 1, 2022), transcript.

[43] Jamaica Kincaid, *A Small Place* (New York: Farrar, Strauss, & Giroux, 1988), 81, emphasis ours. There is a much deeper conversation to have about when slavery truly ends, and the nature of enslavement, of course.

[44] Sales, "Where Does It Hurt?."

To counter this tendency, some might argue for the utility of "strategic essentialism," as suggested by literary scholar Gayatri Spivak and others.[45] However, maintaining a differentiation between the contingent or strategic and the essentializing or normative is often very difficult in practice, and is where we find slippage. This is especially true given the realities of how past and ongoing trauma and violence affect humans on all sides of these relationships—somatically, consciously, and importantly, beneath that which we are conscious of.[46] So the question becomes how to make a different move, not falling back to post-structuralist or post-racial denials of identities and learning to work on slippery terrain in practice without reproducing dualisms. As we will discuss below and then in greater detail in the following chapter, there are key tools or concepts that help traverse this slippery terrain, turning slippages into portals to relational politics.

WORKING ON SLIPPERY TERRAIN: OPENING TO RELATIONALITY

We want to be clear here: we are asking these questions not from some sort of high ground outside the problem, blaming others for bad practice, but because we have ourselves fallen into these very slippages and recognize how challenging a terrain this is. In fact, given the painful and ongoing reality and effects of racism—a reality that is premised on an ontology of fixed categories, identities, property, and a generally zero-sum vision of the world—the challenges of remaining on the slippery terrain of relationality, in which nothing is real or fixed outside of the relationships that constitute them, becomes particularly palpable. The question becomes how to work in a way that acknowledges racism without turning race or whiteness into an immutable reality. How do we move and practice with this understanding, while acknowledging the ways in which racism and "racecraft" still pervade reality?[47]

Anti-racist educator, writer, and activist Ruth King employs Buddhism's "two truths doctrine," to address the difficulty of working in this slippery terrain. She describes the importance of understanding and working from two versions of reality, or two truths: relative reality and ultimate reality. She writes:

> In relative reality, I am a woman, African American, lesbian, great-grandmother, artist and elder. However, in ultimate reality, I'm none of those things. I am beyond conception; I am awareness dancing with the karmic rhythms of life.

---

[45] Gayatri Spivak, "Subaltern Studies: Deconstructing Historiography," in *In Other Worlds*, 197–221 (New York: Routledge, 1987).

[46] Resmaa Menakem, *My Grandmother's Hands: Racialized Trauma and the Pathway to Mending Our Hearts and Bodies*, Illustrated edition (Las Vegas: Central Recovery Press, 2017). For excellent work on the ways in which racialized trauma are embodied.

[47] Karen E. Fields and Barbara J. Fields, *Racecraft: The Soul of Inequality in American Life* (London: Verso, 2012). The Design Studio for Social Intervention in Boston is inspired by a similar realization (see Chapter 5).

> In ultimate reality, there is neither race nor a reason to suffer. We are undivided and beyond definition. But in relative reality, we're all in considerable pain as racially diverse beings driven by fear, hatred, greed and delusion.

It is precisely in this vein that the famous Combahee River Collective statement, "If Black women were free, it would mean that everyone else would have to be free *since our freedom would necessitate the destruction of all the systems of oppression,*" becomes a profound statement of relationality.[48] Black women's liberation means the end of all systems of oppression precisely because all the systems are contingent and mutually constituted and affected by relations internal to them. This suggests that what is important is not the aggregation of oppressions but a relational perspective in which the system is greater than the sum of its interlocking parts, and each part is "reciprocally constitutive of every other."[49] Once those systems of oppression are gone, we no longer have the same relations or even the same categories.[50] And importantly, we cannot know what will come next.

Barbara Holmes, Black theologian and author of *Race and the Cosmos* (2002, 2nd edn. 2020) offers an important insight, on the profound implications of relationality:

> The physics and cosmology revolution that is 100 years old has not been translated into the ordinary world of many of us, and specifically not in communities of color. The world that scientists describe now is so different than the world that I grew up in or even imagined. According to physicists, this is what the world is like: it is a universe permeated with movement and energy that vibrates and pulses with access to many dimensions .... We are all interconnected, not just spiritually or imaginally, but actually ... and the explicate [*or manifested*] order that's all around us makes us think that we're separate. Finally, I learned that ideas of dominance are predicated on a Newtonian clockwork universe. So, like dominoes, you push one and they all fall down, and everything is in order. But quantum physics tells us that the world is completely different. Particles burst into existence in unpredictable ways, observations affect the observed, and dreams of order and rationality are *not* the building blocks of the universe.[51]

48 BlackPast, "The Combahee River Collective Statement," 1977, available online: https://www.blackpast.org/african-american-history/combahee-river-collective-statement-1977/ (accessed January 11, 2021), emphasis ours.

49 David McNally, "Intersections and Dialectics: Critical Reconstructions in Social Reproduction Theory," in *Social Reproduction Theory: Remapping Class, Recentering Oppression*, 1st edn., Mapping Social Reproduction Theory, 94–111 (London: Pluto Press, 2017).

50 McNally, "Intersections and Dialectics." We believe this principle is mostly consistent with the well-established feminist notion of intersectionality, albeit with some important caveats made possible when the ontological is taken into consideration.

51 Barbara Holmes, "Lecture 1, Race and the Cosmos, Unpublished Living School Curriculum," Center for Action and Contemplation, New Mexico, 2019, available online: https://cac.org/daily-meditations/new-language-for-a-new-story-2021-02-15/ (accessed February 15, 2021).

Understanding the distinction between a domino vision of reality and power in which we are essentially working to knock down or build up a row of dominoes that we are already familiar with, on the one hand, and building forms of organization, community, and society, from a truly nondualist perspective, in which things burst or emerge into existence in unpredictable ways, on the other, is key for relational anti-racist practice. It also has implications beyond anti-racism to our very understandings of the aims, scale, temporalities, and domains of politics or social change projects. However, this ontological uncertainty and unpredictability is hard, and goes against many of the most deeply held beliefs and habits of activists, including our belief in a rational mind that can design and create a better collective future.

We recognize that the implications for letting go of the categories of good and bad can seem particularly challenging for activists working within a political framework that is largely premised on the dualisms of winning and losing, good guys (victims, heroes) and bad guys (oppressors, enemies). Whether we are talking about campaigns, elections, revolutions, or the drive to win and defeat the opponent, this often translates into hardened divisions. It continues to produce and reproduce the known world and its dysfunctional systems over and over again, in a vicious and futile cycle. Nothing demonstrates this better than the reality of prisons and the history of attempting to reform them, as the abolition movement has made patently clear (see Chapter 4).

To create a politics that moves beyond these habits, we need to let go of thinking we know what the solution looks like, trying to understand instead the generative nature of radical uncertainty and the reality of emergence. Jack Halberstam's introduction to Stefano Harney and Fred Moten's *The Undercommons*, puts this well:

> We cannot say what new structures will replace the ones we live with yet, because once we have torn shit down, we will inevitably see more and see differently and feel a new sense of wanting and being and becoming. What we want after "the break" will be different from what we think we want before the break and both are necessarily different from the desire that issues from being in the break.[52]

The question becomes then, both how do we get brave enough to accept this uncertainty and allow things to get torn down, and how do we work against our tendencies to mistake our current ways of knowing reality for reality itself, what Wynter calls "mistaking the map for the territory"?[53]

---

[52] Stefano Harney and Fred Moten, *The Undercommons: Fugitive Planning & Black Study* (New York: Minor Compositions, 2013), 6.

[53] Wynter, "No Humans Involved."

CONCLUSION: SLIPPAGES CAN BE PORTALS TO RELATIONAL WORLDS

It is here that we start to recognize the need to move from our discussion of the limits and slippages in current activist practice to more properly discussing what a politics of relationality is and requires, as well as how to get there. Said differently, while we have pointed to many of the obstacles that may get in the way of staying with a politics of relationality, the question of what exactly they are, how they can be achieved and sustained, remain. In the next chapter we move to discussing concrete examples of relational politics. However, before going there, and as a way to bring some closure to this chapter, we want to make an important clarification about slippages lest we slip into another dualism by trying to avoid them.

In our understanding, slippages are part of moving from the old story to the new one. There is no avoiding them. They are part of the uncomfortable, liminal and unknown terrain, what cultural and feminist theorist Gloria Anzaldua calls *nepantla*, or being in between, and part of real transformations. However, we *can* ask how one might move between stories more skillfully. In Buddhism and Yoga, the term "upaya" refers to skillful means, expedient, or skillful action. It refers to acting with wisdom and compassion, rather from the certainty of holding a "correct" or ultimate "truth."[54] As such being skillful does not mean completely avoiding mistakes or slippages, but rather, handling them with compassion and building wisdom from them. Similarly, when we described the ways these slippages have happened historically, say with the civil rights movement or the AGM, we were not suggesting that things should—or could—have gone a different way. This is not a criticism. Slippages are part of the process, and as such, often, the very sites of slippage become the basis for new learning and transformation, and bridges or portals to new worlds. This is also important because being "good modern subjects" we can imagine that some of our readers are already lambasting themselves for continuing to slip, for falling prey to default settings, for not being able exit the old story once and for all. But moving from one story to the next, in the sense we are describing, is not linear and it is not easy.

Relationality invokes a helpful reminder that as we transition between stories—from the Western dualist worldview to the relational one—we need to be mindful of recapitulating linear ideas of progress or getting to the "right" place. As Tibetan Buddhist teacher Pema Chödrön explains, a profound premise of working in this vein is that we need to give up hope:

> If we're willing to give up hope that insecurity and pain can be exterminated, then we can have the courage to relax with the groundlessness of our situation. This is the first step on the path ... In Tibetan there's an interesting word: *ye tang che*. The *ye* part means "totally, completely," and the rest of

---

[54] This does not mean a crude notion of the ends justifying the means, however.

it means "exhausted." Altogether, *ye tang che* means "totally tired out." We might say "totally fed up." It describes an experience of complete hopelessness, of completely giving up hope. This is an important point. This is the beginning of the beginning. Without giving up hope—that there's somewhere better to be, that there's someone better to be—we will never relax with where we are or who we are.

Some may find this depiction of hopelessness to be extremely negative or frustrating, yet in nondualism giving up the idea of *a better place* maybe necessary for actually getting there. This is why we say slippages can become portals, or bridges, to new worlds. A portal does not work in a linear logic of progress.

PART THREE
Remake

4 Autonomy, abolition, and sacred activism: Bridges to remaking life

I wish to live because life has within it that which is good, that which is beautiful, and that which is love. Therefore, since I have known all these things, I have found them to be reason enough and—I wish to live. Moreover, because this is so, I wish others to live for generations and generations and generations and generations.

LORRAINE HANSBERRY[1]

INTRODUCTION: FROM SLIPPAGES TO BRIDGES AND PORTALS

One of the things we have discovered through writing this book is that it is about relationality, yes, but that also means that it is about moving from the old story to the new, and the difficulty of doing so. It is not easy to move from a "One-World world" to a relational one. The last chapter helped us see the way that movements approached a relational politics, but then often missed sustaining it due to slippages back into the modernist onto-episteme and its ways of life. This chapter will explore examples of the political activation of relationality and the navigation of slippages. As we mentioned previously, the goal is not to avoid slippages; they are inevitable. Rather we ask how we might work with sites of slippage more skillfully, so that we may turn them into bridges and portals from this world to the next. Portals and bridges act as relational ways of traversing thresholds, as well as being in the liminal space in between worlds.

---

[1] *To Be Young, Gifted, and Black; Lorraine Hansberry in Her Own Words*, adapted by Robert Nemiroff with original drawings and art by Miss Hansberry and an introduction by James Baldwin (Englewood Cliffs, NJ: Prentice-Hall, 1969), 100.

A few weeks into the global pandemic that served as the backdrop to our writing of this book, Arundhati Roy described the pandemic as both a rupture and a portal:

> Our minds are still racing back and forth, longing for a return to "normality," trying to stitch our future to our past and refusing to acknowledge the rupture. But the rupture exists. ...
>
> Historically, pandemics have forced humans to break with the past and imagine their world anew. This one is no different. It is a portal, a gateway between one world and the next.
>
> We can choose to walk through it, dragging the carcasses of our prejudice and hatred, our avarice, our data banks and dead ideas, our dead rivers and smoky skies behind us. Or we can walk through lightly, with little luggage, ready to imagine another world. And ready to fight for it.

A bridge is also a particularly apt descriptor of relational politics. As Gloria Anzaldúa reminds us in her seminal anthologies, *This Bridge Called My Back* (1979) and *This Bridge We Call Home* (2002), to bridge is at the core of the ontological work of radical transformation:[2]

> Bridges are thresholds to other realities, archetypal, primal symbols of shifting consciousness. They are passageways, conduits, connectors that connote transitioning, crossing borders, and changing perspectives. Bridges span liminal (threshold) spaces between worlds, spaces I call nepantla, a Nahuatl word meaning tierra entre medio. Transformations occur in this in-between space, an unstable, unpredictable, precarious, always in transition space lacking clear boundaries. Nepantla es tierra desconocida, and living in this liminal zone means being in a constant state of displacement—an uncomfortable, even alarming feeling. Most of us dwell in nepantla so much of the time it's become a sort of "home." ... Change is inevitable; no bridge lasts forever.[3]

It is no coincidence that the cultural politics of the Zapatistas, or Zapatismo, that we will describe in greater depth shortly is itself described as a bridge:

> Zapatismo is not a new political ideology, or a rehash of old ideologies. Zapatismo is nothing, it does not exist. It only serves as a bridge, to cross from one side, to the other. So everyone fits within Zapatismo, everyone who wants to cross from one side, to the other. *There are no universal recipes,*

---

[2] Martin Heidegger also spoke of bridges. See Martin Heidegger, *Poetry, Language, Thought*, trans. and intro. Albert Hofstadter, 1st edn. (New York: Harper & Row, 1971); Anne-Marie Willis, "Ontological Designing," *Design Philosophy Papers* 4, no. 2 (June 1, 2006): 69–92.

[3] Gloria Anzaldúa and Analouise Keating, eds., *This Bridge We Call Home: Radical Visions for Transformation* (New York: Routledge, 2002), 1.

lines, strategies, tactics, laws, rules, or slogans. There is only a desire – to build a better world, that is, a new world.[4]

Rather than being a negation, the fact that Zapatismo "does not exist," except to serve as a bridge provides a clear articulation of the ontological principle of relationality and the re-centering of politics onto life and worldmaking. The goal is not the politics themselves, rather, pluriversal politics—another way of naming relational politics—is simply a tool, a bridge, a way of crossing over toward the goal: to make life and ensure that life can be continuously made and remade "for generations and generations and generations." In some senses, all relational projects are bridging projects, and as such they take place on uncertain ground.

A bridge is both materially and conceptually a relational term. Bridges are things, but to bridge is also a verb. To be a bridge is to be in constant flow, to be in process. Similarly, at the heart of relationality is a vision of process, flow, movement; nothing is fixed or permanent, everything needs to be made and remade. Bridges change according to shifting contexts and needs but recognize the fundamental need to get from this world to the next. To bridge, to be relational, is not comfortable; it might even be painful, like facing death. Our goal in this chapter is not to describe solutions, that is, formulas for achieving a politics of relationality. Instead, this chapter seeks to point to the skills and capacities required for bridging—that is, the skills and capacities to withstand the deaths and formlessness that transformation entails. As our society faces a collective moment of apocalyptic rupture and liminality, the need for such bridging skills is more obvious than ever.

In this chapter our examples will highlight the kinds of practices that help transform slippages into portals or bridges. These include the Zapatista project for autonomía, prison abolition and transformative justice projects, as well as a variety of practices that we might call spiritual activism or healing justice. Before moving on to describe these cases in greater detail we first name five *principles of relationality* that undergird many of these projects and practices.

PRINCIPLES OF THE POLITICS OF RELATIONALITY

While not universal or prescriptive, we noticed several common tendencies or principles underlying a relational politics. First, relational politics are contingent and local; that is to say, there is no expression of them outside of concrete, material, and local iterations. Second, they are emergent. This means they are unpredictable, defying linear or mechanistic causal rationality, and they are necessarily complex and collective, in which the whole is greater than the sum of its parts. Third, they exceed easy categorization into boxes or categories; they may seem paradoxical and full of tensions, yet these excesses are generative. Fourth, among

---

[4] The Clandestine Revolutionary Command of the EZLN, quoted in Global Social Theory, "Zapatismo," available online: https://globalsocialtheory.org/topics/zapatismo/ (accessed February 15, 2021), emphasis ours.

the boxes and categories they refuse, is the dichotomy of good and bad. They do not center good and bad per se, but rather the transformative effects of experience: what learning, growth, and so forth, is generated in the process? Fifth, the dimension of the heart or spirit seems to be key to being able to maneuver, know, and be relationally. As we hope will become clear, there are resonances or echoes between these principles and some of the slippages described in the last chapter.

Principle 1: Contingent and local

Describing relational politics is not easy for many reasons. For one, relational politics are always defined vis-à-vis or in relation to something else. They cannot be defined *a priori*, and they cannot be predicted. They can only be defined in concrete instances and places once they have emerged, and often that emergence is not fully intelligible. While a certain practice is progressive or "good" in one context, it might be regressive and problematic in another, depending on histories of power, meaning, and other forms of local relationships. Take for example mass marches. In a totalitarian country where marches were mandated by the State, a massive march with thousands of people might not be progressive. Or take local food. For Black or Indigenous people living under occupation in the American South, the *local* emphasized in the local food movement can represent a harkening back to times of slavery, sharecropping, annihilation. Similarly, somewhere that has no access to basic health care may seek to work on universalizing access, while a place that has a hyper-medicalized society may seek to introduce the idea of de-professionalization of medicine, and the diffusion of DIY wellness practices as alternatives.

There are few things that can be named as relational *a priori* and out of context. This is why when asked how people could contribute to their cause, the Zapatistas would say "fight neoliberalism how it touches down in your place," rather than offering a ten-step program or blueprint for revolution. It is why they say, "*There are no universal recipes, lines, strategies, tactics, laws, rules, or slogans*. There is only a desire." Similarly, abolitionist politics operate from the understanding that everything is an experiment and that there are no one-size-fits-all solutions.

Principle 2: Emergence, complexity, and wholeness

Emergence is a nondualist scientific and philosophical concept in which the basic tenet is that the whole is greater than the sum of its parts.[5] Closely linked to this is the recognition that you cannot predict what that whole will be or

---

[5] There are numerous sources on emergence and complexity, for some of our favorites, which we draw on, see: adrienne maree brown, *Emergent Strategy: Shaping Change, Changing Worlds* (Chico, CA: AK Press, 2017); Joanna Macy and Chris Johnstone, *Active Hope: How to Face the Mess We're in without Going Crazy* (Novato, CA: New World Library, 2012); Brian Goodwin, *Nature's Due: Healing Our Fragmented Culture* (Edinburgh: Floris Books, 2007).

when it will arise. Similarly, the principle of autopoiesis holds that systems self-organize based on the existence and presence of difference. What is more, in an emergent system, individual entities that appear to be acting chaotically on the micro or individual scale can produce an elegant, even stunning configuration and feat at the macro level, seemingly out of nowhere and without any central commander or plan. Emergence is the reality of many living systems—such as ant colonies, amoebas, fungi, beehives, weather systems, our brains, jazz improv, as well as many cities and social systems. From our perspective, it can be seen as a general principle of reality, meaning that reality would be better understood from the perspective of emergence and self-organization rather than mechanistic causality.

Emergence's central notion that the whole is greater than the sum of its parts is a very important corrective to the dualism presumed between collective and individual described in the previous chapter. As a common philosophical adage puts it, reality is "more than one and less than many," troubling the simple dichotomy of collective/individual.[6] In other words, in a relational perspective, rather than seeing the individual as opposed to the collective or the whole, individuality or particularity is determining of it. Importantly, then, the individual, or self, can never be understood as disconnected or separate from the collective, what Macy refers to as a "wider sense of self." Consider these words from Joanna Macy (with co-author Chris Johnstone):

> Interconnectedness is not about merging. Experiencing the wider identity of our connected self does not mean losing our individuality. Quite the opposite: it is through finding and playing our unique role within a community that we feel more strongly part of it. … When you fall in love, you feel incredibly bonded with your loved one and at the same time more uniquely yourself, different from anyone else in the world. The experience of connectedness with a healthy community has similar qualities; it brings out our latent, distinctive gifts.[7]

In a relational worldview, we want more difference for a more cohesive collective. A good example of this, cited by Robin Wall Kimmerer, is that of the "Three Sisters": corn, squash, and beans:

> The most important thing each of us can know is our unique gift and how to use it in the world. Individuality is cherished and nurtured, because in order for the whole to flourish, each of us has to be strong in who we are and carry our gifts with conviction, so they can be shared with others. Being among the [three] sisters provides a visible manifestation of what a community can become when its members understand and share their gifts. In reciprocity, we fill out spirits as well as our bellies.[8]

---

[6] Steven Johnson, *Emergence: The Connected Lives of Ants, Brains, Cities, and Software* (New York: Scribner, 2001).

[7] Macy and Johnstone, *Active Hope*, 92.

[8] Kimmerer, *Braiding Sweetgrass*, 134.

Grown together each enhances the quality and life-chances of the other. Examples from nature abound and are linked to many counternarratives to the traditional biological tropes that comprise Wynter's Man2. In fact, there is a whole stream of biology focused on the notion of evolution as a story of endosymbiosis, rather than competition over scarce resources or a war for the survival of the fittest, not to mention numerous studies of fungi, amoeba, neural networks, and rhizomes that acknowledge the trouble with discerning individuals at all. As the Zapatistas and many Indigenous groups demonstrate, reconceiving of the individual/collective dualism is almost a prerequisite for making forms of life that are relational. Prison abolitionists similarly recognize the crucial importance of holism and fractals as organizing principles for being able to build new worlds from the cellular to the institutional level.[9]

Principle 3: Excess, paradox, and difference:
Radical uncertainty, beyond categories

Some describe relationality as a form of non-dual consciousness that enables you to hold two, supposedly opposed, even paradoxical things without becoming undone. Richard Rohr describes non-dual thinking as:

> our ability to read reality in a way that is not judgmental, in a way that is not exclusionary of the part that we don't understand. When you don't split everything up according to what you like and what you don't like, you leave the moment open, you let it be what it is in itself and you let it speak to you. *Reality is not totally one, but it is not totally two, either!* Stay with that necessary dilemma, and it can make you wise.[10]

Another way people describe this is presence, or simply being with what is.

How we experience this not-knowing is a good example of the difference between a political activation of relationality and a slippage back to the modern settings. In the latter not-knowing is associated with unsettlement, unintelligibility, or even confusion; paradox is seen as a problem rather than the engine of life and change. In the former, in relationality, not-knowing can be positively named as wonder, awe, and curiosity in the face of mystery; mystery and paradox being fundamental to life. This subtle distinction between not-knowing experienced as a lack and not-knowing experienced as wonder is key to opening to relationality.

It is interesting how many things the Western mind deems paradoxical or at odds, but when we reflect on our actual lived experiences these supposed

---

[9] brown, *Emergent Strategy.*

[10] Richard Rohr, "Non-Dual Thinking: There Are Things We Don't Know," *Tiny Buddha* (blog), September 6, 2012, available online: https://tinybuddha.com/blog/non-dual-thinking-there-are-things-we-dont-know/ (accessed April 6, 2021), quotation from transcript, emphasis ours.

contradictions coexist in the dynamic and relational field of life. For example, some people who have terminal illnesses or near-death experiences describe these experiences as leading them to feel more alive. One could say paradox is only an intractable problem *conceptually*, because we seek conceptual resolution. *In practice*, paradox, opposition, tension can just be.

In this view, life is a delicate interplay and constant shifting between dualities. The key being the recognition that the messy and shifting, what some might call the excess, or the incomprehensible, is necessary. Excess, often experienced as pain, grief, or other forms of rupture, are the motor of life and are often essential parts of a bridge or portal to relationality. They are also commonly pathways to the heart (Principle 5). As both cases below will show, the navigation to a politics of relationality often requires traversing painful or unexpected thresholds, including collective deaths, conflicts that seem intractable and a being with radical difference or the seemingly intolerable.[11]

Principle 4: Non-normativity: Beyond good and bad

The principle of non-normativity, beyond good and bad, might be the most difficult aspect of relationality understood as a political project, especially for us moderns with activist propensities. The rejection of any facile distinction between good and bad, positive and negative, gets to the crux of relationality and nondualism.

Compost is an excellent metaphor for getting beyond good and bad. It demonstrates that waste and flowers are literally mutually constituted and neither have a fixed or intrinsic existence. Each becomes the other and makes the other possible.[12] As Thich Nhat Hanh put it, "the gardener who is familiar with organic gardening is constantly on alert to save the waste materials because he knows how to transform them into compost and then transform compost into flowers and vegetables."[13] Similarly, in organic and permaculture practices, rather than focus on *eliminating* "the pests," gardeners seek to increase the biodiversity of the garden so that "pests" don't take over. In so doing, pests are

---

[11] The work of Marisol de la Cadena on this has been pivotal in our understanding this. See,*Earth Beings: Ecologies of Practice across Andean Worlds* (Durham, NC: Duke University Press, 2015); "Uncommoning Nature: Stories from the Anthropo-Not-Seen," in *Anthropos and the Material*, ed. Penny Harvey, Christian Krohn-Hansen, and Knut G. Nustad, 35–58 (Durham, NC: Duke University Press, 2019); "Not Knowing, in the Presence Of .....," in *Experimenting with Ethnography: A Companion to Analysis*, ed. Andrea Ballestero and Brit Ross Winthereik, 246–56 (Durham, NC: Duke University Press, 2021). See also Bayo Akomolafe and Alnoor Ladha, "Perverse Particles, Entangled Monsters and Psychedelic Pilgrimages: Emergence as an onto-Epistemology of Not-Knowing Ephemera," *Ephemera* 17, no. 4 (2017): 819–39, available online: http://www.ephemerajournal.org/contribution/perverse-particles-entangled-monsters-and-psychedelic-pilgrimages-emergence (accessed July 16, 2021).

[12] For more see, Sharma, *Interdependence*.

[13] Thich Nhat Hanh, *True Love: A Practice for Awakening the Heart* (London: Shambhala, 2006), 67–8.

no longer pests, and may even turn out to have some beneficial aspects. Similarly, in many holistic approaches to health, illness itself is not seen as "bad," and health is not simply one thing. Illness can be viewed as a teacher, a sign of deeper imbalance, or a call to attention, and every individual has a different manifestation of health or wellness. Good and bad simply do not work here. Not only because good and bad are not objectively definable, but also because that which is "bad" might have its role to play.

The question becomes how to construct societies where instead of focusing all efforts on securitizing (some) lives against every external harm, we focus also on how harm and trauma can be processed and integrated,[14] where repair can take place as part of the self-regulating aspect of the system, and where the system itself is overall a space for making life, rather than ending it.

Similarly, in much activism having a villain can seem like one of the most motivating factors in compelling political involvement (think of the energy invested in opposing Trump and the Republican Party in the United States). While conflict and anger are not bad and can be extremely generative especially in disrupting stasis and systems of oppression, there is a subtle yet crucial difference between agonistic conflict[15] and personalized, vitriolic positions, or what Michel Foucault calls polemics.[16] Defining enmity as provisional, situational, and contingent is important because it allows for people to change and acknowledges that all of us given certain circumstances and stories are capable of terrible harm and, conversely, great benevolence. While having an enemy can be extremely productive and warranted as a jumping-off point, when we do not move past this to the systems view, there tends to be much collateral damage to all parties. A politics based on oversimplifying enmity underestimates the power of love, care, and compassion. As we will see, prison abolition's commitment to ending police, prisons, and carcerality requires embracing those often defined as unwanted, criminal, disposable and cultivating politics and communities based on care and compassion.

Principle 5: Love and Spirituality: Practicing relationality means being in the heart

One of the ongoing puzzles in the journey to relationality is how we move from a *conceptual* understanding or belief in relationality, to a more thoroughgoing *living* of it, especially given messiness, paradox, and slippage. Another way

---

[14] Prentis Hemphill, "13 Blackness & Belonging—Prentis Hemphill," irresistible (podcast), available online: https://irresistible.org/podcast/13 (accessed June 3, 2022). Prentis Hemphill makes this point about the need for designing systems that can process trauma.

[15] Chantal Mouffe, "Which Public Sphere for a Democratic Society?," *Theoria*, no. 99 (2002): 55–65, available online: https://www.jstor.org/stable/41802189.

[16] Michel Foucault, "Polemics, Politics and Problematizations," in *Ethics: Subjectivity and Truth*, vol. 1, *Essential Works of Foucault*, ed. Paul Rabinow, 111–20 (New York: The New Press, 1994).

to ask this is how do we know and live the radical interdependence of all that is as an embodied ontological premise, not just a nice intellectual or ethical aspiration? According to Thomas Berry, "In the sacred, all opposites are reconciled."[17] Or, as bell hooks puts it,

> Spiritual life is first and foremost about the commitment to a way of thinking and behaving that honors principles of inter-being and interconnectedness. When I speak of the spiritual, I refer to the recognition within everyone that there is a place of mystery in our lives where forces that are beyond human desire or will alter circumstances and/or guide and direct us.[18]

As such, this fifth principle while important in and of itself is in many ways a summation, the ultimate bridging technology.

Another word for this is Love. Martin Luther King Jr. writes of love as a powerful force that is the "supreme unifying principle of life. Love is somehow the key that unlocks the door which leads to ultimate reality."[19] Recalling his articulation of life as an "inescapable network of mutuality," love then, is one of the main bridges or tools to relationality. Love here is not a sentimental or merely personal experience, but, as James Baldwin put it, "a state of being, or a state of grace—not in the infantile American sense of being made happy but in the tough and universal sense of quest and daring and growth."[20] This kind of love is often connected to the ineffable, wondrous, and mysterious.

Another way to explain this principle, is that relationality entails a shift from the mind to the heart; from understanding knowing-being as a rational, mind-based activity, to a heart-based one.[21] Being in the heart entails a form of knowing that does not require proofs and evidence, but a commitment to the Other, without assimilating them or changing them into your version of comprehensibility. It is also only from the capaciousness of the heart that we can handle the radical diversity of life. Arriving to the heart often requires pain and discomfort, the capacity to withstand the heartbreak and myriad small deaths that accompany life.[22] Many of us might be familiar with such intense life experiences that transported and transformed us—often through deep suffering,

---

[17] Carolyn W. Toben and Thomas Rain Crowe, *Recovering a Sense of the Sacred: Conversations with Thomas Berry* (Whitsett, NC: Timberlake Earth Sanctuary Press, 2012), 36.

[18] bell hooks, *All About Love: New Visions*, 1st edn. (New York: William Morrow, 2000), 77.

[19] Martin Luther King Jr. quoted in bell hooks, *All About Love*, 75.

[20] James Baldwin, *The Fire Next Time*, Modern Library edn. (New York: Modern Library, 1995), 94.

[21] Cynthia Bourgeault, "The Way of the Heart," *PARABOLA* (blog), January 31, 2017, available online: https://parabola.org/2017/01/31/the-way-of-the-heart-cynthia-bourgeault/ (accessed November 16, 2018).

[22] Michal Osterweil, "Being with to Discover 'the Love that Will Not Die'," *Michal Osterweil* (blog), January 31, 2022, available online: https://www.michalosterweil.com/blog/being-with-to-discover-the-love-that-will-not-die (accessed March 15, 2022).

forcing us to let go of everything we knew or thought we knew.[23] As wisdom traditions from around the world teach: it is "the heart that breaks open [that] can hold the whole universe."[24]

At the heart of spirituality and the activism that it yields is a distinct way of knowing and being, which is one of the key mechanisms for being able to perceive and stay with relationality, and perhaps most importantly, address the gap between theory and practice that has vexed our movements. This is why we said that the fifth principle is a summation or enactment of all the others. As we describe relational political projects below, the role of the heart, of spirituality, of suffering and rupture as gateways to these, is unmistakable, so much so that relationality and spirituality are often mutually defining.

THE POLITICAL ACTIVATION OF RELATIONALITY: ZAPATISMO AND PRISON ABOLITION

In what follows we explore in greater detail two projects that we feel demonstrate these five principles, albeit in different ways: prison abolition movements from North America, and the Zapatista movement from Chiapas, Mexico. We choose these two examples because in addition to exemplifying the politics of relationality, they demonstrate how different these can look. After describing these projects in greater detail, we engage additional examples of activism that seek to explicitly include spirituality and the heart.

Zapatismo: Changing the world by (re)stor(y)ing power, life, collectivity, and the heart

On January 1, 1994, the day the North American Free Trade Agreement went into effect, an uprising of Indigenous peasants in the Mexican state of Chiapas captivated the world's attention for its reclamation and reframing of the notion of revolution. Led by the Ejército Zapatista Liberación Nacional (EZLN), the movement of Indigenous peasants asserted their right to collectively owned lands, Indigenous forms of self-governance, women's rights, and the rejection of neoliberal corporate-driven economic and extractivist logics in their resource rich lands. Rather than seek to overturn the Mexican State, the communities developed a vision of *autonomía*—or self-governance—based on a mix of Indigenous and leftist visions of democracy and life.[25]

---

[23] Krista Tippett, "Remembering Thich Nhat Hanh, Brother Thay," On Being, aired September 25, 2003, available online: https://onbeing.org/programs/remembering-thich-nhat-hanh-brother-thay/ (accessed January 29, 2022).

[24] Macy and Johnstone, *Active Hope*, 75.

[25] There is no space here to do justice to this movement. In what follows there are excellent sources for further reading.

For Michal and Arturo, the Zapatista movement was one of the first examples of relational politics we encountered long before we began using the terms relationality or recognized the ontological dimension of the political, including their brilliant articulation of interdependence and pluriversality, stated most succinctly in their oft cited slogan, "We want a world where many worlds fit" (*queremos un mundo donde quepan muchos mundos*). The Zapatistas quickly captivated much of the left around the world by the novel reorientations that radically reframed several core assumptions at the heart of traditional leftist revolutionary projects.

While by the 1990s many on both the right and left had bought into the fatalistic notion of "the end of history" and the consequent triumph of capitalism and democracy, implicitly accepting the failure of the leftist imaginary, the Zapatistas reinspired a leftist politics by offering important correctives to troubled political modalities and default settings of the old or traditional left. As autonomist Marxist John Holloway put it, the Zapatistas "reinvented revolution." However, what reinventing revolution truly looks like, especially given the propensity for reading things back into our dominant default settings, was far from clear.

The assumptions of the "old Left" include many discussed in the previous chapters, including a zero-sum, state-centered, and object-based understanding of power; a linear notion of progress and development; a clear-cut, macropolitical understanding of success versus failure, and a rational and secular notion of political ideology. These assumptions originated in binaries such as: revolution versus reform; democracy versus socialism; difference versus collectivity; armed versus nonviolent struggle; struggle versus building life; rule versus subjugation; local versus global; traditional versus modern; culture versus economy (base/superstructure); urgency versus slowness, the list could go on. The Zapatistas turned many of these oppositions on their head, finding a way that was not quite in the middle but that refused to see them as opposed. We can understand this nondualist orientation as Zapatismo, a unique cultural politics, or as we understand it now, a politics operating with a distinct ontology and epistemology.

Here it is important to note an important distinction between Zapatismo and the Zapatistas. The latter refers to the concrete, lived experience of people in Chiapas, Mexico who are Zapatistas. These include the EZLN—the armed political wing of the movement; the autonomous villages—comprising peasant families, children, men, women, and elders; and the caracoles—the physical centers of governance and life-making including the good governance councils and health clinics. The Zapatistas are real-life people creating and living a radically new, yet anciently rooted form of life, with all the messiness, ups and downs that this entails.

Zapatismo, on the other hand, is what can be described as a cultural politics, including the vision underlying it.[26] Some elements that characterize this

---

[26] Manuel Callahan, "Why Not Share a Dream? Zapatismo as Political and Cultural Practice," *Humboldt Journal of Social Relations* 29, no. 1 (2005): 6–37.

culture of politics are: a simultaneously place-based and global orientation—what we have termed "place-based globalism";[27] the centrality of women and women's demands; the paradoxical yet untroubled inclusion of Indigenous *and* modern approaches in various realms including health, education, economy, and governance; and their commitment to "walking while questioning" or embracing uncertainty, contingency, and the messiness of practice. Perhaps one of the most challenging for Westerners is their emphasis on "walking at the pace of the slowest"; walking at the pace of the slowest not only runs counter to the urgent temporality of most social change activists, in so doing it challenges the temporal assumptions of modernity. Taken together, these elements constitute the Zapatista project of autonomy, or autonomía. Importantly, while Zapatismo and the Zapatistas are distinct, they cannot be understood separately from one another.

The principle of contingency/locality can be seen at play in multiple ways. The Zapatistas posited that it was only at local, material and grounded scales that radically different worlds can coexist without needing to either subjugate or resolve these differences. This key insight was captured in the phrase: "We want a world where many worlds fit." These spaces wherein relational and nonrelational worlds experience themselves simultaneously can also be understood as what in the next chapter we call pluriversal contact zones—a key space for transitioning to relationality—and demonstrates Principle 3 of paradox, uncertainty, and excess.

This multiplicity or unity in diversity can been seen in numerous ways. From the moment the man who came to be known as Subcomandante Marcos arrived in the jungle to "organize" the Indigenous peasants, the soon to be named Zapatistas became involved with the inspiring project of translating between worlds. That project is ongoing in terms of both the global movements they have inspired and their own elaborations of Zapatismo for their communities.

While the Zapatistas are largely constituted by Indigenous peoples from Chiapas, one of the things that made the Zapatista project so potent and popular especially in the late 1990s and early 2000s, the heyday of the AGM, was that it was integrally and from its inception a project of pluriversal amalgamation of the political cosmovisions of Indigenous communities from southeast Mexico with those of leftists from the city, then globally. In the early 1980s Marxist-Leninists from Mexico City set out to organize the Indigenous of the state of Chiapas—a state they saw as having the poorest and most exploited peoples. Upon arriving to the jungle, they were met with the more radical political practices and life philosophies of the Indigenous people there. In other words, the inspiring vision of radical democracy that eventually came to be called Zapatismo or Zapatista autonomía was a result of what some have called the "clash," or what we might see as the copresence of these two not fully separate worlds. These

---

[27] Michal Osterweil, "Place-Based Globalism: Theorizing the Global Justice Movement," *Development* 48, no. 2 (June 2005): 23–8, available online: https://doi.org/10.1057/palgrave.development.1100132.

encounters fostered a generative not-knowing, that turned out to be one of the keys to enabling the shift to a relational worldview.

Relatedly, Zapatismo included a crucial reframing of leftist politics and global solidarity work. Key to this reframing was the recognition that what worked in one place, at one time, might not work elsewhere (Principle 1: contingency). When the Zapatistas would post their communiques or invite people to "Encuentros" in the Selva Lacondona, they were not after some new unified program for the left or recreation of solidarity politics such as those of the 1970s and 1980s. One of their most famous slogans was a riff on Lilla Watson's, "If you have come here to help me, please go home. If you have come because your liberation is bound up with mine, then we can work together." While they did accept support of different kinds, their most common request for those interested in furthering their cause was to fight neoliberalism in their own places.

One of the most important concepts they shared globally was the importance of *caminar preguntando*, walking while questioning. No maps or ten-point programs, simply humility and a road made by walking.[28] This was true for their own local practices and suggested a more general understanding that it is only through humble practices—however partial or imperfect—that progress can be made.

The project of autonomía: Lekil kuxlejal

Autonomía is often used as a synonym for the cultural politics of the Zapatistas. We call it *autonomía* to distinguish it from the liberal understanding of "autonomy" that is non-collective and opposed to interdependence. In reality, autonomía and interdependence go hand in hand. While the Zapatistas are some of the most important theorists of autonomía, many Indigenous movements, as well as other radical activist configurations (particularly the Italian tradition of autonomía in the 1960s and 1970s) also developed instructive visions of autonomía. Key to all of these is a vision not only of reinventing politics but also, as we shall describe, of helping to cultivate the conditions for existence or "making life." As Sylvère Lotringer and Christian Marazzi describe it, "[autonomy] is not only a political project, it is a project for existence."[29] Specifically, this is a collective and dignified existence, what the Zapatistas call *lekil kuxlejal—the life that is good for everyone*. In fact, for the Zapatistas and many others, reinserting the

---

[28] As Anzaldúa put it, "*Caminante, no hay puentes, se hace el puente al andar* (Voyager there are no bridges, one builds them as one walks)." Gloria Anzaldúa, "Foreword," in *This Bridge Called My Back: Writings by Radical Women of Color*, ed. Cherrie Moraga and Gloria Anzaldúa, 2nd edn. (New York: Kitchen Table/Women of Color Press, 1983), v.

[29] Sylvère Lotringer and Christian Marazzi, eds., *Autonomia: Post-Political Politics* (Los Angeles, CA: Semiotext(e), 1980).

political into the quotidian and healing the fragmented view of life, is key to any liberatory praxis, and is therefore integral to autonomía.[30] Overall, autonomía is an excellent example of the political activation of relationality, for its redefining of power, life, and collectivity.

Lekil kuxlejal is reminiscent of the terms *sumaq kawsay* and "suma qamaña" or "buen vivir," created by Indigenous movements in Bolivia and Ecuador as a response to pressures and assumptions that the good life could only be defined as an economically developed life.[31] This points to another crucial dimension of the political activation of relationality: the emphasis on the *work* of *making life*, life that is good for everyone—where everyone is not limited to the human, or the "desirable" kind of human. The stress on radical inclusivity rather than political opposition, and on life, not just politics, are counterintuitive in a Western political milieu in which the emphasis is on winning for the interests of certain people—that is, the working class, the poor, the marginalized—and on politics rather than life. While improving life for the marginalized is crucially important, the difference in emphasis is notable; it stresses the need for a form of governance that takes everyone's definition of "the good" into account, while challenging the political-economic as that over which struggle takes place, opening up the struggle to all of life.

Tseltal scholar Juan López Intsin speaks of "lekil kuxjelal" "as a basis for transforming a sense of humanity based on a social life of plenitude, dignity, and justice as part of another world mediated not by power but by the power to be, or what he terms, *el poder sentirsaber-sentirpensar* (the power or ability to be feel-know and to feel-think)." Or as Mariana Mora puts it, "When the act of living affirms the power to be rather than the power over something or somebody, then living becomes a political act in itself than ensures the socio-cultural and biological continuation of life."[32]

Restor(y)ing power relationally

To understand autonomía means to reorient one's view of power and the raison d'être of a social movement or social change projects more broadly. One of the most radical and novel reorientations the Zapatistas offered was their view of

---

[30] Mariana Mora, *Kuxlejal Politics: Indigenous Autonomy, Race, and Decolonizing Research in Zapatista Communities* (Austin: University of Texas Press, 2017). For a powerful explication of the meaning of Zapatista autonomy see the above reference. Mora also translates it as "a good way of living," referring "not only to an individual but to that being in relation to a communal connection to the earth, to the natural and supernatural world … thus constantly honored" (19).

[31] Eduardo Gudynas, "Buen Vivir: Today's Tomorrow," *Development* 54, no. 4 (2011): 441–47, available online: https://doi.org/10.1057/dev.2011.86; Ashish Kothari, Federico Demaria, and Alberto Acosta, "Buen Vivir, Degrowth and Ecological Swaraj: Alternatives to Sustainable Development and the Green Economy," *Development* 57, no. 3–4 (December 2014): 362–75, available online: https://doi.org/10.1057/dev.2015.24.

[32] Mora, *Kuxlejal Politics*, 19–20.

power, which was inextricably linked to their understanding of the collective and relational basis of making life. Rather than seek to "take power" by overturning the Mexican state, the Zapatistas articulated a novel project what Holloway has described as "chang[ing] the world without taking power."[33] Instead of treating power as some *thing* to be possessed and exercised over people, or power-over, the Zapatistas understand it as power-with or power-to.

In this vein, the Zapatistas sought to build communal life by reclaiming their power over various facets of making life. This included but was not limited to radically democratic forms of governance—the good governance councils, caracoles, and the assembly form—but also involved creating commissions for health, education, economy, and food, as well as fashioning systems that did not reproduce the capitalist forms of these, but rather built forms of life from Indigenous wisdom. In this vision, power is not scarce or finite, it is a force that resides in relation to the not-yet.

An important part of the redefinition of power, then, has to do with recogniz-ing the notion of intrinsic or latent power, which in turn points to the emergent or collective dimension. Think of a seed and the power that it possesses to burst through the earth. Until that moment the power is purely potential. And it goes even deeper. In many ways autonomía inheres notions of self-realization that can be understood as a sort of inner power. Leanne Betasamosake Simp-son describes such inner power in a different, but related, context: "From this standpoint it doesn't matter who is president or prime minister, because our most important work is internal, and the kinds of transformations we are compelled to make, the kinds of alternatives we are compelled to embody are profoundly systemic."[34] This inner dimension points to the nondualism of the individual and collective, and to the emergent and complex nature of systems, or the whole.

Said somewhat differently, the Zapatista project can be understood as a social-ontological project for reclaiming and reasserting the communal basis of all life—outside the prescribed terrain of politics reduced to seizing the reigns of the State. So, on the one hand, it is about refusing to play into a vision of reality limited by current categories, but, on the other, it is also about recon-stituting life and governance from below without the forms of alienation and separation prescribed by modernity.

Autonomía can be seen as a true solution to the political and ontological problem of separation and alienation. While in conversation with traditional leftist theory, the project of autonomía goes way beyond the traditional analysis of alienation in the realm of labor; as a recent text on Zapatista governance

---

[33] John Holloway, *Change the World without Taking Power*, New edition (London: Pluto Press, 2010).

[34] Simpson, *As We Have Always Done*, 6. While we have focused on Zapatistas here, it is noteworthy that many Indigenous movements and decolonizing liberation projects share similar visions and principles of autonomy.

put it, Zapatismo addresses the aporias of individualism and the division between life and politics:

> A form of political existence in which there is no separation between autonomous government and the communities, where everyone participates in governance and is prepared to take a turn in a governing body in the Caracol, the municipality and the community. This reflects an awareness that social alienation is only in part the result of a separation between producers and their labor and the products of their labor. *It is also the result of the separation between the community and all the products of its communal activity.*[35]

Collectivity and democracy

In addition to revisioning power and governance, then, autonomía is also a nondualist alternative to modernist versions of the collective. For the Zapatistas life is always and necessarily a collective endeavor; in this way, they counter the production of non- or anti-relationality and the myth of individuals, which as we saw in the last chapter, must be actively produced. That being said, Zapatista understandings of the collective involve a certain belief in concepts of self-actualization and voluntary free association rather than the more coercive and conformist understandings of collective from the modernist visions of the left.

As described in the previous chapter, modernist versions of the collective (i.e., communism, socialism, or even anarchism not steeped in communal culture) tend to view the individual as pitted against the collective and communal, much like capitalism is pitted against communism. The autonomist vision of collectivity, on the other hand, like Buddhist, Emergence, and Indigenous visions, sees difference and singularity as necessary for a healthily functioning collective. As John Clark puts it, "the Zapatista political ideal is a society based on voluntary cooperation, with autonomy and individuality of each person and group protected and expanded through collective action that serves the good of the whole."[36] But, and quite importantly, the self-actualization is premised on a profoundly distinct ontology of interdependence, in particular interdependence of the heart and potentiality. "For the Zapatistas, dignity, autonomy, and democracy for each people as well as the creation of this people as a collectivity arises through the growth of the heart, through bringing one another into one collective heart."[37]

---

[35] Dylan Eldredge Fitzwater and John P. Clark, *Autonomy Is in Our Hearts: Zapatista Autonomous Government through the Lens of the Tsotsil Language* (Oakland, CA: PM Press, 2019), xxvii, emphasis ours. We are very grateful to Matt Meyer for introducing this book to us!

[36] Fitzwater and Clark, *Autonomy Is in Our Hearts*, xxviii.

[37] Fitzwater and Clark, *Autonomy Is in Our Hearts*, 36.

In *Autonomy Is in Our Hearts*, Dylan Fitzwater explores core tenets and practices of autonomous governance in Chiapas through a close engagement of the Tsotsil language, specifically the Tsotsil that many Zapatistas speak and has thus been co-created with Zapatismo.[38] What follows is a beautiful slice of this complex book attempting to translate this profound political project:

> Creating collectivity in Tsotsil is understood as the reciprocal process of the growth of the heart (o'on) and of the potentiality (ch'ulel). The education promoters have described this process using the phrase *ichbail ta muk*, which means to bring (ichil) one another (ba) to largeness or greatness (ta muk) and implies the coming together of a big collective heart. I have also seen this phrase translated simply as "democracy." Furthermore, this process of bringing one another to greatness is understood as the creation of *lekil kuxlejal*, which literally means the life that is good for everyone, but which is usually translated as autonomy or dignified life. *For the Zapatistas, dignity, autonomy, and democracy for each people as well as the creation of this people as a collectivity arises through the growth of the heart, through bringing one another into one collective heart, through ichbail ta muk*.[39]

There is no way to succinctly cover Fitzwater's inspiring argument; however, it is worth noting the centrality of two terms *ch'ulel* (soul) and *o'on* (heart). "Every entity in the world has ch'ulel that defines its potentials and shapes its relationships to other entities."[40] According to Xuno López Intzin, a contemporary Tzeltal intellectual and activist, "That which all existing beings share is ch'ulel. From this understanding of the ch'ulel in everything, the human being established relations with all that exists."[41] These profoundly relational terms speak to a dimension not often included in Western understandings of politics (or perhaps even of the human and life)—namely, the heart. Moreover, in Tsotsil, thoughts and feelings (*sentipensamientos*) are understood as one and the same and reside in the heart. So, when Zapatistas speak of truth or reason, which they do frequently, it is not a logocentric version of either but one guided by the heart.

Finally, the state of the community is largely depicted as the wholeness or fragmentation of the collective heart, and not surprisingly the state of each

---

[38] Fitzwater and Clark, *Autonomy Is in Our Hearts*, 9. Fitzwater's is noteworthy among English-language books about Zapatismo because it centers the profoundly distinct sensibility of the Indigenous worldviews expressed through their language. "Tsotsil political concepts ... do not represent some timeless or unchanging Indigenous wisdom, rather they are contemporary political concepts shaped by Tsotsil people's reflections on their participation in the everyday struggles of building Zapatista autonomy."

[39] Fitzwater and Clark, *Autonomy Is in Our Hearts*, 36, emphasis ours.

[40] Fitzwater and Clark, *Autonomy Is in Our Hearts*, 33.

[41] Quoted in Fitzwater and Clark, *Autonomy Is in Our Hearts*, 33.

person's ch'ulel is part of the overall state of the communal heart.[42] In Chiapas, the growth of this collective heart is described to have taken place with the collective recognition of sadness and pain—not as something bad to be avoided or solved, but as that which enlarged the collective heart enabling the creation of the collective struggle:

> There was so much pain in our heart, our sadness and death were so much that they no longer fit … Our pain and sadness were so big they no longer fit in the heart of a few, and it began overflowing and began filling other hearts with pain and sadness."[43]

As Fitzwater goes on to explain the collective sadness was that which brought them "together in the shared space of a single heart."[44] Sadness and pain are seen as catalysts or mechanisms for political activation. Not coincidentally, in many contemporary forms of spiritual or sacred activism, the beginning is allowing for, even calling in, our grief for the world. Pain, sadness, suffering, are all points of access, what we might term portals to the political activation of relationality. This is not to romanticize pain or loss, but to highlight that these are, for many, direct portals into a space or mode of consciousness that allows us to be in between, and often, to recognize, experientially (not just conceptually) our radical interdependence with all that is.

It is no coincidence that many potent examples of the political activation of relationality come from peoples bearing the brunt of oppression, marginalization, and pain in contemporary capitalism. As we have described here, Zapatismo as a political theory and as a material project of life-making, demonstrates all the principles of relationality, inextricably linked to one another, and visible often in contrast to the dominant ways of being and doing politics we are more accustomed to.

PRISON ABOLITION: BUILDING BRIDGES INWARD, RADICAL INCLUSIVITY, AND ARCHITECTURES OF ACCOUNTABILITY

Like Zapatismo, prison abolition is a bridge project. It demands the courage and willingness *to be with* the unknown, the wounded, and the different as we cross to the other side, to the next world. Abolitionists do not pretend to know all the answers; in fact, their main goals are to ask better questions and to stop repeating the life-annihilating version of reality most people take as given. If Zapatismo asks how to bridge the old world to the new in terms of governance, labor, and

---

[42] This is a very complex set of ideas shared in chapter 2 of Fitzwater's book. Many books and ethnographies on Zapatismo, although excellent and admittedly part of our own education on it, have failed to integrate fundamental notions such as spirit, heart (o'on), and even the soul/potentiality (ch'ulel) into a truly transformative politics.

[43] Quoted in Fitzwater and Clark, *Autonomy Is in Our Hearts*, 31.

[44] Fitzwater and Clark, *Autonomy Is in Our Hearts*, 34.

making life that is good for everyone, abolition asks us to explore what kinds of mechanisms or bridges we need to design to be able to build capacities and structures inside ourselves and our communities for achieving true liberation. Abolitionists are asking how to redesign and re-story life in places, many urban, wrought from violent histories of slavery, segregation, white supremacy, settler colonialism, and industrial capitalism. This means building and reconstituting communities produced out of violence and displacement, then destroyed many times over through ongoing projects of segregation, criminalization, drug wars, gentrification, and neoliberalism. It also means confronting some of the deepest foundational myths and institutions, as well as values and laws of the modern settlement, among the privileged—who supposedly benefit from this system—and the oppressed alike.

The central question of abolition is, then, how to build and sustain diverse communities without prisons or carceral logics, while acknowledging and reckoning with the violent histories that have led us here. This means not only coming to understand the values and institutions that underpin the carceral society we currently live in, but also cultivating communities of care and forgiveness that are not based on logics of disposability or exclusion; that refuse simplistic binaries of victims and perpetrators; and that embrace not-knowing, love *and* nonviolent forms of accountability.

Prison abolition: A brief introduction[45]

Prison abolition is one of the movements and political projects that we believe best embodies relational politics and designing relationally, especially within the context of the United States. In this piece we will refer in particular to the vision of abolition articulated and promoted by Critical Resistance and numerous projects that emerged from it in the late 1990s. Notably, however, Critical Resistance builds on the foundational work of activists of the 1960s and 1970s, following the Attica Prison riot (1971) in Attica, New York, as well as other radical movements for prison reform and then abolition.[46] These in turn were based on the ideas and organizing of Black nationalists and other radicals on the left from the "long 1960s"—many of whom were imprisoned for their activism.[47] As Angela Davis, one of the recognized founders of contemporary prison abolition

---

[45] We are indebted to Matthew DelSesto for his help on the history of prison abolition.

[46] Prison Research Education Action, ed., *Instead of Prisons: A Handbook for Abolitionists*, Critical Resistance (1971; 2005); Dan Berger, ed., *The Hidden 1970s: Histories of Radicalism* (New Brunswick, NJ: Rutgers University Press, 2010); Liz Samuels "Improvising on Reality: The Roots of Prison Abolition," in *The Hidden 1970s: Histories of Radicalism*, ed. Dan Berger, 21–38 (New Brunswick, NJ: Rutgers University Press, 2010).

[47] Samuels, "Improvising on Reality"; Robert Dellelo Jamie Bissonette with Ralph Hamm, *When the Prisoners Ran Walpole: A True Story in the Movement for Prison Abolition* (Cambridge, MA: South End Press, 2008).

notes, the ideas for prison abolition can in turn be traced back to W.E.B. Du Bois' notion of abolition democracy.[48]

Acknowledging these longer and crucial histories, we start with Critical Resistance because of their work in making visible and consolidating this vital work for liberation in more recent years (intersecting with the AGM and affine politics at times). Critical Resistance was formed in 1997 when "activists challenging the idea that imprisonment and policing are a solution for social, political, and economic problems came together to organize a conference that examined and challenged what we have come to call the prison industrial complex (PIC)."[49] The shift from speaking about abolishing prisons to abolition of the prison industrial complex was one of their core contributions. As they put it:

> PIC abolition is a political vision with the goal of eliminating imprisonment, policing, and surveillance and creating lasting alternatives to punishment and imprisonment.
>
> From where we are now, sometimes we can't really imagine what abolition is going to look like. Abolition isn't just about getting rid of buildings full of cages. It's also about undoing the society we live in because the PIC both feeds on and maintains oppression and inequalities through punishment, violence, and controls millions of people. Because the PIC is not an isolated system, abolition is a broad strategy. An abolitionist vision means that we must build models today that can represent how we want to live in the future. It means developing practical strategies for taking small steps that move us toward making our dreams real and that lead us all to believe that things really could be different. It means living this vision in our daily lives. Abolition is both a practical organizing tool and a long-term goal.[50]

Over 3,500 academics, activists, former prisoners, youth, and policymakers from all over the United States, gathered in Berkeley over three days in 1997 and launched the movement for prison abolition. The movement included projects that worked directly to improve (or save) the lives of current or former prisoners, and with organizations aimed at changing policy and culture; and these projects include both local and smaller-scale initiatives—such as *A New Way of Life*, to be described below[51]—and larger movements of cultural reorientation and system change that in turn include numerous reframing of the goals of

---

[48] Angela Y. Davis, *Abolition Democracy: Beyond Empire, Prisons, and Torture* (New York: Seven Stories Press, 2005).

[49] "History," *Critical Resistance* (blog), available online: https://criticalresistance.org/mission-vision/history/ (accessed June 8, 2022).

[50] "What Is the PIC? What Is Abolition?," *Critical Resistance* (blog), available online: https://criticalresistance.org/mission-vision/not-so-common-language/ (accessed June 1, 2022).

[51] Susan Burton and Cari Lynn, *Becoming Ms. Burton: From Prison to Recovery to Leading the Fight for Incarcerated Women*, with a foreword by Michelle Alexander (London: New Press, 2017).

social justice work to include holistic and nondualist understandings of change. Whereas the former category involves concrete efforts to help formerly incarcerated, currently incarcerated, or vulnerable populations in the United States with the basics of survival, the latter seeks to transform communities and US society writ large to help design and build non-carceral worlds.

Prison abolition has become increasingly tied to much social justice and anti-racist organizing in the United States today, especially in the wake of the 2020 anti-police violence protests following the murders of George Floyd, Breonna Taylor, and Ahmaud Arbury (among others). While many people are familiar with #Black Lives Matter, the movement for prison abolition that is behind much of the longer-term organizing for it is less known. The hashtag #BLM and the related movement network emerged in 2013 as a response to the acquittal of George Zimmerman in the killing of Trayvon Martin, and grew in 2014 with the murder of Mike Brown by police officer Darren Wilson. It was, however, in May of 2020 with the murder of George Floyd that the movement became a household word, and perhaps more significantly for our purposes here, when the vision of many BLM activists to defund and dismantle the police and PIC started to be more openly recognized. However, it was also in the wake of these massive uprisings, that the call for abolition was often dismissed as "too radical," scary, or simply *unrealistic*. This last criticism is more crucial than we might realize.

In fact, one of the biggest hurdles facing abolitionists is the attachment to the current version of reality—which includes the belief that creating a world without police and prisons is both unrealistic and impossible—and the limits of our imagination. While in the wake of these massive protests and the murders that catalyzed them numerous Americans have come to espouse an anti-racist politics *in principle*, actively protesting for the value of Black lives, most still cannot comprehend or imagine the idea of a world without police. This is certainly true among white Americans, but also among many communities of color. People often ask: Where would we put criminals? What would we do about violent crime? Who would maintain order? While most people agree that police may need to be trained differently and that prisons could be run differently, maybe even that drugs should be decriminalized, the idea of not having police at all triggers fears of chaos and anarchy. In conversations about abolition, deep attachments to the institutions of police and prisons—the main kind of institutions and worlds we are familiar with—are often revealed.

When interviewed about abolition, scholars and activists almost always acknowledge that "we can't just go to abolishing police and prisons in one fell swoop." In other words, abolition is consciously a bridge project. A bridge project that asks fundamental questions about how to get from the current white supremacist carceral capitalist society to one in which these institutions are no longer (seen as) necessary. One of the most profound things about these questions is that they are asked while recognizing the deep uncertainty underlying it all: the recognition that we cannot really know what will and will not work, and that the obstacles in the way range from thoughts about the inevitability of policing and prisons, as well as deeper, gut-and-marrow-level things, such as certain thought-forms and founding myths of scarcity, worth, inclusion/exclusion, good guys/bad guys, punishment/revenge that live in us.

Key to being able to reimagine, however, is understanding what prisons are and what they do. While many think of them as natural and inevitable parts of any society, police and prisons were invented in Europe and the United States not so long ago in order to control specific populations including vagrants, poor people, slaves, and those who might rebel. From their inception, the prison and police were not meant to keep people safe or to rehabilitate the imprisoned; they were meant to control or remove certain populations. As Foucault demonstrated, the "humanizing" of the prison was an extremely significant and powerful transformation that signaled a shift in how the world was structured, resulting in a veritable disciplinary, carceral society peculiar to the modern age. This also went hand in hand with Enlightenment-supported colonial projects seeking to curb who was considered part of humanity. As he put it in a 1973 interview in the *New York Times*:

> The monotonous tumbling of locks and the shadow of the cell block have replaced the grand ceremonial of flesh and blood. The condemned culprit's body is concealed rather than being placed on exhibition. We no longer want to cause the criminal pain; we want to train him; we want to reeducate his "spirit."
>
> The change took place throughout Western civilization in less than a century. The Middle Ages had its prisons and jails but it was unfamiliar with anything resembling the rigid system of regimented, fastidious detention that developed between 1780 and 1820 as Europe and the New World became covered with penitentiaries.
>
> It is not enough to say, with the 18th-century "reformers," that "humanization" and "progress" explained and justified this radical change in the penal system.
>
> The shock of corporal punishment and the silence of reclusion are not simply two isolated and opposed phenomena; nor are their differences only on the surface. They stand for a change from one kind of justice to another, a profound change in the organization of authority.[52]

Or as long-time abolitionist Mariame Kaba puts it when asked, "what would we do without prisons? Whatever it takes to build a society that does not constantly rearrange the trappings of annihilation and bondage while calling itself free."[53] In other words, prisons and police were important to creating and justifying a certain kind of society.

---

[52] Michel Foucault, "On the Role of Prisons," *New York Times*, August 5, 1975, available online: https://archive.nytimes.com/www.nytimes.com/books/00/12/17/specials/foucault-prisons.html (accessed June 1, 2022). See also Michel Foucault, *Discipline and Punish* (New York: Vintage Books, 1979).

[53] Mariame Kaba, *We Do This 'til We Free Us: Abolitionist Organizing and Transforming Justice*, Abolitionist Papers (La Vergne, TN: Haymarket Books, 2021), 62.

Overall prison reform, which until recently entailed the majority of activism around issues of police and prison injustice, in the name of "humanization and progress," has further naturalized and entrenched the current PIC. In so doing, it has played a huge part in creating a system and worldview in which the exclusion or disposability of millions of people, particularly Black, Brown, and poor people, labeled "criminals," seems natural. This naturalization, building on the biological notion of scarcity, not only relegates millions of our citizens to horrific conditions inside and outside the prison; it means *we cannot imagine a world in which this would not be necessary.* Not coincidentally, it also depends fundamentally on the belief in the "individual"—both in terms of police and criminals, who are both seen as "bad apples," responsible for their own actions—rather than seeing the histories and systems that create the conditions for certain behaviors.

Importantly, the "prison is not unique" and works with other seemingly immutable institutions of modernity to create this naturalized vision:

> It [prison] is positioned within the disciplined society, the society of generalized surveillance in which we live. … our prisons resemble our factories, schools, military bases, and hospitals-all of which in turn resemble prisons.[54]

Drawing attention to the ways in which these diverse institutions work to produce a particular vision of life, and the centrality of certain aspects of the story to them is one layer of abolitionist work. This work is particularly challenging because of how foundational these institutions are to understandings of life and reality. But this is also what makes abolition so exciting. As feminist scholar and anti-violence activist Andrea Smith puts it:

> I think the politics of abolition is a positive politics, is a positive vision and not really a negative vision. I think when people hear prison abolition they freak out and think you're saying tear down all the walls tomorrow … Whereas what I think it is, it's about crowding out these things with positive alternatives. So, for instance back to the anti-violence movement, I don't think the question we're asking is should somebody call the police if they're under attack. Because I think they gotta do what they gotta do. The question is why do they have no other options but to call the police. So, I think our goal is to proliferate these alternatives until they squeeze out the prison industrial complex and squeeze out the state.[55]

---

[54] Michel Foucault, "On the Role of Prisons."

[55] *Visions of Abolition: From Critical Resistance to a New Way of Life,* directed by Shigematsu Setsu (Pottstown, PA: MVD Entertainment Group, 2012), DVD.

Practicing relationality: Holism, emergence, healing, and radical inclusivity

We see abolition as one of the most promising examples of the politics of relationality because of four main components that run counter to the dualism implicit in many other social change projects. They also embody the principles described above: (1) Abolition is holistic (systemic); rather than tweak broken institutions it seeks to build new ones. (2) Abolitionists articulate the ways systems and cycles of violence and harm comprise both institutions *and* individuals' trauma, feelings, and bodies: they have a fractal view of systems and reality. (3) Abolitionists are very aware of the tendency for social change projects to recapitulate oppression by focusing on enemies, rather than systems, or by privileging "systemic" change at the cost of human kindness and healing: they believe in radical inclusion and designing a world in which everyone and everything belongs. This is an important reminder that at the heart of a relational worldview, and in strong contrast to the world of scarcity and monohumanism we have been socialized into, is radical inclusion. (4) Finally, abolitionists are unafraid of straying from the known. They embrace uncertainty, experimentation, failure, and the possibilities of healing with and through wounds rather than trying to find perfect solutions.

Holism

There is nothing new under the sun, but there are new suns.

Octavia Butler

Many abolitionists are informed intellectually by Black feminism and Black radical traditions writ large. It is no wonder then that, like the Zapatistas, the central goal of abolitionists is the need to build new systems rather than tweak what is already there. As the Zapatistas put it, "To change this world, that's too hard, let's build new ones." This requires a deep analysis of the State, capitalism, and power. Although winning political battles at the level of the State (like defunding the police) can be important, abolition *also* requires working at the smallest "cellular level", seeking ways to foster and cultivate the kinds of people and institutions that can respond to both the good and bad of their communities more holistically and embrace the complexity of it all.[56]

The abolitionist approach to "reform" is relational rather than binary. Abolitionists assert a difference between "non-reformist reforms" or "urgent reforms"—reforms that do not preclude the comprehensive transformation or elimination of the PIC—and the kinds of reforms that solely deflect attention from the true problems while further entrenching the PIC and perpetuating a world in which certain people are seen as disposable, and in which violence,

---

[56] We borrow the term "cellular level" from Prentis Hemphill. See Hemphill, "13 Blackness & Belonging—Prentis Hemphill."

abuse, and other forms of harm perpetuate and augment cycles of harm, feeding more people into the PIC.

Sometimes we have to engage in the politics of survival and urgent reform because some people will simply be gone, in the sense both of being locked up for a long time or of being dead, if we are not taking those practices seriously. So, this makes the on-the-ground rendition of abolitionist politics very difficult, complex, and challenging.[57]

Abolition also means creating conditions that allow people not to see punishment and retribution as the only ways to respond to wrongdoing. It also means understanding the ways in which harm and the PIC are rooted at different scales or points of the system.

Emergence

How we are at the small scale is how we are at the large scale.

adrienne maree brown

Abolitionists understand system change not in traditional leftist terms that see work on smaller scales as "not radical enough." Rather, abolitionists know that the smallest level impacts and inheres the largest. Systems are articulated less like Newtonian blocks built upon one another and more like fractals, mycelium, rhizomes. As adrienne maree brown explains in *Emergent Strategy*, "Fractals are infinitely complex patterns that are self-similar across different scales."[58] And, "How we are at the small scale is how we are at the large scale."[59] Or "The micro reflects the macro and vice versa ... The tiniest most mundane act reflects the biggest creations we can imagine."[60] For abolition, this applies to addressing the multiple scales and sites where carcerality is upheld, from the largest institutions to our everyday habitual responses to harm and wrongdoing.

Abolitionist practices range from smaller-scale projects working with incarcerated, formerly incarcerated, or vulnerable populations to strategies aimed at policy and culture change more broadly. The smaller-scale organizations are a particularly poignant example of the fractal nature of reality, both in carceral and abolitionist iterations.

A New Way of Life is an organization that supports formerly incarcerated women and their children to get the skills and auxiliary support they need after being in prison. While residential, and like transitional housing in some senses, the organization's commitment to feminist and abolitionist principles and analyses distinguishes it from others. Rather than simply put a band-aid over the deep wounds that both lead to and are caused by incarceration, the organization seeks

---

[57] Dylan Rodriguez quoted in *Visions of Abolition*.

[58] brown, *Emergent Strategy*, 51.

[59] brown, *Emergent Strategy*, 52.

[60] brown, *Emergent Strategy*, 51.

to cultivate communities where, "people are able to reconnect with themselves, with their true selves, their sense of self. The ownership of who they are and not what they have [had] to become because of their environment." This means raising political consciousness and addressing through therapy and other modalities the individual and collective traumas the women have lived through. The vision behind it is to build "a society that actually had meeting people's needs as its first priority rather than profits and the greed driven system."[61]

The organization was founded in the late 1990s by Susan Burton, a formerly incarcerated woman. Burton, who has been called a modern-day Harriet Tubman, has a remarkable personal story that "hits every statistic there is about the life of a poor Black girl in America: From childhood sexual abuse to alcohol and drug struggles, it highlights just how the U.S. fails Black people daily."[62] After a youth of sexual abuse and violence, Burton was incarcerated several times when, following the killing of her five-year-old son by a police vehicle, she spiraled into a cycle of addiction to cope with the deep depression the loss of her son triggered, as well as the sense of powerlessness from the fact that the officer who killed her son was never held accountable. Not long after its founding Burton encountered Critical Resistance and began to integrate their political education and consciousness raising workshops into the programming of A New Way of Life.

The film, *Visions of Abolition*, captures her story as well as testimonies from women she and the organization have helped, and she has written a book on her life-story.[63] In *Visions of Abolition*, women who became a part of A New Way of Life and Critical Resistance express profound analyses of systems and cycles of violence, as well as the possibilities for rehabilitation and forgiveness even after their own tragic losses. One woman, Patricia Naqi, describes dealing with the murder of her son and mother aided by the analysis of Critical Resistance and argues that she understands that nothing is helped by having the murderer in jail, that he, like everyone else, had simply snapped. Unlike most Americans, her go-to is not wanting retribution or revenge, but rehabilitation.

Healing society means healing ourselves

As Angela Davis puts it, at the core of abolition is an understanding of the multiple scales of reality in which the prison and policing are rooted: from the most personal and internal to the institutional:

> If we shift the register a bit and talk about what it means to be an abolitionist, how one has to rethink not only modes of justice that happens at

---

[61] Susan Burton quoted in *Visions of Abolition*.

[62] Stephanie Sengwe, "Pain to Passion: Susan Burton Finds a New Way of Life for Herself and Other Formerly Incarcerated Women," PureWow, June 20, 2021, available online: https://www.purewow.com/wellness/susan-burton-a-new-way-of-life (accessed March 15, 2022).

[63] Burton and Lynn, "Becoming Ms. Burton."

institutional levels, but how we personally think about our relations with one another. In this country and in the West in general we have come to think about revenge as the only possible response when one is the target of wrongdoing. Or once when something bad is done to us our first response is to think about how to get back at the person who did it. So how do we change that idea?

...

So you might say that what people in Critical Resistance call abolitionist values requires us to rethink our own emotional responses. So alternatives would involve different forms of justice: reparative justice, restorative justice, justice that does not rely on retribution and revenge.[64]

Similarly, for Mariame Kaba "restorative and transformative justice takes into account the needs of those affected by an incident of harm, the contexts that produced or shaped harm, and seek to transform or rebuild what was lost rather than view punishment as a final resolution."[65] Moreover, transformative justice is

> a community process developed by anti-violence activists of color ... to build support and more safety for the person harmed, figure out the broader context we set up for harm to happen, and how the context can be changed so that harm is less likely to happen again ... It is not grounded in punitive justice, and it actually requires us to challenge our punitive impulses, while prioritizing healing, repair and accountability.[66]

In other words, the micro and macro reinforce one another, such that beliefs and impulses live in people, in our bodies, and simultaneously, systems perpetuate certain behaviors, often resulting in trauma and wounding. In other words, our systems are themselves based on certain cultural assumptions that they then perpetuate. Consider again the words of Angela Davis:

> I can say now that I am totally convinced that this broken prison system ... is in large part responsible for the pandemic of child abuse, child sexual abuse, in this country. Because where we assume that a person who has committed such a horrible act against a child only needs to be thrown away into prison, that means we abdicate our responsibility of thinking about what has produced this individual who has committed this horrendous act. If we think about that, usually we discover that this person was at one time in his or her life, a victim of child abuse him or herself. If we simply assume that using the prison system to deal with it is going to be the solution, we're actually perpetuating the problem. And we're allowing that generational dynamic to continue over and over again.

[64] *Visions of Abolition.*

[65] Kaba, *We Do This 'til We Free Us*, 79.

[66] Kaba, *We Do This 'til We Free US*, 59, emphasis ours.

In other words, it is not only about eliminating harm, but changing the ways in which violence and harm are both perceived and addressed by individuals and their communities. It is also about recognizing the fundamental uncertainty underlying this endeavor and the importance of asking different questions. This leads us to the fundamental humility at the heart of abolition. Like caminar preguntando of the Zapatistas, this is not a humility to be gotten over once we figure things out, but a general ethos. As Andrea Smith, puts it,

> our movement has to be a little more humble …. If anybody really knew what to do, they probably would have ended global oppression by now. So, let's just say that we don't know what we're doing. And let's just try stuff out. But obviously we can't go from here to prison abolition in one swoop. So we're going to have to try things. And the things we try may not work. Or it may seem like it was going to work at the time, but it turns out it doesn't.[67]

It also means digging deeper to understand the beliefs that keep us tied to carcerality, including how we work in organizations, manage conflict, and manage difference more generally.

Radical inclusivity

Disposability might be our most villainous concept.

adrienne maree brown

Fundamental to this multi-scalar work, is working against the deeply embedded notion that some people, when categorized as criminal, drug addict, or thug, are expendable or even undesirable. More positively, this means, coming to embrace a principle of radical inclusion, the recognition that "It takes all kinds of people to make a world," as Isoke Femi puts it.[68] Like the Zapatista concept of lekil kuxlejal, many abolitionists grapple and actively work against the kinds of social justice orientations that build on the idea of the enemy, the bad guy, not only when it works against them but also when it might seem to help their cause.

Mariame Kaba points out the challenges facing many communities when what she calls the criminal punishment system actually punishes the "bad guys." Referring to the famous case of a rapist—a bad guy—who is successfully prosecuted and sentenced harshly, Kaba raises concerns. She cautions abolitionists against falling prey to the easy binaries that simply keep the system in place, even when you "like" the decision the system produced. As she puts it,

---

[67] *Visions of Abolition.*

[68] Bayo Akomolafe, interviewed by Isoke Femi, "A Crack in Time Can Heal the World: A Conversation on Roots, Repair & Reimagining," *Thrive East Bay*, November 20, 2021, YouTube video, 1:34:18, available online: https://www.youtube.com/watch?v=4ggkGY1mNAQ (accessed March 10, 2022).

we decry the system and advocate for change that is long overdue. *Yet when the system ensnares people we loathe, we may feel a sense of satisfaction.* When we see defendants as symbols of what we most fear and that which we greatly despise we are confronted with *a true test of our belief that no justice can be done under this system.*[69]

In other words, being an abolitionist means being against the system even when powerful white men or others that usually benefit from the system receive "justice."

Similarly, adrienne maree brown gently and thoughtfully challenges activist communities to consider propensities toward vilifying or ostracizing people with call-outs, cancel culture, or even calls for imprisonment. In an interview about her recent book, *We Will Not Cancel Us*, she explains:

What I'm making a case for is that disposability is a concept that might be the most villainous for our species: to think that there's some way we can get rid of people who commit harm, and that will remove the harmful behavior and the harmful belief systems from our communities. And when it doesn't— it hasn't—at a certain point we have to ask ourselves, what are we doing? And what are some alternative ways we could be spending that time to help us actually stop harm from happening, deepen our relationship with each other and grow movements that can hold difference, that can hold conflict, that can recover from misunderstanding, that can fundamentally make a case that abolition is really possible?

Stopping harm means so much more than punishing those who cause harm. It means allowing people to heal from the wounds and traumas that have led them to cause harm, and it also means building systems and communities that can *both* hold difference and conflict differently *and* are based on healthy relationships and forms of the collective. Returning once more to the cellular level, it is not possible to create safety without healthy relationships, healthy forms of attachment, and the capacity to feel loved and to love.

Overall, we can say that abolitionist work has a dual emphasis: to create and build new models of justice and material practices for addressing conflict, harm, and the conditions that lead to incarceration, on the one hand; and, on the other, recognizing, unlearning, then learning anew the ways in which these systems reside in us. Like the Zapatistas, abolitionists understand that necessary for a *new world*—a non-carceral world—are new capacities, including the ability to hold radical inclusivity, both within and outside of ourselves, in turn linked to compassion and forgiveness for ourselves and others. In other words, it requires linking the view of changing external systems with skills for understanding and changing our inner systems and landscapes. It is no coincidence, then, that like in Zapatismo and among many Indigenous movements, many

---

[69] Kaba, *We Do This 'til We Free Us*, 59, emphasis ours.

abolitionists have developed frameworks that point to spirituality, healing, and the heart as key to their social justice work.

RETURNING TO THE HEART: SPIRITUAL ACTIVISM
AND AN EPISTEMOLOGY OF LOVE

> White people in this country will have quite enough to do in learning how to accept and love themselves and each other, and when they have achieved this—which will not be tomorrow and may very well be never—the Negro problem will no longer exist, for it will no longer be needed.[70]

James Baldwin

The turn to the heart or spirituality is not limited to abolitionists, the Zapatistas or other Indigenous movements. The connection to spirit and heart has been at the core of many transformative movements historically—think Gandhi's satyagraha, Martin Luther King Jr.'s Beloved Community, not to mention the Catholic Worker Movement, among many others. Today more and more practitioners are moving with an integrated analysis of how suffering and liberation manifest in individual leadership, organizational culture, movement activity, collective systems, and responses to injustice in the world at large. There is a fundamental recognition that it is not sufficient to fight for political, social, or structural shifts of external systems; the transformation of individual capacity and presence is equally vital for lasting change; as social justice leader Grace Lee Boggs said, "We have to change ourselves in order to change the world."[71] Claudia Horwitz and Jesse Maceo Vega-Frey, co-founders of the Stone House in North Carolina and leaders in the movement for spiritual or transformative activism, describe the emergence of new forms of activism in this way:[72]

> We are moving toward a doing that grows more deliberately out of being; an understanding that freedom from external systems of oppression is dynamically related to liberation from our internal mechanisms of suffering. It provides us with a way to release the construct of "us versus them" and live into the web of relationship that links all. Instead of being limited by the reactions of fight or flight, we encounter a path that finds fullness in presence. The humility of not-knowing allows truth to appear where fear once trapped us. We recognize the pervasive beauty of paradox, the dynamic

---

[70] James Baldwin, "James Baldwin: Letter from a Region in My Mind," *The New Yorker*, November 9, 1962, available online: https://www.newyorker.com/magazine/1962/11/17/letter-from-a-region-in-my-mind (accessed May 15, 2022).

[71] Boggs, *The Next American Revolution*, 100.

[72] Huge thanks to Claudia Horwitz. This section builds on collective research and writing Michal and Claudia did together but never published. See also Claudia Horwitz, *The Spiritual Activist: Practices to Transform Your Life, Your Work, and Your World* (New York: Penguin Compass, 2002).

tension between two simultaneous truths that seem contradictory. We enlarge our capacity to hold contradictions and be informed by them. And our movements for change are transformed as a result.[73]

Said differently, activists are moving from the recognition that it is not sufficient to fight for political, social, or structural change of *external* systems if they do not also address how those systems are created, internalized, and maintained *within* organizations, as well as in activists' bodies, hearts, souls, and minds. Relatedly, healing justice insists that it is impossible to fight for the transformation of large systems without tending to and caring for—offering healing to—those who continue to bear the brunt of these toxic and violent systems.[74]

Central to distinguishing these practices from other forms of social change is the recognition that both identity politics and materialist analyses of power and oppression are insufficient frameworks for making sense of people's pain or their liberation. In addition to spiritual activism, people have described this trend as "transformative organizing," or Deep Change work. Transformation is not easy or comfortable, and unlike change, there is no turning back; as such it is in the nature of most humans, and the systems we have built, to resist it.

As Reverend angel Kyodo williams, Sensei in the Zen Buddhist tradition and founder of the Center for Transformative Organizing puts it:

> For us to transform as a society, we have to allow ourselves to be transformed as individuals. And for us to be transformed as individuals, we have to allow for the incompleteness of any of our truths and a real forgiveness for the complexity of human beings and what we're trapped inside of, so that we're both able to respond to the oppression, the aggression that we're confronted with, but we're able to do that with a deep and abiding sense of "and there are people, human beings, that are at the other end of that baton, that stick, that policy, that are also trapped in something. They're also trapped in a suffering." And for sure, we can witness that there are ways in which they're benefiting from it. But there's also ways, if one trusts the human heart, that they must be suffering. And holding that at the core of who you are when responding to things, I think, is the way—the only way we really have forward—to not just replicate systems of oppression for the sake of our own cause.[75]

---

[73] angel Kyodo williams, ed., *Framing Deep Change: Essays on Transformative Change* (Berkeley, CA: Center for Transformative Change, 2010).

[74] Importantly this healing is both literally offering health care (ranging from massage, acupuncture, mental-health support and other medical treatment) to addressing systems of trauma, etc. See Astraea Lesbian Foundation for Justice, "What Is Healing Justice?," Advocate, May 16, 2019, available online: https://www.advocate.com/commentary/2019/5/16/what-healing-justice (accessed July 6, 2022).

[75] angel Kyodo williams, interview by Krista Tippett, "angel Kyodo williams—The World Is Our Field of Practice," On Being, aired April 19, 2018, available online: https://onbeing.org/programs/angel-kyodo-williams-the-world-is-our-field-of-practice/ (accessed June 18, 2022).

We could spend an entire chapter telling the story of this exciting strand of movement work, unpacking the quote above, or simply defining spirituality and spiritual activism.[76] The uniting threads, however, are unmistakable. There is no way to do transformative work—to be transformed—without doing inner work and engaging the heart and the spirit, both of which are intimately tied to the body. She continues:

> To do our work, to come into deep knowing of who we are—that's the stuff that bringing down systems of oppression is made of. And so capitalism in its current form couldn't survive. Patriarchy couldn't survive. White supremacy couldn't survive if enough of us set about the work of reclaiming the human spirit, which includes reclaiming the sense of humanity of the people that are the current vehicles for those very forms of oppression.[77]

Like Zapatismo and abolition, the recognition is that transformation will happen if we focus on cultivating the inner planes and restoring or reclaiming the innate goodness and wholeness at the core of humanity. Whereas the old paradigm of revolution is a product of modern dualism and its progressivist temporality, this vision of transformative change is relational and looks more like healing or restoring to wholeness, which in turn rests on an understanding of the fundamental interconnectedness of life. Finally, this work holds all humans with compassion and open heartedness, without denying the importance of accountability and ending harm.

Spirituality?

The terrain of spirituality has been rather taboo in academia and social movement studies, except by and large in anthropology and the study of religions; alternatively, it has been relegated to "new age" or treated as unscientific woo-woo. It is not a coincidence, however, that spirituality has been taken seriously by thinkers and activists who are not only committed to transformation but also experientially steeped in alternative epistemologies and aware of the aporias of secular, disembodied Western thought. Among these is the hugely influential feminist anthologies, *This Bridge Called My Back* and perhaps even more-so, its sequel, *This Bridge We Call Home*, and the works of bell hooks, M. Jacqui Alexander, and numerous other feminists of color. We feel it worth quoting from Keating's opening essay to *This Bridge We Call Home* in which she sees in "spiritual activism"—a term coined by Gloria Anzaldúa in the early 1980s—a possible solution to the insufficiencies of feminism:

> My experiences have taught me that the recognition of our radical interconnectedness offers a vital key to long-term individual/collective change, a

---

[76] We first encountered the term spiritual activism with the work of Gloria Anzaldua and Claudia Horwitz.

[77] williams, "angel Kyodo williams—The World Is Our Field of Practice."

crucial point of departure in our work for social justice: if we're all radically interconnected, then the events and belief systems impacting my sisters and brothers in South America or Central Park or Jerusalem have a concrete effect on me. *Spiritual activism insists that we rise or sink together …* Viewed within the Soul's presence there's no "me" or "you". There's just "us." And yet, this "us" has been shattered and fragmented—split into a multiplicity of pieces marked by the many forms our identities take. I believe, with all my heart, that spiritual activism can assist us in creating new ways to move through these boundaries.[78]

Like Martin Luther King Jr.'s "network of inescapable mutuality," our radical interconnectedness becomes the basis for activism, at the same time as it is the description of reality. Notably, in response to Keating's distress over how to reconcile a tension she felt between identity politics and a more transformative spiritual activism, Anzaldúa reminds her friend of the "belief that we're living in a place/time of nepantla, a point where we're exiting from the old worldview, but have not yet entered or created the new one to replace it." Agreeing, Keating astutely writes, "Do we choose to enter into and cross over this threshold, or do we continue clinging desperately to the place we're now at?"[79] Again the recognition here is that we need bridges between stories. Spiritual activism is one of the bridges to living relationally; it is also a bridge to a more holistic understanding of the obstacles to achieving it.

Reframing obstacles to relationality as spiritual, not just material or identity-based, becomes key. As Ruby Sales described it, her practice of social change transformed radically one day, when, talking to a young woman who had suffered an extreme amount of trauma, she realized that to truly address the woman's pain, to understand "where it hurts," she needed a much larger frame of analysis than the one Marxism or materialism afforded her. Sales goes on to describe racism itself as a "spiritual malformation and social pathology that requires all of us to diminish our humanities and become pale images of who we are as human beings."[80] Similarly, Buddhist teacher and activist Ruth King describes racism as a "heart disease."

Toward an epistemology of love: "The gap between theory and practice is the heart"

At the heart of spiritual activism is a distinct way of knowing and being, one of the key mechanisms for being able to perceive and stay with relationality, and perhaps most importantly, address the gap (and slippages) between theory

---

[78] Anzaldúa and Keating, *This Bridge We Call Home*, 19, emphasis ours.

[79] Anzaldúa and Keating, *This Brige We Call Home*, 19.

[80] Quoted in Quinn Soleil Osment, "Working to Heal White Supremacy: Spiritual Ontologies and Anti-Racist Activism," (Honors Thesis, UNC Chapel Hill, 2019).

and practice that has so vexed our movements. This again is why we said that Principle 5—love and spirituality—is the ultimate bridge technology and a summation of all the others.

The heart has special capacities to connect the abstract with the concrete, to hold paradox and to unite. This speaks to the unique way the heart, as opposed to the mind, knows, allowing us to be with radical uncertainty, contradiction, and the messy, often painful realities of the world; but also, the capacity of the heart to love—despite everything. In many traditions, the heart is understood as a "spiritualized mind" that knows more fully:

> According to the great wisdom traditions of the West (Christian, Jewish, Islamic), the heart is first and foremost *an organ of spiritual perception*. Its primary function is to look beyond the obvious, the boundaried surface of things, and see into a deeper reality, emerging from some unknown profundity, which plays lightly upon the surface of this life without being caught there: a world where meaning, insight, and clarity come together in a whole different way.[81]

In a related but distinct proposal, Bayo Akomolafe describes the call for "sacred activisms"—part of an agenda he calls post-activism and that he defines primarily through a recognition of the need for new questions and for wonder:

> Sacred activism is not activism + spirituality – not in an additive sense; it is what I call "post-activism," or the kinds of commitments that invite us to ask new questions not only about what we are doing with the world but what the world is doing with us in the same gesture. In a posthuman relational world, the logic of the familiar is composted and the limitations involved in co-producing the "next" are acknowledged. Rabbi Abraham Heschel notes that "to be spiritual is to be amazed." It's an important point to make – wonder corrodes fences and encourages transgressive boundary-crossing gestures. A sense of wonder infuses our ways of thinking about change, blowing it open to accommodate other modes of acting and becoming – making new capacities possible. This is what I think a sacred activism mode of engagement affords us: "new" ways of meeting the universes that shake us from our firm tethering to victory.[82]

Awe, wonder, amazement, these are all generative ways of being with uncertainty that differ quite drastically from the modernist tendency to both condemn not-knowing and render us blind to the larger field of life. As we also learned from

---

[81] Cynthia Bourgeault, "The Way of the Heart, by Cynthia Bourgeault | Parabola Essay," PARABOLA (blog), January 31, 2017, available online: https://parabola.org/2017/01/31/the-way-of-the-heart-cynthia-bourgeault/ (accessed November 16, 2018), emphasis ours.

[82] Bayo Akomolafe, "Sacred Activisms Writings—Bayo Akomolafe," available online: https://www.bayoakomolafe.net/post/sacred-activisms (accessed June 3, 2022).

Zapatismo and abolition, in addition to embracing uncertainty, the heart can only know in practice: out of doing and being with what is, rather than an abstract or conceptual knowing. It is why the heart and love are central to traversing the slippages and gaps between theory and practice. Roshi Kyodo williams again:

> The way that I think of love most often these days is that love is space.
>
> It is developing our own capacity for spaciousness within ourselves to allow others to be as they are—that that is love. And that doesn't mean that we don't have hopes or wishes that things are changed or shifted, but that to come from a place of love is to be in acceptance of what is, even in the face of moving it towards something that is more whole, more just, more spacious for all of us. It's bigness. It's allowance. It's flexibility … Really it is about expanding our capacity for love, as a species.[83]

But the thing is, this takes practice. We need to grow our muscles and capacity for love. As bell hooks points out in *All about Love*, love is not simply a feeling, it is a verb. It is a practice. One cannot love abstractly, but through specific experiences one can gain access to the universal force of love. Many philosophers, gurus, activists, religious leaders from traditions too numerous to name have long held that expanding our capacity for love is literally the point of life on Earth, as we also discovered with Maturana and Verden-Zöller in Chapter 2. We are struck by the ubiquity of this insight, that at the root of it all is the presence or absence of love.

CONCLUSION

In this chapter we have shown how the politics of relationality can and do exist in contemporary projects, including among the Zapatistas and other Indigenous movements, especially those for autonomía; among prison abolitionists and a network of activists doing transformative and spiritual work. By embracing principles of relationality, including contingency; complexity and emergence; radical uncertainty; non-normativity; and a heart-based knowing and being, change projects have the capacity to build bridges toward becoming relational beings and systems.

The Zapatista vision of autonomía suggests that rather than attempting to take over the Mexican State, these Indigenous communities are building good governance, good education, health, farming—autonomy or democracy and life from below—so that the power of the Mexican State can no longer dominate them. Autonomy necessarily looks different in different places and cannot be described outside concrete histories, contexts, and practices. Similarly, while many like to depict the project of prison abolition as being about abolishing prisons and eliminating police, the real project of abolition is about creating a society in which police and prisons are no longer necessary. This

---

[83] williams, "angel Kyodo williams—The World Is Our Field of Practice."

means that rather than focusing solely on what is "bad," what activists do not want—namely, taking down the prison, police, and so on—abolitionists seek to "crowd out" the institutions, cultures, and practices that lead to crime by cultivating the conditions that lead to care, dignity, and community. While certainly prisons, police, and state oppression are seen as unwanted, the project's focus is on growing and creating that which is wanted. It is about recognizing that treating people as disposable, as criminals, shutting them away "outside of society," simply reproduces the problem, perhaps deferring its effects.

Finally, both projects can be turned into a series of questions for making life (or designing): How do we build a world where many worlds fit? "If we are to imagine a world without prisons, what then do we have to do? What then are our relationships? What then are our institutions?"[84] It is a question of how to design worlds where the prison is not necessary, where the bad governments are not the only game in town. This then is a question of designing for radical inclusion, but also for emergence and the visions of power and change that accompany these.

---

[84] Angela Davis paraphrased by Prentis Hemphill in a 2018 interview "13 Blackness & Belonging—Prentis Hemphill."

5 Designing relationally: Envisioning paths toward pluriversal transitions

INTRODUCTION: DESIGNING IN THE CONTEXT OF WORLDMAKING

A recent session convened under the rubric of "Designing for an Ontological Turn," held at the Participatory Design Conference organized in Manizales, Colombia, in June 2020, started with the following question: "Can there be a design culture and practice that stops being anthropocentric and embraces the idea of radical interdependence, and is capable of operating in the reality of the contemporary world?" It continued:

> Today's environmental emergency requires specific efforts in terms of thinking/acting in designing. The consequences of anthropocentric ways of producing, consuming, and living are becoming painfully clear. Design has contributed in many ways to this anthropocentric mindset, considering human interests as separate from those of the planet. Design is hence obliged to recognize its risks and consequences. In this regard, designers are currently, and increasingly, becoming aware that an *ontological shift* is needed.[1]

In this chapter, we suggest ways for design/ing to become attuned to the political activation of relationality. As the quote above suggests, this is already happening

---

[1] The session, entitled "The Politics of Nature: Designing for an Ontological Turn," was organized by Virginia Tassinari, Ezio Manzini, Arturo Escobar, Liesbeth Huybrechts, and Annalinda De Rosa; see DESIS Philosophy Talks, "DESIS Philosophy Talk #7.2 The Politics of Nature. Designing for an Ontological Turn," June 3, 2020, video, 1:42:51, available online: https://www.desis-philosophytalks.org/desis-philosophy-talk-7-2-the-politics-of-nature-designing-for-an-ontological-turn/ (accessed July 19, 2023). For an important antecedent on relational designing, see Alastair Fuad Luke, "Designing for Radical Relationality: 'Relational Design' for Confronting Dangerous, Concurrent, Contingent Realities," in *Emerging Practices in Design*, ed. Ma Jin and Lou Jongai, 43–72 (Shanghai: China Building Industry Press, 2014).

in some quarters within critical design studies and practice. Our main question is: given its historical role as a practice linked to anthropocentrism and monohumanist capitalism, can designing become a pluriversal and effective praxis for sustaining life?

Approaching this question requires situating design (as a professional practice) and designing (in the extended sense in which we are using it here, that is, as an open-ended capacity and a mode of acting in the world) within the much more encompassing processes of worldmaking and pluriversal transitions. Our guiding questions thus become: can there be a practice of worldmaking that (a) stops being anthropocentric; (b) embraces radical interdependence; and (c) is capable of operating effectively in the reality of the contemporary world? These are the crucial questions framing the chapter.

We start with a brief discussion of two aspects of ontological dualism that have been essential for design/ing as we have known it: the centrality of the "object," on the one hand, and its relation to representational epistemologies based on the separation between subject/object and observer/observed, on the other.

This initial discussion leads us to ask, is a design/ing practice without "object" conceivable? This seemingly inconspicuous question will enable us to examine the tension-ridden encounters between object-centered and life-centered worldmaking practices, while discussing the implications for designing as an ontological praxis of making and restor(y)ing life.

The next section examines the emergence of novel narratives of life in Latin America that decenter the liberal, secular story of bioeconomic man. Taken as a whole, they may be seen as de facto enacting a relational story of life articulated in terms of six concepts: territoriality, communality, autonomy, re-existence, pluriversal transitions, and politics in the feminine. This conceptual tapestry constitutes the architecture of an emergent *pensamiento*. We introduce this story of life to develop further one of the central insights guiding this book from the outset: that of being in between stories. This Latin American story of life enables us to explore the idea that worldmaking—and, hence, designing— could be reimagined as a praxis of transitioning between stories. To this end and drawing also from Latin American struggles against extractive forms of development, we propose the concept of *pluriversal contact zones*, defined as tense interfaces where relational (the emergent story) and nonrelational (the dominant story) narratives of life and worldmaking meet. We end this section by outlining six strategies for the practice of pluriversal transitions based on the conceptual tapestry previously summarized.

The conceptual tapestry and strategies for transition provide an entry point for the final section, devoted to discussing some examples or moments of designing that may be seen as embodying them, drawing both from design literature and from broader inquiries concerning commons, food, and cities as domains where alternative practices attuned to relationality are emerging. In keeping with the insights from the previous chapter, we ask whether these moments could be seen as portals or bridges where the refusal of simple binaries is at play through the building of diverse worlds and communities of care. Throughout the chapter, we come back to the idea that relationality needs to be actively produced and cultivated, while being mindful of the slippages encountered along the way because of our habitual return to the prevailing version of reality. We end the chapter with a series of propositions on pluriversal designing as a praxis for imagining and creating portals for restor(y)ing and remaking life.

FROM OBJECT-ORIENTED DESIGN TO LIFE-CENTERED DESIGNING

Designing is becoming attuned to relationality, first and foremost in its reorientation toward the earth but also in its growing attention to the communal, place, and the local. Why is this so? Because as a practice, designing is "thrown" into the world (in the Heideggerian sense), which means that given the contemporary crisis it cannot but encounter the implications of the denial of relationality face-to-face. Of course, most design has been performed nonrelationally. The very concepts of designer, user, object, project, and interface reveal the nonrelational structure of design. At the same time, one may argue that designing is emerging as an important domain for thinking anew about life and worldmaking.

There is no doubt that design has played an important role in the consolidation of an ontology of inherently existing objects and of individual subjects intent on creating and using them, rendering them into "scarce" commodities, extracting value from them, hoarding them, turning them into waste, and so forth. This ontology surely goes beyond design, pervading the entire gamut of globalized capitalist worldmaking practices. Its consequences are visible everywhere: in the treatment of most humans, Earth, and life as things, resulting in a world of obscene social inequalities, untold ecological destruction, rampant consumerism, and staggering levels of waste. While waste often remains unremarked, it is a *sine qua non* of modern capitalist design. As Zygmunt Bauman revealingly put it, "modernity is a condition of compulsive, and addictive, designing. Where there is design, there is waste."[2]

The question becomes: What happens to designing when it begins to consistently include more of life? Can designing, as a mode of acting, move, *in practical (not just theoretical) terms*, toward a non-objectifying understanding of humans and the world? Can it contribute to weakening those ways of making that prioritize measurement, optimization, and consumption? Can it further a sort of "ontological detox" through forms of being that engage with object-centered and waste-producing worldmaking-as-usual while creating bridges to relational life? These questions have no easy answer, for there is a tight relationship between objects, making, and unmaking, as Elaine Scarry has tellingly conjectured: "Knowledge about the character of creating and created objects is at present in a state of conceptual infancy. Its illumination will require a richness of work

---

[2] Zygmunt Bauman, *Wasted Lives: Modernity and its Outcasts* (Cambridge: Polity Press, 2004), 17.

far beyond the frame of any single study: like the activity of 'making,' the activity of 'understanding making' will be a collective rather than a solitary labor."[3] This chapter could be seen as part of such collective historical investigation.

One of the foundational features of the ontology of intrinsically existent objects and things is the representationalist understanding of knowledge—that is, the idea that sound knowledge must be separate from the knower (see the Appendix). Second-order cybernetics and the early notion of ontological design by Winograd and Flores undermined such framing. Second-order cybernetics argued that it is impossible to separate the observer from the observed. As one of its founders, Heinz von Foerster, put it, the observer is "a participant actor in the drama of mutual interaction of the give and take in the circularity of human relations";[4] concomitantly, objectivity "is a popular device for avoiding responsibility." As he eloquently put it, the reason for the adherence to the principle of objectivity "was fear; fear that paradoxes would arise when the observers were allowed to enter the universe of their observations."[5]

Understanding Computers and Cognition: A New Foundation for Design deepened this challenge of the representationalist tradition by weaving three theoretical threads into a novel account of knowledge and action: (1) the autopoietic theory of Maturana and Varela; (2) speech act theory (philosophy of language), with its emphasis on the centrality of commitment in communication, as opposed to information transmission; and (3) hermeneutics, with its accent on the tacit shared background that enables understanding. The resulting approach sees human action as realized by a living body that preserves its basic constitution (its autopoiesis), although in permanent reinvention of itself; as initiated by situated, embodied persons capable of responding to others through linguistic commitments; and as taking place in a space of norms and past traditions (the horizon of historical pre-understanding). As living, speaking, and interpreting beings, humans are always in the present, engaged in all three temporalities. The ability to coordinate in language, granted by living in spaces of relevance opened by the nervous system, enables humans to attend to what is going on. By making sense and listening to each other around particular concerns (the domain of Martin Heidegger's "Dasein"), speakers are always immersed within realms of practice and coordination for action in language.[6]

Maturana and Varela's work on autopoiesis and cognition provided an important pillar for moving beyond the notion of "objects" that are "represented" in the mind. As mentioned in passing in Chapter 2, for these authors the purpose of the cognitive system is not to construct mental representations of an

---

[3] Scarry, The *Body in Pain*, 280.

[4] Heinz von Foerster, *Understanding Understanding: Essays on Cybernetics and Cognition* (New York: Springer Verlag, 2010), 293.

[5] Foerster, *Understanding Understanding*, 288–89.

[6] Terry Winograd and Fernando Flores, *Understanding Computers and Cognition: A New Foundation for Design* (Norwood, NJ: Ablex, 1986). For a substantial discussion of ontological design, see Arturo Escobar, *Designs for the Pluriverse* (Durham, NC: Duke University Press, 2018).

alleged external reality but to provide possibilities for embodied action within the world; succinctly, to be alive is to be attuned to a situation. Living beings coordinate actions and move around by relying only partly on representations. The representationalist tradition celebrates an ontological gulf separating us from our world, leaving no place for a functional co-generative interweaving of world, body, and self. But our entire biological being (not just the brain or the mind) participates in the creation of our being-in-the-world; our bodies are our opening onto situations through the braiding of languaging and emotioning since human emotions and moods are the foundation of our making sense of our worlds through our attunement to situations.[7]

From these reformulated foundations there arises Winograd and Flores's definition of ontological design: "We encounter the deep question of design when we recognize that in designing tools we are designing ways of being."[8] Hence the need to address "the broader question of how a society engenders inventions whose existence in turn alters that society."[9] Every tool or technology is ontological in the sense that, however minutely, it inaugurates a set of rituals, ways of doing, and modes of being, thus contributing to shape what it is to be human (digital devices are a dramatic case in point). Another sense in which design is ontological is that in designing objects, tools, and institutions humans design the conditions of their existence and, in turn, the conditions of their designing. "Design designs," is the apt formula given to this circularity by Anne-Marie Willis; "we design our world, while our world acts back on us and designs us."[10]

Toward the end of their book, Winograd and Flores summarize their plea for an ontological approach to designing:

> The most important design is *ontological*. It constitutes an intervention in the background of our heritage, growing out of our already-existent ways of being in the world, and deeply affecting the kinds of beings that we are … Ontologically oriented design is therefore necessarily both reflective and political, looking back to the tradition that have formed us but also forwards to as-yet-uncreated transformations of our lives together. Through the emergence of new tools, we come to a changing awareness of human nature and human action, which in turn leads to new technological development. The designing process is part of this "dance" in which our structure of possibilities is generated.[11]

"In ontological designing," to quote one final time, "we are doing more than asking what can be built. *We are engaging in a philosophical discourse about*

---

[7] Maturana and Varela, *The Tree of Knowledge*.

[8] Winograd and Flores, *Understanding Computers and Cognition*, xi.

[9] Winograd and Flores, *Understanding Computers and Cognition*, 4–5.

[10] Willis, "Ontological Designing," 80–98.

[11] Winograd and Flores, *Understanding Computers and Cognition*, 163.

the self—about what we can do and what can be."[12] Succinctly, ontological designing is about the making of the world and the human.

Tony Fry's design ontology develops some of these ideas further by tackling the consequences of living under the structural unsustainability brought about by modernity. For Fry, one of the most serious effects of modernity is what he calls "defuturing." Modernity "did not just take the future away from the peoples it damaged and exploited, but set a process in motion that negated the future and defutured both the born and the unborn."[13] The dialectic of defuturing and futuring brings forth the need to move from the Enlightenment to the Sustainment, a new imaginary of being and doing capable of countering modernity's defuturing effects. Sustainment involves the destruction of that which destroys, via "elimination design," and this applies to the hegemonic category of the human. As he puts it, "'we' are travelling toward a point at which we will have to learn how to redesign ourselves. This is not as extreme as it sounds, for we have always been a product of design—albeit unknowingly … In essence, what is being suggested here is action towards the relational development of a new kind of 'human being.'"[14]

By raising the stakes concerning the nature of designing, Winograd, Flores, Willis, and Fry shift the emphasis from a representationalist paradigm to the praxis of worldmaking. Can the nonrepresentationalist framework become a grounding for a different type of designing? What would become of designing if it were to be based on the fundamental insights that, first, the world does not exist "out there," separate from us and, second, that the world is always the result of our actions, even if within a complex dynamic of emergence, contingency, and historical drift? And finally, that Earth is "not a collection of objects, but a communion of subjects"—a comingling of nonseparable entities (including objects)—as ecologist and theologian Thomas Berry powerfully put it?[15] These questions will remain with us for the remainder of this chapter. For now, we have posited the possibility of nonobjectifying worldmaking practices as a prelude to any futuring, life-centered praxis.

THE POLITICS OF RESTOR(Y)ING LIFE: AN EMERGENT IMAGINARY FROM LATIN AMERICA

Throughout this book, we have emphasized the notion of transitioning between stories. Whether in the domains of theory, politics, or designing, we proposed that "we" (moderns) no longer have good narratives for belonging to the earth. Crafting a new narrative surely is a transgenerational endeavor, involving coalitions around compelling new narratives for belonging to the planet. From

---

[12] Winograd and Flores, *Understanding Computers and Cognition*, 179, emphasis ours.

[13] Tony Fry, *City Futures in the Age of a Changing Climate* (London: Routledge, 2015), 23.

[14] Tony Fry, *Becoming Human by Design* (London: Berg, 2012), 37 and 162.

[15] Thomas Berry, "The Determining Features of the Ecozoic Era," in T. Berry, *Selected Writing on the Earth Community*, 142–44 (Maryknoll, NY: Orbis Books, 2014).

the previous chapters we may infer that new stories cannot come only, or even primarily, from academic thinking, no matter how persuasive, nor can we invent them at our whim; we also suggested that powerful narratives are emerging at the multiple boundaries between the older ontology and a slew of new or renewed ontologies, cosmovisions, and practices linked to struggles for social justice and the defense of the earth, whether humble grassroots struggles for survival and sufficiency or self-conscious postcapitalist alternatives. The emergence of new stories is thus necessarily a struggle with entrenched discourses, powers, and institutions. It is a centerpiece of the political activation of relationality.

In this section, we outline what we believe is a promising narrative emerging during the past three decades at the interface between territorial struggles and activist and academic debates in Latin America; it is finding cogent articulation through a series of salient concepts: territoriality, communality, autonomy, pluriversality, re-existence, and politics in the feminine. Our hypothesis is that these provide the grounding for a different story of life and an alternative basis for action. These concepts are not just abstractions; rather, they are the result of theoretical-practices infused with the knowledge and wisdom of struggles. As discussed in the previous two chapters, these practices are an important dimension of what many social movements do, and hence a crucial element in the politics of relationality. In fact, these concepts are derived from struggles that instantiate the principles of relational politics developed in Chapter 4: struggles that are contingent and local, emergent, generative, that resist good–bad binaries and, above all perhaps, bridge the gap between theory and practice by appealing to epistemologies of *sentipensar*, where heart and mind are not separated.[16]

Finally, the conceptual tapestry stems from contested spaces where ontologies of separation and of relationality meet and get entangled in multifarious ways. Building on the previous work of de la Cadena and Escobar, we refer to these interfaces as pluriversal contact zones, a salient example of the generativity of ontological excess, another important principle of relationality. We outline this latter concept before moving fully to the Latin American discussion, which we will introduce through a contemporary Colombian example.

Worldmaking and designing relationally as the creation of pluriversal contact zones

If designing involves the creation of interfaces (traditionally understood as bringing together tool/object, user, and task/purpose), it follows that when faced with overlapping life stories, we encounter an interface designing of a

---

[16] On the notion of social movements' theoretical-practices, see Michal Osterweil, "The Italian Anomaly: Place and History in the Global Justice Movement," in *The European Social Movement Experience: Rethinking "New Social Movements", Historicizing the Alterglobalization Movement and Understanding the New Wave of Protest*, ed. C. Fominaya and L. Cox, 33–46 (London: Routledge, 2013).

different kind.[17] In fact, the interfaces are often already there, in the multiple power-laden entanglements that exist amongst stories and their worlds. Anthropologist Marisol de la Cadena has proposed a useful conceptualization in this regard, that of "pluriversal contact zones" (PCZs).[18] These are most clearly visible in the ontological conflicts often present alongside environmental conflicts. Let us take a simple example: some Indigenous and Black communities in Latin America defend rivers, lakes, or mountains against large-scale mining or hydroelectric dams on the basis that they are *one with* the river, lake, or mountain, that they do not exist separate from them; sometimes this takes the form of stating that the river, lake, or mountain, is a sentient being, or that it is alive. From a modernist ontological perspective, this is nonsense: everybody knows that the mountain is an inert being, a piece of rock, or at most an ecosystem, and as such can be mined (destroyed) for profit or for the good of the nation or managed through environmental conservation. But there is much more at stake than meets the eye in these conflicts. To quote de la Cadena:

> My proverbial example is the defense of Ausangate in Cuzco, Perú against a mining corporation by a coalition of environmentalists and Indigenous peasants. Ausangate is a complex entity; it is a mountain and not only such. It is also an earth being. In the alliance, urban activists defended the mountain, Indigenous peasants defended the earth being. Their ontologically divergent interests converged in a common interest: their opposition to the conversion of the complex space that Ausangate occupies into an open pit mine.[19]

Borrowing a phrase from Isabelle Stengers, de la Cadena refers to these cases as instances of relation between worlds in which they have "interests in common that are not the same interest." Another cogent example comes from Luz Enith Mosquera Perea, a young Afrodescendant environmental engineer and activist in the movement to declare Colombia's third largest river, the Atrato, which traverses the northern half of the Pacific Rainforest, as subject of rights, in an attempt to defend the territory from deforestation and attenuate the forced

---

[17] Lara Penin, *Bui Bonsiepe: The Disobedience of Design* (London: Bloomsbury, 2022). Gui Bonsiepe emphasized the centrality of the interface to all designing. See the substantial anthology of his writings edited by Lara Penin.

[18] Marisol de la Cadena, "Not Knowing: In the Presence of ….," in *Experimenting with Ethnography: A Companion to Analysis*, ed. Andrea Ballestero and Britt Winthereik, 146–56 (Durham, NC: Duke University Press, 2021); Marisol de la Cadena and Arturo Escobar, "Notes on Ontological Excess: Towards Pluriversal Designing," in *Design for More-than Human Futures: Towards Post-Anthropocentric Worlding*, eds. M. Tironi, M. Chilet, C. Marín, and P. Hermansen (London: Routledge, in press).

[19] de la Cadena, "Not Knowing," 146.

displacement of the region's Black inhabitants.[20] The struggle, as Luz Enith vividly described, was based on the notion that "We are all the Atrato; we need to defend the river we all are. And we all mobilize together for the life of all." As with Ausangate, "the Atrato" emerges from these movements as a communitarian entanglement that is only partly understandable by the State. In fact, "We are all the Atrato" simply *cannot be* in the ontological eyes of the State, since the State ineluctably separates "humans" from "river" and "individual" from "community"; a community that involves more-than-humans is unthinkable. The language of "rights of nature" thus emerges *as an onto-epistemic interface and portal that enables that which cannot be to emerge in politics.* Such politics involve the tense co-emergence of diverse ways of worlding, one stemming from the inseparability between river, territory, and humans, and another that thrives in their separation. In the PCZ thus opened, what is uncommon to both worlds meet (often, through the mediation of environmental discourses and practices) as an instance of an interest in common (the protection of the river) that is not the same interest. We believe these cases are auspicious pluriversal openings.

Pluriversal contact zones interrupt, temporarily at least, the coloniality of practices that make the world one. They hint at unknown forms of together-ness that diverse worlds must learn. Scary as this endeavor feels, it needs to be undertaken, for if we open our senses to current events, we may feel the presence of the pluriverse and its portals proliferate. Opportunities at feeling them follow the attempts at their destruction by practices of terricide. Pluriv-ersal contact zones are genuinely emergent, especially where open political struggle is at play; they make newly visible the ontological stakes embedded in designing and in the political activation of relationality. The approach of PCZs, portals, and slippages offers clues and possibilities for designing pluriversally.

Designing spaces for life and happiness amid
territorial conflict: A Colombian example

Take a careful look at almost any territory in Latin America and the Caribbean at present and you will find a complex history of terricide and popular struggles to contain it. We find a good example of this dynamic in the long-standing territo-rial defense of a region located along the banks of the Sinú River in northwest Colombia and inhabited by Indigenous, peasant, and fishing communities.

The lower Sinú River basin (approximately 170,000 hectares) is an amphib-ian territory composed of wetlands, swamps, rivers, and estuaries, with cyclic rains that determine periods of flooding and dryness that locals have learned

---

[20] Marisol de la Cadena and Arturo Escobar, "Sentidos de las ecologías políticas del Sur/Abya-Yala," CLACSO's Political Ecology Working Groups, April 9, 2021, with presentations by Luz Enith Mosquera, Marisol de la Cadena, and Arturo Escobar; CLACSO TV, "A 20 años del Grupo deTrabajo: Sentidos de las ecologías políticas del sur/Abya-Yala". 2° encuentro," April 9, 2021, YouTube video, 1:53:33, available online: https://www.youtube.com/watch?v=xWmJdIvwcIM (accessed July 19, 2023).

to inhabit since pre-Columbian times. The result has been a *cultura anfibia*, or amphibian culture, with people's livelihoods depending on agriculture, fishing, hunting, and handicraft making, including gold, ceramics, and basketry. The Spanish Conquest and colonization brought threatening changes to this tapestry of living, beginning with the destruction of food gardens to undermine people's self-sufficiency, the introduction of patriarchal mores in lieu of matrifocal organizations, and the destruction in the nineteenth century of the network of canals that the Zenúes (Zenú Indigenous people) had constructed, to pave the way for tobacco cultivation, cattle ranching, gold mining, and forest extraction. Local Indigenous, Black, and mestizo peasants were relegated to the region's margins, where they attempted to survive autonomously, adapting new lands for the cultivation of staple crops such as cassava and plantains. The twentieth century brought additional dramatic changes to the territory as the struggle for land became fiercer with the intensification of large-scale cattle raising and the fencing of large holdings with barbwire. The 1970s saw a wave of struggles for the recuperation of land, prompted by the expansion of Green Revolution monocropping of cotton, maize, and sorghum. A final blow was added in the 1990s with the construction of a large hydroelectric dam up the Sinú River (the Urrá Dam) and with the arrival of the armed conflict between guerrillas and paramilitaries, with the latter enforcing a remorseless strategy of forced land dispossession.

Even this brief sketch is enough to illustrate that this region "has seen it all." Peasant resistance of yesteryear gave way in the 1990s to a steady process of collective thought and strategy, led by the *Asociación de Campesinos, Pescadores e Indígenas del Bajo Sinú* (Asprocig, Peasant, Fisherfolk, and Indigenous Association of the Lower Zenú River). These grassroots organizing efforts took place in the context of the presence of State and non-governmental organization (NGO) experts who, especially in the early years, often failed to understand local perceptions and skills. What followed was a slow and collective "conceptual reconstruction that emerged daily out of the dialogue of forms of knowledge amongst all of us," as an Asprocig activist and technician described it.[21] The organization's conceptualization centered on a notion of the territory in terms of ancestral knowledges and autonomy, all in the context of the history of territorial affectations, from the Conquest to the Urrá Dam. Ancestrality encompassed the retrieval of the memory of a whole series of practices concerning Zenú dwelling in the territory, long-standing livelihood strategies, customary hydraulic technologies, and local seeds, all of which became important elements in the perspective of autonomy.

The resistance relied on a vision of the territory and the river as sources of life. Asprocig's goal was to strengthen peasant landholdings through the reconstitution of the interrelations among wetlands, forests, fields, agriculture,

---

[21] Tatiana Roa, "El camino de las resistencias hacia las alternativas al desarrollo. Tres experiencias colombianas" (PhD dissertation, University of Amsterdam, 2023). This account is based on a draft of chapter 4 of Tatiana Roa's excellent doctoral dissertation from which the quotes are taken.

and local culture. Gradually, the initial productivist orientation centered on livelihoods gave way to a relational understanding that saw knowledge as collective, paving the way for ecological, ludic, and spiritual concerns. Among the many initiatives introduced by the association were the reconstruction of dikes for redressing river erosion and climate change mitigation, communal aquaculture, the creation of "agroecological spirals"; the restoration of forests, rice cultivation, and local milling; and the commercialization of agroecological products, all of which were understood as elements of an *economía propia* (an alternative local economy). More ambitious but real goals included a significant transformation of patriarchal relations, beginning with the organization itself; the recovery of collective practices of decision-making in community assemblies; and collective leadership. The resulting livelihood strategies, under the rubric of "diverse agroecosystems," entailed the articulation of reconstituted peasant practices with market-oriented activities. The political orientation, however, was decidedly toward *la defensa de lo propio y con lo propio* (the defense of one's own and through one's own means), with lack of land as a continuing bottleneck.

The Sinú case exemplifies the steady erosion of the relational weave of life by colonialist interventions and heteronomous design from above, from the colonization period to the development age. These interventions may be seen as the making of an anthropocentric world in its multiple entanglements with capitalist patriarchy and colonial modernity. Conversely, going beyond resistance, local actions and practices could be interpreted as a counter-designing in relation to the State and agroindustrial development, based on a sophisticated weaving of ancestral and new knowledges, intelligent political struggle, the crafting of alternative livelihoods, and the building of action capacities and skills through explicit forms of organizing.

While nurtured by collective organizing and research, Asprocig's approach was the result of the interaction with external experts, such as agroecologists; what ensued, as Roa concludes, was a "reconstruction of social, economic, political, ecological, spiritual, and cultural relations in ways conducive to more harmonious relationships among humans and between these and the natural environment." Asprocig's decision to work within the existing constraints, particularly their disadvantageous power relations vis-à-vis capitalist landlords and the State, led them to develop a complex understanding of the coexistence of multiple worlds in the territory, motivating a shift of strategy from an all-out struggle of open confrontation to a partial but significant negotiated reconstitution of local livelihoods. Here, pluriversality thus means keeping a world partially alive in the face of tremendous violence, even if the latter prevents the full blossoming of such worlds.

Could the novel practices involving the reconstitution of autochthonous hydraulic technologies, forests, and communal agroecology, among others, based on the local amphibian culture and the coevolution of communities with the river, be seen in terms of the political activation of relationality and as autonomous forms of designing? To address this question, we now introduce a series of concepts that suggest that what might be at stake in this case is the enactment of a story of life entangled with, but altogether different from, capitalist monohumanism. We take an additional cue from Asprocig when they state that: "*Nosotros conservamos la vida, así no dé utilidades*" ("We conserve life, even if it might not yield profits"). As they see it, their experience evinces the collective articulation of an alternative way of making life, rather than just a movement against a dam, agroindustrial development, greedy capitalists, or violent landlords, even if these, too, are at play.

A tapestry of concepts: An emergent narrative of life at
the interface of activist praxis and social theory

The case of Asprocig, as so many other cases of peasant, Black, Indigenous, and popular struggles, demonstrates the centrality of the territory to the struggle. Equally important is the emphasis on communal concerns and a political praxis of organizing from below to ensure a modicum of autonomy over the conditions of existence. It is in this context that the reconstitution of local worlds and livelihoods needs to be understood. Activists often refer to this strategy in terms of going beyond resistance to enable re-existence, meaning a continued reconstruction of the conditions of existence in contexts of domination that allows locals to go on with their lives by reinventing themselves permanently. In short, Asprocig may be seen as a concrete example of our hypothesis about the emergence of a conceptual tapestry that embodies a more relational story of life.

Territoriality, communality, autonomy, re-existence, pluriversality, and politics in the feminine are novel concepts with complex genealogies; they are the subject of complex debates. The concepts overlap and irradiate each other, which is why we prefer to speak about a tapestry of concepts. Together, they provide the basis for a relational narrative of life conducive to making life in re-embodied, re-communalized, re-localized, and re-earthed manners. Taken as a whole, this conceptual assemblage constitutes a platform for thinking about post-development, post-extractivist transitions and transitions to the pluriverse, with Buen Vivir (good living, or collective well-being) as a guiding star—all important dimensions of the active production of relationality. These concepts have been emerging over the past two to three decades from multiple sites throughout the continent (and, we believe, in many other parts of the world in other ways, as some of the cases discussed in previous chapters suggest); they have been arrived at through collaborative epistemologies and collective research and action. Very importantly, we are talking about a reconfiguration of categories that *enable novel constellations of practice* in place. What follows is a succinct statement on each of the concepts.[22]

To start with *territory*: this concept emerged among Indigenous and Black movements in the Andean countries in the early 1990s, to overcome the perceived

---

[22] For the sake of brevity, we will cite sparingly in this section. See Escobar, *Pluriversal Politics*, for the main references on these concepts.

limitations of land-centered peasant movements. As an Afro-Colombian elder, Don Porfirio, from the Pacific rainforest put it in 1993, "anybody can own land, but territory is something else altogether."[23] The territory is seen as the collective and historically constituted space where humans and nonhumans (often including spiritual worlds), place and identity, culture and politics, livelihoods and all other activities, take place. Territories harbor unique worlds—hence the expression, often voiced in activist circles, of *territorios de vida y diferencia*, or territories of life and difference. Over the past two decades, this conception of the territory has become decidedly relational. Working with Indigenous groups in the Sierra Nevada de Santa Marta in northwestern Colombia, anthropologist Astrid Ulloa concludes that the purpose of relational territoriality is to ensure the circulation of life through practices involving knowledge, sacred sites, seeds, and rituals.[24] Another key notion is the unbroken continuity between the body and the territory, conceptualized by feminists through the notion of *cuerpo-territorio* (body-territory), derived from observing women-led territorial struggles against extractive operations where the inseparability of body and territory becomes patently clear.[25]

Territoriality goes hand in hand with a renewed emphasis on the communal dimension of existence. The neologism of *comunalidad*, or communality, coined by Indigenous intellectuals in Oaxaca in the 1970s, best embodies the ineluctability of being communal. Communality names a collective "We" as the subject of all activities in a particular place, from eating to learning. "The communal," says Oaxacan activist-intellectual Arturo Guerrero, "is not a set of things, but an 'integral' fluidity"; this fluidity is life itself, "the spiral of existence," pluriverse, an openness to "all beings and forces ... a mutual hospitality," within the context of place in its relation to an exterior socioeconomic context.[26] The result of this perpetual interaction with the exterior is *lo propio*, what is one's own, or the We. Communality invokes a different way of being persons, always from the We, that includes land and soil and the timeless sediment of life and death. Communality is enacted through collective agreements, a "communalocracy." To live is to exist *nosótricamente*, in a We-manner, abiding by the communal option. Here we find an objectless ontology centered on rooted existence rather than on stand-alone entities. This concept continues to be profusely enriched, particularly through research-action programs in Mexico, Guatemala, and Colombia; it names those

[23] Arturo Escobar, *Territories of Difference: Place, Movements, Life, Redes* (Durham, NC: Duke University Press, 2008), 111.

[24] Astrid Ulloa, "Los territorios indígenas en Colombia: De escenarios de apropiación transnacional a territorialidades alternativas," *Scripta Nova* 16 (2012): 65.

[25] A movement led in 2014 by Francia Márquez, current vice president of Colombia, to defend her community's river against gold mining, coined the powerful slogan: *El territorio es la vida y la vida no se vende, se ama y se defiende* (the territory is life, and life isn't sold, it is loved and defended).

[26] Arturo Guerrero, "*Comunalidad*," in *Pluriverse: A Post-development Dictionary*, ed. Ashish Kothari, Ariel Salleh, Arturo Escobar, Federico Demaria, and Alberto Acosta, 130–33 (Delhi: Tulika/AuthorsUpfront, 2019).

variegated forms of communal existence that are neither a return to the past nor a continuation of the present, but that reveal a fight over the conditions for the collective production of life in common.

The struggle over the collective production of life is a central aspect of *autonomy*. We discussed at length Zapatista *autonomía*, which continues to inspire notions of autonomy in many parts of the world. As we argued, autonomía harbors a strong sense of interdependence and enacts novel practices of making life and politics. It challenges modernist notions of power, politics, and collective action. To restate, autonomy refers to a communal politicity.[27] Its thrust is to lessen dependence on global markets and the State and the creation of institutions where self-rule, non-hierarchy, and direct forms of democracy prevail—those in which common people can assume their own power. Autonomous struggles attempt to counter the ontology of scarcity imposed by economic society, creating openings for reconstituting the making of life on the principles of sufficiency and conviviality. Autonomy also refers to communities' ability for changing traditions traditionally, instead of heteronomously from above. Communities striving for autonomy, it is said, engage in the democratic organization of the art of hope and dignity. This notion of autonomy can be interpreted as the autopoietic production of communitarian tapestries, a theory of interbeing, or as a political practice for pluriversal designing.[28]

Autonomy and interdependence, though in tension, are co-constitutive. This co-constitution is inherent to the notion of the pluriverse. We arrive at this conclusion from the perspectives of both biology and activism. Maturana and Varela's concept of biological autonomy suggests that each living being (from the cell on) creates boundaries and an organization or network of relations among its key components, in such a way that their continued interaction produces the living being in question; in other words, living beings are self-producing. Otherwise, the organism ceases to exist as such. There is a certain "operational closure" at play here, but this does not mean that the organism is self-sufficient, for it needs exchanges of matter and energy with its environment through "structural coupling."[29] Politically, a given local world (say, an Indigenous community) similarly needs a certain closure to ensure their permanence in time, albeit always in interaction with the State, corporations, and other actors, whereas these actors undermine autonomy by rupturing the system of relations among

---

[27] Raquel Gutiérrez Aguilar, "Producir lo común: entramados comunitarios y formas de lo político," in *Comunalidad, tramas comunitarias y producción de lo común*, ed. Raquel Gutiérrez Aguilar, 51–72 (Oaxaca: Pez en el árbol, 2018).

[28] Gustavo Esteva, "The Hour of Autonomy," *Latin American and Caribbean Ethnic Studies* 10, no. 1 (2015): 34–145; Xochitl Leyva-Solano, "Zapatista Autonomy," in *Pluriverse: A Post-development Dictionary*, ed. Ashish Kothari, Ariel Salleh, Arturo Escobar, Federico Demaria, and Alberto Acosta, 335–38 (Delhi: Tulika/AuthorsUpfront, 2019); Ana Cecilia Dinnerstein, *The Politics of Autonomy in Latin America: The Art of Organizing Hope* (London: Palgrave Macmillan, 2015).

[29] Humberto R. Maturana and Francisco J. Varela, *Autopoiesis and Cognition: The Realization of the Living* (Boston, MA: Reidel, 1980).

key components (e.g., among territory, ancestors, locally generated livelihoods, spiritual or sacred practices, and communal rituals). We may conclude that *the pluriverse is the result of the dance between autonomy and interdependence that living beings and many place/territory-based communities perform* to keep themselves and the pluriverse going. At its best, autonomy is a praxis of inter-existence.

Territoriality, communality, and autonomy constitute the basis for the notion of *re-existence*. Activists connected with Black and Indigenous struggles in Northern Cauca (Colombia) started to speak of re-existence in the late 1980s to stress the connection among their long-standing practices of ancestrality, collective memory, resistance, marronage, and the affirmation of their distinct "cosmovision." In the context of the intense political organizing going on in the region, the notion has become a cornerstone for insurgent pedagogies and mobilizations. Re-existence takes both old and new practices of livelihood, politics, and culture of subaltern communities as the living archive from which "to reinvent and dignify life in order to continue being while changing"; it is an answer to the question of "what are we going to invent today in order to go on living," while confronting the attempts to exterminate them as distinct worlds.[30] For racialized women, such politics involves the peaceful reconstitution of their territories of life, as the Afro-Colombian philosopher Elba Palacios suggests in her work with Black women in Cali's popular neighborhoods; these women teach us that "to re-exist means much more than resist; it involves the creation of autonomy in defense of life, through a sort of contemporary urban marronage that enables them to reconstitute their negated humanity, reweaving communities in the historical diaspora."[31]

As in much of the world, conversations on *pluriversality* and *transitions* are in the air in Latin America. From a political ontology perspective, pluriverse signals the multiple struggles against the One-World world by relational ways of worlding. Post-development and post-extractivist transitions are essential for a movement beyond the globalized capitalist model to a peaceful, though tense, reconstitution of national and global governance along plural civilizational foundations.[32] Pluriversal transitions evince

---

[30] Adolfo Albán, "Pedagogías de la re-existencia," in *Pedagogías decoloniales. Prácticas insurgentes de resistir, (re)existir, y (re)vivir*, Vol. 1, ed. Catherine Walsh, 443–68 (Quito: AbyaYala, 2013); Betty Ruth Lozano, *Aportes a un feminismo negro decolonial* (Quito: Abya Yala, 2018); Lina M. Hurtado and Carlos Walter Porto Gonçalves, "Resistir y re-existir," *GEOgraphia* 24, no. 53 (2022): 24–53.

[31] Elba M. Palacios, "Sentipensar la paz en Colombia: Oyendo las reexistentes voces pacíficas de mujeres Negras Afrodescendientes," *Memorias: Revista Digital de Historia y Arqueología desde el Caribe colombiano* 38 (May–August 2019): 131–56.

[32] Ashish Kothari, Ariel Salleh, Arturo Escobar, Federico Demaria, and Alberto Acosta, eds., *Pluriverse: A Post-development Dictionary* (Delhi: Tulika/AuthorsUpfront, 2019); Maristella Svampa, *Las Fronteras del neoextractivismo en América Latina* (Guadalajara: Universidad de Guadalajara, 2019); Eduardo Gudynas, *Extractivismos* (Cochabamba: CEDIB/CLAES, 2015).

the *gigantic and global confrontation* between diverse and plural *entramados comunitarios* (communitarian entanglements), with a greater or lesser degree of relationality and internal cohesion, on the one hand; and, on the other, the most powerful transnational corporations and coalitions among them, which saturate the global space with their police and armed bands, their allegedly "expert" discourses and images, and their rigidly hierarchical rules and institutions[33]

A holistic conception of Buen Vivir and *ubuntu* ("I am because we all are," because all else exists) is often taken as the goal of the transitions.

Our last concept, *politics in the feminine*, gathers the previous notions together. It refers to those personal and collective practices required for actively desiring and constructing non-patriarchal, noncapitalist, and relational modes of living—in other words, practices of dis-identification with capitalism, masculinism, racism, and with the ontologies of separation integral to all forms of oppression. A politics in the feminine centers on the social production and reproduction of life, building on women's capacity to create forms of counter-power based on their living bodies.[34] Politics in the feminine opposes the "minoritization" of women that has accompanied the de-communalization of nonmodern worlds, in favor of a politics that reclaims the "ontological fullness" of women's worlds. As discussed in Chapter 2, patriarchal ontologies are not only the oldest form of domination and the expropriation of value, they continue to be at the root of most forms of violence, resulting in a "pedagogy of cruelty" functional to the deepening of dispossession.[35] This ontological mandate must be dismantled by building on the relational and communal practices that still inhabit, albeit in fragmentary and contradictory ways, many marginalized and subaltern worlds. It is instructive to quote from Rita Segato to bring the exposition of these concepts to a close:

> We need to remake our ways of living, to reconstruct the strong links existing in communities with the help of the technologies of sociability commanded by women in their domains; these locally rooted practices are embedded in the dense symbolic fabric of an alternative cosmos, dysfunctional to capital, and proper of the *pueblos* (peoples) in their political journey that have allowed them to survive throughout five-hundred years of continued conquest. We need to advance this politics day by day, outside the State: to re-weave the communal fabric as to restore the political character of domesticity proper of the communal .... *To choose the relational path*

---

[33] Raquel Gutiérrez, "Pistas reflexivas para orientarnos en una turbulenta época de peligro," in *Palabras para tejernos, resistir y transformar en la época que estamos viviendo*, ed. Raquel Gutiérrez, Natalia Sierra, Pablo Davalos, Oscar Olivera, Héctor Mongragon, Vilma Almendra, Raúl Zibechi, Emmanuel Rozental, and Pablo Mamani, 9–34 (Oaxaca: Pez en el Árbol, 2012).

[34] Raquel Gutiérrez Aguilar, *Horizontes comunitarios-populares* (Madrid: Traficantes de Sueños, 2017); Verónica Gago, *La potencia feminista* (Buenos Aires: Tinta Limón, 2019).

[35] Rita Segato, *La guerra contra las mujeres* (Madrid: Traficantes de Sueños, 2016), 16.

is to opt for the historical project of being community. It means to endow relationality and the communal forms of happiness with a grammar of value and resistance capable of counteracting the powerful developmentalist, exploitative, and productivist rhetoric of things with its alleged meritocracy. *La estrategia a partir de ahora es femenina* (The strategy, from now on, is a feminine one).[36]

It should be emphasized that feminine in this context is intended to revalue women's historical links to body, place, and community and women's ethics of care, but within a thoroughly depatriarchalized perspective. It unsettles the patriarchal imposition on women to be relational caretakers while denying them autonomy over their bodies and economies. If capitalism cannot exist without patriarchy, the corollary is that the entire economy needs to be depatriarchalized and reconstituted under the principle of the care of life for all.[37] This politics in the feminine is not just local; it is concrete and place-based but also potentially plural and generalizable through rhizomatic expansion.[38]

The concepts sketched above reverberate in territorial struggles against extractive operations such as mining or large-scale infrastructure projects and plantations. The interfaces from which they arise share some features: they are spaces of thought construction centered on the re/production of life in common; the knowledge produced is not Eurocentric, even often involving academic categories; it is non- or a-disciplinary, questions the human/nonhuman divide, and is resistant to the observer/observed separation; it positions the ancestrality of struggles as contemporary forces in the making of life at present. The notions stem from a *sentipensante* praxis that weaves experiences collectively through their difference; such praxis deindividualizes knowledge production and privileges collective research and writing, collaborative epistemologies, and practices of "walking the word" and "walking while asking" in the territories; art, music, graphic design, and performance are often part of the effervescence of the struggles within which these knowledges are being produced, so are expressions of spirituality and the sacred.[39]

The emergent Latin American narrative conveys an understanding of humans as embedded in land, place, and territory; continuously co-creating

---

[36] Segato, La *guerra contra las mujeres*, 106, emphasis ours.

[37] Natalia Quiroga, *Economía pospatriarcal. Neoliberalismo y después* (Buenos Aires: Cooperativa La Vaca, 2020).

[38] Lucia Linsalatta, "Repensar la transformación social desde las escalas espacio-temporales de producción de lo común," in *Comunalidad, tramas comunitarias y producción de lo común*, ed. Raquel Gutiérrez Aguilar, 365–74 (Oaxaca: Pez en el árbol, 2018).

[39] There is a vast literature on the epistemologies and methodologies of collective struggles. See, for example, the volumes coordinated by Xochitl Leyva-Solano in Mexico, *Prácticas otras de conocimiento(s): Entre crisis, entre guerras* (San Cristóbal de las Casas: Cooperativa Editorial Retos, 2015); Catherine Walsh in Quito, *Pedagogías decoloniales*, Vol. 2 (Quito: Abya Yala, 2017); and Patricia Botero, *Resistencias: Relatos del sentipensamiento que caminan la palabra* (Manizales: Universidad de Manizales, 2015) and Astrid Ulloa, ed., *Mujeres indígenas haciendo, investigando yreescribiendo lo político en América Latina* (Bogotá: Universidad Nacional, 2020), in Colombia.

the communal tapestry to which they belong; and enduring as the world they want to be by constantly reinventing what or who they are. It is a far cry from the anthropocentric and patriarchal story that humans are somehow special, separate from place, territory, community, spirit, sacredness, Earth. The two stories embody different civilizational projects. While the latter enacts the historical anthropocentric project of *las cosas* (objects, things), the former sustains the historical Earth-based project of *los vínculos* (links, relationality).

There will be multiple new beginnings and paths toward the regeneration of relational worldmaking stemming from multiple emergent stories. To a greater or lesser extent, many of us move in our everyday lives according to several old and emerging stories. No single proposal exhausts the field of possible paths and practices, or the ways of thinking about possibility. Could it be the case that these movements are riding, and constituting, a wave of re/emergent relationality?

SIX STRATEGIES FOR PLURIVERSAL TRANSITIONS

Bridging nonrelational and relational worldmaking is a complex process but one that, we argue, is already underway to a greater or lesser extent in many of the alternatives being set into place by groups all over the world. These concern livelihoods, alternative and community economies, commoning, energy transitions, the small- and medium-scale production of wholesome food, transition towns, degrowth, rewilding, urban gardens and forests, autonomous communities, ecovillages, environmental justice, rights of nature, defense of water, permaculture, slow movements, and in many of the actions fostered by the ideas of ecofeminism, eco-anarchism, bioregionalism, regeneration, earth spiritualities, Black liberation, Indigenous resurgence, transfeminisms, and so forth.

To provide a map of the plethora of ongoing movements and proposals that embody the restor(y)ing of life, however partially and contradictorily, would require an entire book and more, but it is possible to enumerate some strategies variously at play in many of them, from the perspective of the conceptual tapestry described above and the principles of relational politics stated in Chapter 4. Each of these strategies is connected to pressing issues and open questions in activist practice, social theory, and designing, which are beyond the scope of this book. Their overall guiding principle is the need to reclaim the power over making life based on the awareness of radical interdependence. These strategies are the recommunalization of social life; the relocalization of activities; the strengthening of autonomies; the depatriarchalization, de-racialization, and decolonization of social relations; the reintegration with the earth; and the support for self-organizing networks among transformative alternatives. They are inextricably related to each other. We are only able to present a brief outline of them here.[40]

---

[40] For more substantial discussion on this topic, see Arturo Escobar, "Reframing Civilizations," *Globalizations* (2021), available online: https://doi.org/10.1080/14747731.2021.2002673.

The recommunalization of social life

Globalization has entailed an uncompromising war against everything that is communal and collective. But the communal condition of existence is an essential dimension of the co-emergence of living beings and their worlds; we exist in communal entanglements that make us kin to everyone that is alive. Oaxacan activists refer to this dynamic as the *condicion nosótrica de ser*, the we-condition of being. If we see ourselves *nosótricamente*, we cannot but adopt the principles of care as ethics of living, starting with home, place, and community. Recommunalization does not entail isolation but is rather a condition for rooted sharing that is more collective and integrated with the entire span of nonhumans. This orientation toward *compartencia* ("sharingness") applies to the ideas needed to foster new communities.

The relocalization of social, productive, and cultural activities

Human communities have historically experienced movement and regroupings. Delocalizing pressures, or the unchosen movement of people from their lands (often through force), however, has increased exponentially with global capitalism and development. Given the ecological and social costs of globalization (made evident by the COVID-19 pandemic), it is imperative to relocalize life-essential activities back in the places where we live. While not everything can be relocalized (think about selective relocalization), in the last instance relocalization points at the need to regain the capacity for producing our own lives more autonomously. Food sovereignty, agroecology, seed saving, community economies, commons, transition towns, and urban gardens are just some of the well-known instances of the will to relocalize. As Helena Norberg-Hodge and Vandana Shiva, pioneers of the worldwide relocalization movement, put it, a new path forward for the human is necessarily a path that localizes, not globalizes. The social, cultural, ecological, and economic benefits of relocalization are increasingly undeniable when put side by side with the costs of global monocultures. Relocalization has become a matter of survival for most communities.[41]

The strengthening of autonomies

Without autonomy, recommunalization and relocalization are easily reabsorbed into newer forms of delocalized globalization. Designing practices can be recentered on the autonomous production of life through designing coalitions that enable

---

[41] See the excellent documentary, *Planet Local: A Quiet Revolution* (2022), featuring prominently Norberg-Hodge and Shiva, and Norberg-Hodge's project: Local Futures, "Home," available online: https://www.localfutures.org/ (accessed July 19, 2023).

selective de-globalization; by meeting social needs and livelihoods more locally, they would lessen dependence on the dominant economies. This implies the notion that every community practices the designing of itself. In some places, autonomy is explained in terms of the substitution of nouns (education, health, food, housing, and so on), which create dependency on experts and the State, for verbs that bring back personal and collective agency: learning, healing, eating, dwelling.

Strategies of recommunalization, relocalization, and autonomy must be place-specific and take existing local power relations into account. Each social group and locality will have to come up with its unique set of strategies, attuned to place, landscape, and diversity. Whether in the Global South or the Global North, in rural or urban territories, every social group is bound to reweave its internal relations and relations to others based on care and respect. It is a fact that communities today are ineluctably open, connected, and traversed by de-communalizing economic and digital pressures; this makes the process difficult but also enlivening.

The depatriarchalization, de-racialization, and decolonization of social relations

The civilizational project of patriarchal capitalism is naturalized in our desires and subjectivities and in the designs of the worlds we inhabit. We are reminded of the stakes at hand by the Latin American feminist dictum that there is no decolonization without depatriarchalization and de-racialization of social relations. This feminist and anti-racist optic is essential for healing the tapestry of interrelations that make up the bodies, places, and communities that we all are and inhabit, guided by the question of "what type of practices are capable of depatriarchalizing and decolonizing here and now"?[42] There are potential synergies between depatriarchalization and recommunalization, underlined by Mayan and Aymaran communitarian feminists, such as Gladys Tzul Tzul, Julieta Paredes, and Lorena Cabnal. For Tzul Tzul, the reconstitution of life's web of relations in a communitarian manner is one of the most fundamental challenges faced by any transition strategy, since any major infrastructure of modernity enacts a nonrelational, patriarchal ontology. [43] Transitions must be communalitarian and post-patriarchal or they will not be. This feminist relational politics needs to be actively incorporated into designing practices.

The re-earthing of life

Earth constitutes an emergent horizon for a renewed living praxis; it is the basis for the essential human act of dwelling. There are many expressions of the intensely felt need of reintegrating with Earth at present, going beyond

[42] Gago, *La potencia feminista*, 91.

[43] Tzul Tzul, *Sistemas de gobierno comunal indígena*.

prevailing idioms of sustainability—for instance, under the rubric of regeneration. The Nasa Indigenous people of Northern Cauca in the Colombian southwest
speak of the Liberation of Mother Earth as essential to weaving life in liberty.
They invite us to *disoñar* ("dreamagine") different worldings, propitious to the
reconstitution of the entire web of life, the sustainment of the territories, and
communalized forms of economy, wherever we are. Newer forms of Earth-wise
design and of re-earthing cities, to be discussed in the next section, reflect a felt
need for designing to reencounter with Earth and, in some cases, for resacral-
izing designing.[44]

The construction of meshworks among transformative initiatives and alternatives

This last strategy points to the need to encourage the convergence of genuinely
transformative alternatives, particularly from below. There is a growing recognition of the need to build bridges among "radical alternatives," meaning those
based on nonhierarchical, relational, and pluralistic worldviews. The project of
fostering the creation of self-organizing meshworks, or networks of networks,
among such alternatives is being tackled by a growing number of collective
undertakings and constitutes a key factor in any politics of transition.[45]

These strategies aim at the creation of dignified lives in rural and urban
territories. They intuit the end of globalization as we know it and constitute an
impulse toward the pluriverse. While our hypothesis is about the emergence
of novel stories of life focused on Latin America, we suggest that they are at
play in many parts of the world, even if often falling back into nonrelational
practices and infrastructures, but also fostering bridges to more decidedly
relational modes of being, knowing, and making. It will be up to each group
engaged in the task of transitioning in between stories to reflect on their practice from this perspective.

DESIGNING RELATIONALLY

The above conceptual tapestry and transition strategies inform the strategies
for relational designing to be discussed in this section, to the extent that these
too rely on practices that strengthen the communal and the place-based, revalue
care, recognize the importance of relocalizing practices of autonomy, and aim
to buttress the potential of local ways of worlding in the face of globalizing
one-worldism.

[44] On the Nasa movement, see Escobar, *Pluriversal Politics*.

[45] See, for instance, The Global Tapestry of Alternatives ("Main page," available online:
https://globaltapestryofalternatives.org [accessed July 19, 2023]), and Adelante: Dialogue
of Global Processes ("About ADELANTE," available online: https://adelante.global/
[accessed July 19, 2023]).

In what follows, we review some trends we find particularly revealing from the perspective of rethinking designing. We seek to buttress the awareness that it is impossible to sustain the "natural world" while the "human world" remains separate from it. Humans must decidedly commence our journey toward reconstituting ourselves as beings existing within the ceaseless stream of life. There are many developments in areas such as participatory design, co-design, ecological design, transition design, biodesign, fashion design, just design and design with justice, regenerative design, decolonial design, and designs from the South that could guide the inquiry into relational designing. We can only point at a few of them here from an ontological perspective.

Rather than seeing them as isolated "case studies," however, we ask readers to consider them as interventions that configure an open territory of experimentation in alternative worldmaking practices—to give the sense that this designing is in the service of worldmaking—a territory that will need to be populated collectively with other instances where the shift from nonrelational to relational worldmaking is being pursued. We have chosen these areas largely because of our familiarity and active interest in them. Some point to general designing tendencies, while others refer to local and place-based experiments. We believe that they are particularly salient at present, both politically and in terms of designing theory and action. Our examples come from the areas of design for social innovation, commons, food sovereignty, and the re-earthing of cities.

Design for transformative social innovation

A good place to start is the evolving framework of design for social innovation (DSI) spearheaded by Ezio Manzini and Virginia Tassinari in Milan, Italy, since it explicitly links designing with transformational social change while foregrounding place, communities, and autonomy. In recent works, Manzini and Tassinari ably infuse the DSI framework with relational and non-anthropocentric dimensions, within an alternative modernity conception.[46] Manzini introduces an ensemble of notions such as collaborative life projects, enabling ecosystems, fluid communities of place, design activism, designing coalitions, collaborative economies, and project-centered democracy; these notions capture the contemporary sense of individuals relearning to come together to produce "transformative social innovations" capable of systemic change in particular areas of social life. Given the generalized uprootedness that prevails at present, Manzini is mindful of the fact that relational approaches involve a tension: the greater the degree of relationality, the greater "the commitment they call for and the vulnerability they produce."[47] This tension is at the heart of attempts at building portals toward designing relationally.

---

[46] See the DESIS Philosophy Talk series curated by Tassinari, available online: https://www.desis-philosophytalks.org/ (accessed July 19, 2023).

[47] Ezio Manzini, *Politics of the Everyday* (London: Bloomsbury, 2019), 30; *Design when Everybody Designs* (Cambridge, MA: MIT Press, 2015).

At the heart of Manzini's proposal is the notion of autonomous life projects, defined as those that break "with dominant ideas and behaviors, moving outside the rules of the game, and deciding to collaborate with others … [by] adopting ways of thinking and doing things that contrast with prevailing ones."[48] Actualizing this opportunity requires tools that favor bricolage, dialogic and collaborative approaches, unprecedented forms of design activism, and practices of distributed agency and augmented locality. Many of his examples evince these principles (e.g., co-housings, collaborative living, relocalized food production, urban transportation, digital platforms, cities). They show the variegated ways in which "the local and the everyday are the theater of life for human beings, but they are also the open construction site in which this theater is openly rebuilt and adapted and sometimes radically transformed."[49] Everyday actions can become transgressive: "system change on a local scale."[50] This strategy often requires a small, creative group of people to jumpstart the process and continued vigilance so that the emerging trajectories are not reconverted into mainstream choices. As they interweave with like-minded projects, they widen the field of participatory democracy, creating the possibility of influencing larger scales. Manzini envisions articulations between citizens' diffuse design capabilities and expert design, stressing the need for a collective design intelligence propitious to imagining alternative futures.

Manzini's and Tassinari's DSI approach resonates with the vision crafted by the Design Studio for Social Intervention (DS4SI), a practice-based collective in Boston, United States. Their primary contention is that the social and ecological emergency poor people face today is the result of long-standing and naturalized arrangements. Hence, it is imperative for activists and designers to become attuned to the task of redesigning the social by understanding how the broad injuries of discrimination are embedded in entrenched sets of interlacing ideas, arrangements, and effects that lock communities in certain states. This demands a capacity to examine those arrangements where naturalized forms of power are busy at work. In their work with poor and racialized communities, the DS4SI strives to enact the principle that design is not just about problem-solving within existing paradigms, it is about world building. "We believe it's essential," the authors state, "for people who care about social justice to see themselves as designers of everyday life." As they conclude, "we use social interventions as signals, suggestions and invitations to galvanize others into this work of rearranging and changing ideas and relations."[51]

A key element in the ideas-arrangements-effects (IAE) framework is the principle that "effects don't naturally send us to inspecting arrangements."[52]

---

[48] Manzini, *Politics of the Everyday*, 44–5.

[49] Manzini, *Politics of the Everyday*, 73.

[50] Manzini, *Politics of the Everyday*, 82.

[51] Design Studio for Social Intervention (DS4SI), *Ideas, Arrangements, Effects: Systems Design and Social Justice* (Colchester, MA: Minor Compositions, 2020), 118.

[52] DS4SI, *Ideas, Arrangements, Effects*, 20.

Racism is a case in point; confronted with the myriad instances of racial discrimination in daily life (racism's "effects"), we jump to the Big Idea ("Racism"), missing altogether the crucial domain of the arrangements that serve as relays between the big "-isms" and their mundane but at times lethal effects. Here we find DS4SI's designerly imagination at its best: in helping us see the multiple and often subtle mediations, the smaller ideas and practices that harbor the petty, but insidious, daily forms of discrimination, from schools to the media, from beliefs to infrastructures, and from government routine procedures to the enduring practices of the economy. As the authors put it, "We believe the IAE framework can both deepen *our understanding* of the social contexts we hope to change and improve, as well as *expand our capacity* for designing the world we truly want."[53] The IAE vision constitutes a framework that articulates a radical sense of politics with a practicable set of concept-tools for enacting such politics in concrete settings.

Transformative social innovation and design for social intervention provide routes to "disclosing new worlds"[54] and bringing them into existence. For the former, the key issue is "collaboration and the capacity to reconnect people and places, and in so doing to produce relational values and social commons."[55] For DS4SI, this translates into a tangible guide: "Wherever you want to start, think small and think big. Question the small arrangements that shape everyday life. Imagine big arrangements and the impact we could have. What profound rearrangements are you yearning for?"[56] These are principles for rearranging the social ontologically; by directing our attention to those power relations where individual and communities get locked, they make visible the spectrum of slippages that await activists and designers and that get in the way of the fundamental rearrangements that, as they eloquently put it, many of us are yearning for.

An ontological shift toward the commons

Rearranging the social and transformative social innovation at myriad places are paths to reorienting designing. Three areas of significant activity in this regard are food, cities, and the commons. A recent inspiring, hands-on volume on the commons, *Free, Fair and Alive*, ably demonstrates why commons and commoning involve manners of rearranging the social from a perspective that transcends the individualist ontology.

---

[53] DS4SI, *Ideas, Arrangements, Effects*, 22, emphases in the original.

[54] Charles Spinosa, Fernando Flores, and Hubert Dreyfus, *Disclosing New Worlds: Entrepreneurship, Democratic Action and the Cultivation of Solidarity* (Cambridge, MA: MIT Press, 1997).

[55] Manzini, *Politics of the Everyday*, 126.

[56] DS4SI, *Ideas, Arrangements, Effects*, 15.

Commons "are living social systems through which people address their shared problems in self-organized ways."[57] Commons denote a different paradigm of governance, provisioning, and cooperative social practice. Look at any thriving alternative social practice and you will find commoning at work. A constellation of experiences is emerging from such patterns—a pluriversal "Commonsverse" (e.g., farmers' movements, collaborative platforms and federated wikis, housing commons, co-ops, seed saving, energy localism, collective rights, creative appropriation of public resources, commons-public partnerships, and community charters). The Commonsverse, however, demands an OntoShift away from the OntoStory of the Modern West. "Commoning has a different orientation to the world because its actions are based on a *deep relationality* of everything."[58] This OntoShift is an important dimension of the political activation of relationality, for which the book provides a working toolbox; this begins by exposing the stale categories that sustain the current worldview (e.g., citizen, development, innovation, participation, scarcity, etc.), replacing them with "commons-friendly" terms, such as "Nested-I," care, complex adaptive systems, convivial tools, "do-it-together" (DIT), emergence, open source, heterarchy, interoperability, semi-permeable membranes, mutualizing, peer governance, pluriverse, provisioning, *ubuntu* rationality, and vernacular law.

Commoners engage in worldmaking in a pluriverse by linking three spaces: Social Life, Peer Governance, and Provisioning. Each term evinces a relational designing orientation. On the side of *Social Life* (not an exhaustive list), we find "Cultivate shared purpose and value," "ritualize togetherness," "practice gentle reciprocity," "trust situated knowing," "deepen communion with nature," and "reflect on your own governance." *Provisioning* is associated with "make and use together," "support care and decommodified work," "pool, cap, and divide up," "trade with price sovereignty," "convivial tools," and "rely on distributed structures." Finally, on the side of *Peer Governance*, we find "bring diversity into shared purpose," "create semi-permeable membranes," "rely on heterarchy," "relationalize property," and "finance commons provisioning."[59] Each of these notions contain useful clues for detecting nonrelational designing while creating reality-based hope for disrupting capitalist value chains and strengthening communal-based value networks.

One question remains: can the Commonsverse be cultivated? Can it grow larger and transform the prevailing political economy and ontology? In Helfrich and Bollier's view, this requires rethinking property and the State through four strategies: to emulate and build collaborative networks and shared infrastructures; to pursue intercommoning that enable diverse commoners to come together; to

---

[57] David Bollier and Silke Helfrich, *Free, Fair and Alive* (Gabriola Island: New Society Publishers, 2019), 17. For a related approach centered on community economies, see J.K. Gibson-Graham, Jenny Cameron, and Stephen Healy, *Take Back the Economy* (Minneapolis: University of Minnesota Press, 2013).

[58] Bollier and Helfrich, *Free, Fair and Alive*, 41.

[59] See Bollier and Helfrich, *Free, Fair and Alive*, 98, for a summary diagram. Designers will find in this book a practicable guide for designing for commoning.

construct a shared language; and to prevent re-enclosure through longer-term protective legal strategies. The expansion of the Commonsverse relies on "the deeper wisdom of the commons, which accepts the idea of distributed, local, and diverse acts of commoning whose very aliveness produces the creativity and commitment to develop solutions adapted to every context."[60] Digital tools—for example, blockchain and holochain technologies—are central to many of these efforts; not only do they foster digital commons, they provide infrastructures to commoning economies, languages, and cultures. This "deeper wisdom of the commons" constitutes portals into relational designing.

Food sovereignty

That making life relationally is the best option for living well together is amply attested in the domain of food. In the north, movements for local food, slow food, community supported agriculture (CSA), permaculture, and ecovillages reflect a salient trend. Localizing food is an important dimension of transition town movements, commoning, and degrowth.[61] In the Global South, the category that best embodies this thrust is food sovereignty. For food sovereignty activists, food production is much more than about food; it is embedded in an entire territory, involves an intricate relation between humans and nonhumans, and relies on place-based, communal processes; it involves everything, "from bread to freedom." The contrast between making life versus outsourcing it takes literal meaning when it comes to food. From an onto-epistemic perspective, relationalizing the making of food is one of the most complex socioeconomic and political endeavors any group can undertake. This is because food sovereignty involves an intricate tapestry of interdependencies in which history, memory, soils, seeds, water, climate, energy, farmers, knowledge, biodiversity, markets, laws, and a host of nonhumans are deeply entangled.

The transnational peasant movement *La Vía Campesina* (The Peasant Way) defines food sovereignty as "the right of peoples to healthy and culturally appropriate food produced through ecologically sound and sustainable methods, and their right to define their own food and agriculture systems."[62] The concept originated in the 1990s from the struggles of communities around the world against the corporate food system. Food sovereignty and autonomy became a rallying cry for a wide range of struggles by peasants, fisherfolk, pastoralists, urban farmers, women, youth, and Indigenous peoples, including

---

[60] Bollier and Helfrich, *Free, Fair and Alive*, 205.

[61] Giorgos Kallis, Susan Paulson, Giaccomo D'Alisa, and Federico Demaria, *The Case for Degrowth* (Cambridge: Polity Press, 2020).

[62] La Via Campesina, *Food Sovereignty and Trade: Nyéléni Declaration* (2007), available online: https://nyeleni.org/spip.php?article290 (accessed July 11, 2023). La Via Campesina is an impressive network of peasant organizations representing over 200 million farmers in more than eighty countries, for more, see La Via Campesina, "Home," available online: https://viacampesina.org/en/ (accessed July 19, 2023).

struggles against land, water, and seed grabbing; agrotoxics; the corporatization of land and food; the patenting of life forms; and for biodiversity conservation and nature's rights; farm workers' rights; and food provision in urban centers, among others. Under this paradigm, everything that sustains materially and spiritually a people in a territory—seeds, land, water, knowledge, biodiversity—is considered a commons. The movement embodies a radical transition from corporate agrifood systems to models based on the defense of the knowledges, practices, and territories of food producing peoples.[63]

Women farmers play a crucial role in food sovereignty movements. Women's groups are fundamental in the conservation, recovery, exchange, and development of native seeds through networks of seed custodians, community seed banks, and "transgenic free zones." Food sovereignty contests the biohegemony of Western agrotechnology, law, and science.[64] In South Asia, villagers set into motion recommunalization strategies in rural communities, *adivasi* territories, and popular urban neighborhoods. Central to them is the concept of *swaraj* or "self-rule." As they connect with each other, they foster a form of radical local ecological democracy, or *eco-swaraj*, with potential larger-scale governance envisaged "as clusters or federations of villages and towns with common ecological features, larger landscape-level institutions, and others that in some way also relate to existing administrative and political units."[65] They do so through face-to-face and digital networking, often producing their own visual and audio media.

Food sovereignty is related to a slew of initiatives that go under the banner of "regeneration." Regenerative designing is emerging as a powerful framework and set of practices for transitioning between the story of separation to the story of interbeing. Regenerative designing calls for transformative social innovation beyond current notions of sustainability; is centered on a living systems' understanding of society and the economy; relies on collaborative and communal-oriented practices; and aims at the constitution of regenerative cultures with the potential to change significantly the purpose and character of designing. This is a very promising trend at the heart of critical design studies, including serious attempts at bringing the paradigm of regeneration to businesses and NGOs.[66]

---

[63] Laura Gutiérrez Escobar, "Food Sovereignty and Autonomy," in *Pluriverse: A Postdevelopment Dictionary*, ed. Ashish Kothari, Ariel Salleh, Arturo Escobar, Federico Demaria, and Alberto Acosta, 185–88 (Delhi: Tulika/AuthorsUpfront, 2019); Philip McMichael, "Rethinking Land Grab Ontology," *Rural Sociology* 79, no. 1 (2013): 34–55.

[64] Laura Gutiérrez Escobar and Elizabeth Fitting, "La *Red de Semillas Libres*: Contesting Biohegemony in Colombia," *Journal of Agrarian Change* (2016): 711–19.

[65] Ashish Kothari and Pallav Das, "Power in India: Radical Pathways," in *State of Power* (Amsterdam: Transnational Institute, 2016), available online: https://www.tni.org/en/publication/power-in-india-radical-pathways (accessed July 19, 2023), 193.

[66] Wahl, *Designing Regenerative Cultures*; Josie Warden, "Regenerative Futures: From Sustaining to Thriving Together" (London: RSA, 2021); and the consultancy on regenerative futures, Solvable, "Home," available online: https://www.solvable.ca/ (accessed July 19, 2023).

Re-earthing cities

Cities have been historically built on the banishment of nature and rural life beyond their borders. Other modes of dwelling need to be created by recasting architecture and urban design as onto-epistemic, technical, and political practices for pluriversal forms of inhabiting. Some clues in this regard are found in the "relational turn" in urban studies, which sees the city as a constellation of assemblages made up of multiple peoples, nonhumans, materialities, and so forth. An awareness of the effects of the modern city on human sociality is growing; as former UN-Habitat director Joan Clos put it, "we have created the city, but what we have not thought enough about is how the city is recreating us."[67] This becomes ever more important with the polycrisis for, as Tony Fry argues, we can expect abandoned cities, pervasive food and climate riots, mass deaths, fierce struggle for survival, and all kinds of human-induced disasters as the modern city unravels under the effects of climate change. This generalized unsettlement constitutes the condition for any attempt at remaking the city.[68]

To this end, Fry proposes a framework for urban metrofitting following the exhaustion of the European city as design paradigm. Metrofitting involves seeing the city as a relational, historical, and metabolic designing event. For Fry, the remaking of the city stands upon its unmaking, which in turn implies "embracing the ontological status of the city assemblage as post-natural environments of difference together with regimes of ordering and disordering (the formal and the informal, the informational and metabolic, the industrial and post-industrial, the spectacular and hidden)," in short, a different type of post-urbanism.[69] The reorientation of planning and design in domains such as renewable energy, urban food, transportation, biowaste management, air and water quality, housing, and so forth, are essential to this goal. Newer visions of the city as open, permeable, and always being un- and redone are auspicious elements for this remaking.

Biophilic urbanism provides another starting point. It involves the massive re-earthing of cities—their infrastructure, institutions, and governance. Biophilic cities are envisioned as places profusely endowed with accessible and abundant nature, enticing residents into integration with nature through multisensory environments. For biophilic designing, urban metabolism must be based on closed-loop philosophies, bioregionalism, and ecological restoration, with cities harboring natural shapes and forms, all of these at the levels of building, block, street, neighborhood, community, and region.[70] These trends counteract the continued dependence of the city on fossil fuels. Indeed, a "carbon-form" of

---

[67] Richard Sennett and Joan Clos, "A Conversation," in *The Quito Papers and the New Urban Agenda*, ed. R. Sennett, 150–73 (New York: Routledge, 2018).

[68] Fry, *City Futures in the Age of a Changing Climate*.

[69] Fry, *Becoming Human by Design*, 88.

[70] Timothy Beatley, *Handbook of Biophilic City Planning and Design* (Washington, DC: Island Press, 2016).

the city—a subset of the larger carbon-modernity—has dominated the modernist city since the Industrial Revolution. An ontological metrofitting of cities would need to transcend this onto-epistemic and infrastructural energy background if it wants to pursue a path toward an Earth-form of the city.[71]

Social critics rarely take notice that modern Man exists in a designed space. Calls for remaking the city from the perspectives of "the multiplicity of Others" and "multispecies urbanism" challenge monohumanist norms and forms of the urban environment. Contesting the dependence of urban freedom for the privileged on the unfreedom of racialized and gendered forms of labor and a whole range of "undesirable bodies" is but a place to start. Other cities are possible when imagined from the perspective of the multiplicity of the others that inhabit it. This realization applies to nonhumans, with multispecies urbanism as a spatial practice extending the right to the city to more-than-humans, inspired in urban plants, living soils, and urban and peri-urban agroecology. The aim is to devote the urban surface and subsurface as habitat and food to the extent possible.[72]

We find a cogent example of this idea in the design vision by the architect from Cali, Colombia, Harold Martínez Espinal, whose proposal for "a new fusion of country and city" rests on a deeply relational perspective. His explicit starting point is the crisis of habitability stemming from occidental modes of dwelling. Martínez's architectural and design proposal calls for multistory buildings fitted with open-air corridors with movable shelves for planting foodstuffs (vegetables, herbs, and other plants), and surrounded by food gardens and green areas, with social centers for collective gatherings. The idea is to establish a circulation "from the garden to the corridor and from this to the kitchen and the dining table." Martínez's vision of rurbanization is based on the notion that to inhabit is to live communally, crafting and sustaining an environment. By seeing the human as the inhabitant of a living universe, rather than the occupier of a passive soil, he articulates a cogent framework for transitions to cities that challenge the human/nonhuman binary, moving decidedly into a post-dualist conception of the city.[73]

Worldwide, middle-class, gated communities continue to be the default setting of urban development, but they constitute profoundly anti-ecological

---

[71] Elisa Iturbe, "Two Modernities in One: Carbon Form and the Reduction of Ecological Space," in *Non-Extractive Architecture: On Designing without Depletion*, ed. Grigory Cheredov and Polina Filimonova, 27–41(Berlin: Sternberg Press, 2021).

[72] Afaina de Jong and Debra Solomon's manifestos, presented at the Dutch Pavilion for the 2021 Venice Biennale, see Afaina de Jong, "Manifesto: The Multiplicity of Other," *Who Is We*, available online: https://whoiswe.nl/works#de-jong-multiplicity-of-other (accessed July 19, 2023); Debra Solomon, "A Multispecies Urbanism Manifesto: 12 Tenets of Brief," *Who Is We*, available online: https://whoiswe.nl/works#solomon-multispecies-urbanism (accessed July 19, 2023).

[73] The full architectural and design proposal can be found in Harold Martínez Espinal and Grupo CU:NA, *La fusión campo-ciudad desde un nuevo concepto de Vivienda* (Cali: Universidad del Valle, 2023). For a fuller discussion, see Arturo Escobar, "Habitability and Design," *Geoforum* 101 (2019): 132–40.

spaces of de-communalized, de-localized, and de-sacralized life, posing a huge designing challenge. They deny that interdependence is created through collective entanglements in everyday life, as it still tends to happen in popular neighborhoods. Manzini's recent advocacy for cities of proximity, "in which everything that people need for daily life is just a few minutes away by foot from where they live," begins to provide a corrective to this situation. A remaking of the city under a paradigm of relationality and care based on proximity, as he demonstrates, is not only desirable but essential for a functional, place-based, and Earthwise human sociality. The notion of proximity challenges head on the isolating tendencies of post-pandemic living, providing workable clues to counter the de-localizing and de-communalizing effects of the modernist "city of distance" and the seductive "everything at/from home" model enabled by virtuality.[74]

To be applicable to cities in the Global South, the infrastructures of proximity need to be thought about in tandem with questions of mobility, informality, and access to urban space and services for the often-racialized urban poor. Generally speaking, a city that cares needs to be reconceived from the perspective of non-anthropocentric, nonliberal and noncapitalist spatialities, namely, those that do not intrinsically privilege the individual citizen, private property, the capitalization of urban space, global connections, and the separation from the natural environment, all of which assume unlimited growth of energy and materials. These features of the political activation of urban relationality are essential to vying for the political agenda of the futures of the city, currently hijacked by land speculators and urban development cartels, often with the complicity of urban professionals.

This cursory description of some hopeful trends should serve to make us aware of the potentiality of redesigning design. The cases presented involve general, system-wide sets of emergent criteria linked to social innovation and intervention, food, commoning, and cities, but all of these must find their appropriate scale and conditions for each specific locale, group, and place (as some of the Latin American cases suggest). The conceptual tapestry, the six strategies for transition, and the principles of relational politics provide some guides for the task of localizing, as it were, the multiple paths for relational designing. Going back to our initial questions for this chapter, the various cases contribute to illustrate practices of worldmaking that (a) question the anthropocentrism of design/ing; (b) embrace the idea of radical interdependence; and (c) demonstrate that they are capable of operating effectively in the contemporary world.

While we have focused on shifting our understanding of the terrain of the possible, we do not want to paint a rosy picture, particularly for communities

[74] Ezio Manzini, *Livable Proximity: Ideas for the City that Cares* (Milan: Bocconi University Press, 2022). The Italian architect Paola Viganò is developing a perspective of metropolitan regions as made up of networks of villages on a living soil; see Institute of Technology in Architecture, ETH Zurich, "ITA on Designing for New Climate with Paola Viganò," May 5, 2022, YouTube video, 1:14:29, available online: https://www.youtube.com/watch?v=k020IvP7EJc&t=2021s (accessed July 19, 2023).

in the Global South who live under incredibly intense pressures for surviving, often under atrocious capitalist conditions and violence. For many in the Global North, the liberal spatialities of middle-class urban living ("my room," "my space," "my house") is a particularly key area of slippage into the nonrelational. Imagining other modes of dwelling is essential to the overall political activation of relationality. There is also a wide array of challenges in moving along transition paths if one wants to avoid irreparable slippages back into the ontologies of separation embedded in so many seductive and seemingly sensible modernist solutions (such as eco-modernism; sustainable development; green economies; and smart, competitive, and global cities), even if some slippages will inevitably occur along the way.

There is one more challenge specific to designers brought to the fore by Colombian design theorist Alfredo Gutiérrez who arrives at unanticipated conclusions in examining the links between representation, object, and project. For him,

> modern design monopolizes the relationships with tomorrow under the idea of 'project.' The future can only be reached through project, which ends up capturing every possibility of existence … But in the lands of prefiguration, many plant species distinct from 'design' grow; in the other worlds, which do exist, many things are relationally brought into life by the others of design, by design with other names[75]

In other words, Gutiérrez warns against reducing "other-than-Western design" to second-class design, or to the category of "craft." In bringing into light an entire new domain of alternatives *to* design rather than alternative designs, and by going beyond "designorance" (by which he means what design ignores and what it ignores it ignores) he invites designers to a decolonial reflection that heals design/ing from its "Occidentosis" while opening to multiple other traditions for bringing entities relationally into life.

CONCLUSION: PLURIVERSAL DESIGNING AND MOBILIZING FOR NEW WAYS OF DWELLING ON THE EARTH

Nosotrxs no pedimos la propiedad de la tierra, nosotrxs proponemos otro arte de habitar en la tierra (we do not demand property over land; we propose a different art of inhabiting the earth).

Moira Millán[76]

[75] Alfredo Gutiérrez, "When Design Goes South: From Decoloniality, through Declassification to Dessobons," in *Design in Crisis*, ed. Tony Fry and Adam Nocek, 56–73 (London: Routledge, 2020), 57.

[76] Pensamiento Ambiental, "Moira Millán y el Buen Vivir originario," May 22, 2016, YouTube video, 17:04, available online: https://www.youtube.com/watch?v=JOiRYUW8R08 (accessed July 19, 2023).

We have barely scratched the surface of the rich experimentation going on in designing fields from relational and pluriversal perspectives. Nevertheless, our account gave us the opportunity to arrive at poignant questions. Can designing be reconceived in relation to struggles over making life? What would it mean to design outside the hegemony of the liberal, secular, modern notion of the human? Designing practices based on the insight that the world does not exist "out there," separate from us, but that we co-construct it with every one of our actions, should contribute to challenge the power of a globalizing economy where only One World and One Human fit. Such designing might become a force in transitions to the pluriverse, with a multiplicity of others and all living forms.

We live in an age that requires ways of being and thinking capable of enabling collective processes of mobilizing for other ways of dwelling on the earth. This historical circumstance calls for an "ontology of navigation" apt to seeing the world as a site of the historical drift of emergencies, contingencies, and emergences rather than in terms of simple causality, prediction, and control. This ethos of navigation requires refining our capacity for observing the world. It goes to the heart of the unprecedented challenge of reimagining how we should share the planet, as we take seriously the magnitude of the changes that will take place over the next fifty to one hundred years, due to accelerating technological change, the climate emergency, deepening social crises, and changes in the geopolitical global balance.

The navigation ontology proposes a major interpretive shift from an ontology and epistemology of representation, knowledge, prediction, and control to one of embodiment, observation, anticipation, and attunement to situations that include awareness of emotions and moods. It fosters an openness toward a pluralistic sharing of the world based on the conviction that we exist in domains of conversation and action through which we co-invent ourselves, the world, and our capacity to care (or not) with others.[77]

The notion that we are all designers, and designed by our designs, means we need to take responsibility for the worlds we create with others, humans and not, anytime, anywhere. This implies interrupting the globalizing project of fitting all worlds into one. Designing, in this way, might become a praxis of healing the web of life, a sketch, a stitch, a loop at a time, collectively: designing as a mindful and effective weaving and repairing of the web of life.

Designing pluriversally means designing from, with, and within a world of many worlds; it implies designing based on the premise that life is constituted by radical interdependence among all existing entities; its goal is the reconstitution, healing, and caring for the web of interrelations that make up the bodies, places, and landscapes that we are and inhabit. Designing pluriversally contributes to repair the social, ecological, existential, and emotional damage done by the relentless individuation, de-localization, de-communalization, de-placing, and

---

[77] The navigation ontology framework is being developed by Fernando Flores and B. Scot Rousse, partly through group conversations with Terry Winograd, Don Norman, and Arturo Escobar.

defuturing effected by modern forces; conversely, it aims to heal the ontological uprootedness from body, place, and landscape through forms of making that contribute to re-embodying, re-placing, and re-earthing life.

Designing pluriversally entails regaining the capacity for making life autonomously, instead of outsourcing it to institutions, experts, the State, and the capitalist economy. It does so while fostering non-anthropocentric modes of being human, in connection with the rest of life. It creates spaces for reimagining ourselves as Earth, pluriverse, and community.

Designing pluriversally contributes to dismantle the mandate of masculinity that is at the core of the dualistic and object-driven ontology of modernity; it emphasizes collective modes of making and acting, pragmatically privileging communitarian forms of social existence. It takes seriously the struggles for social justice, respect for the earth, and the rights of human and nonhuman entities. This goal could be partially pursued by collaborating with those who are still nourished by relational existence, as they rise in defense of their life territories, strengthening their life projects and autonomy.

Designing pluriversally requires a renewed awareness of how the creation of conditions for life-sustaining coexistence will necessarily have to engage with the dominant logic of unsustainability and defuturing. It goes beyond problem-oriented formulations, particularly when dealing with civilizational challenges such as climate change, which resist the modernist framing of problems and solutions. Finally, one can surmise that designing pluriversally could become a key agency in the civilizational transitions from toxic to healing existence. This reorientation of designing will take a lot of work. Only slowly will pluriversal designers discover the considerable potential of acting from interdependence and care.[78]

---

[78] The recently created Pluriversal Design SIG (Special Interest Group) within the Design Research Society (DRS) aims to illuminate a theory and practice of designing that resonates closely with these ideas. The group is convened by Lesley-Ann Noel and Renata Leitão. See Design Research Society, "Pluriverse Design Sig," available online: https://www.designresearchsociety.org/cpages/sig-pluriversal-design (accessed July 19, 2023).

Conclusion

As we arrive at the end of our journey, we recall that the last thing we wanted our book to be was just another academic treatise full of dense theory and jargon, even if theory, too, was part of our language and a tool to re-narrativize life. Nor did we want it to be a manifesto in the tradition of modern leftist social movements, and even less a blueprint or model for transition, for these might only emerge as they are collectively constructed. Our wager in this regard was to bet also on the poetic, including emotioning and feeling-thinking, as part of our journey. As we struggled, laughed, and sometimes pulled our hair out trying to get this book onto paper, we were guided by a core question: Can we be for the reader what the experiences that moved us to create this book were and are for us? So that the reader too will be moved to create—design—relationally? At this stage, readers, of course, will have the last word in this regard.

REMAKING AND RESTOR(Y)ING LIFE: THE PROBLEMATIZATION OF LIFE, WORLD, AND THE HUMAN

We started out by considering the thought that the socioecological crisis—what some now call a "polycrisis," that is, an entanglement of crises with potentially powerful nonlinear and cascading interactions among them—demands from us a significant revisiting and problematization of what life, the human, and the world have come to be because of the ways of knowing and making that have characterized the modern era.[1] While the polycrisis discourse does not broach these underlying questions for the most part, it is stirring up concerns about dramatic upheavals, catastrophes, and civilizational collapse. We find the open discussion of these potential futures telling. A new sense of historical

---

[1] On the notion of the polycrisis, see The Cascade Institute, "Institute Overview," available online: https://cascadeinstitute.org/about/overview/ (accessed July 19, 2023) and its related Resilience Funders Network, Omega, available online: https://omega.ngo/ (accessed July 19, 2023). See also the repository on the concept, Polycrisis, available online: https://www.polycrisis.org/ (accessed July 19, 2023).

mission seems to be on the rise. It is clear that the time for collective meditation and horizontal organizing for the ending of a civilization premised on infinite growth, ruthless competition, and extractive capitalism is here. The revered Buddhist teacher Thich Nhat Hanh invites us to actively contemplate this possibility: "Breathing in, I know that this civilization is going to die. Breathing out, this civilization cannot escape dying."[2] More than a death after which nothing remains, of course, this would be a phasing out of a civilizational project, for many of its realizations will go on, as elements of other configurations of Earth, life, world, and the human.

Awareness about being earth-bound and finite is intensifying, fostering a lexicon centered on notions such as resurgence, regeneration, repairing, healing, caring, re-earthing, reconnecting, reweaving, reanimating, and so forth, as we have seen. These categories recenter human action on the defense, care, and reconstitutions of life—a poetics and politics in the feminine. New paradigms of relation between humans and the earth find unexpected inspiration in nonhuman living beings, including, notably, fungi, mycelia, rhizomes, forests, and sacred plants,[3] and in cultures and ontologies that have lived with the strong awareness that the earth is alive, such as animistic and other Indigenous ontologies.[4] In between the world of human design—the One-World world—and the autopoietic Earth, a vast space is opening for inquiries and transformative practices of making life otherwise, inspiring a great deal of work at the interface of art, language, architecture, design, activism, social justice, and the earth.[5]

The current problematization of life and the human is fostering ideas and practices for transforming customary ways of being, knowing, mobilizing for change, and designing. Many of these emergent ways have to do with regaining the ability to see and act relationally. This observation is at the basis of our claim that the transitions are already happening, as we tried to substantiate throughout this book. We started out with an onto-epistemic analysis of some of modernity's most naturalized constructs, including the human, reality, science, politics, and

[2] Thich Nhat Hanh, *The World We Have: A Buddhist Approach to Peace and Ecology* (Berkeley, CA: Parallax Press, 2008), 46.

[3] Suzanne Simard, *Finding the Mother Tree* (New York: Alfred Knoff, 2021); Monica Gagliano, *Thus Spoke the Plant* (Berkeley, CA: North Atlantic Books, 2018); Iván Vargas, "Forests on Trial: Toward a Relational Theory of Legal Agency for Transitions into the Ecozoic," in *Liberty and the Ecological Crisis*, ed. Christopher Orr, Katie Kish, and Bruce Jennings, 139–55 (London: Routledge, 2020).

[4] Andreas Weber, *Sharing Life: The Ecopolitics of Reciprocity* (Delhi: Heinrich Böll Stiftung, 2020); and Tim Ingold, *Being Alive: Essays on Movement, Knowledge and Description* (London: Routledge, 2011). The current revival of interest in animism is not coincidental.

[5] See the creative exhibit, *In Search of Pluriverse*, at the Het Nieuwwenin Instituut in Rotterdam, curated by artists Sophie Krier and Erik Wong (Het Nieuwwenin Instituut, "In Search of Pluriverse," available online: https://pluriverse.hetnieuweinstituut.nl/en/exhibition [accessed July 19, 2023]); Dawn Danby and David McConville (Spherical, "Home," available online: https://spherical.studio/ [accessed July 19, 2023]); Serpentine Galleries, "Back to Earth," available online: https://www.serpentinegalleries.org/whats-on/back-to-earth/ (accessed July 19, 2023); Futuress, "Design without Design," available online: https://futuress.org/stories/design-without-design/ (accessed July 19, 2023).

the economy, all of which are heavily implicated in the causation of the polycrisis. This exploration led us to a diagnosis of where "we"—modern humans, and by extension most other humans to varying degrees—have been and are at present: within the categorical and experiential space of bioeconomic man and the damaging loops of living deployed by dualistic thought in its capitalist entanglements.

For us, this exercise was essential for seeing anew the modes of operation and consequences of nonrelational living and, concomitantly, to provide a clearing for the incredible potential of relationality to become visible. Understanding what "we have made" civilizationally was the first step in our journey, as we followed Wynter's autopoetic turn ("*that which we have made*, we can unmake, then, *consciously* now, remake"). We hope our readers have felt as rejuvenated by this aspect of our journey as we have.

The realization of the critical role of narratives in shaping what modernity has made of life and the human ushered in the second dimension of the journey; it led us to raise the question of how to choose consciously and purposefully between such narratives. Coming to terms with the designing force of foundational narratives guided us to the formulation of restor(y)ing life and the human against dualistic narratives of separation, scarcity, and supremacy, arriving at the idea of *transitioning between stories* as a purposeful descriptor and enabling formulation of the task confronting us at present. Changing the foundational myths that silently but effectively have constructed much of the world, placing it at the edge of the abyss, arose for us as a crucial aspect of all transitions.

Succinctly, as Wynter put it, the taken for granted bioeconomic notions of the human, life, and knowledge "have to go"—Wynter's heresy: to dare to be a different kind of human by shifting naturalized civilizational myths and practices. Fortunately, as we realized, the reservoir of life (and of the human) is infinitely vaster than what modernity has imagined and made of it—vaster than its economic, technoscientific, and even most philosophical narratives—which led us to focus on telling cases of restor(y)ing life and their concomitant attempts at changing the infrastructures and practices based on such narratives and ontologies. This was the third aspect in our journey's horizon: "remake." We discussed some salient bridges to remaking life otherwise in politics, social mobilization, sacred activism, and designing.

"Remaking" goes hand in hand with the contention that we all make our worlds all the time through our day-to-day interactions and through the structures of thought that we inhabit and that inhabit us, largely without our realizing it. Whether one thinks of oneself as a designer or not, today more than ever we confront the need to overcome the inertia of simply acting out of the toxic loops in which we are enmeshed because that is how things have always been; we need to become self-aware designers who understand where we have been (remembering), then skillfully and consciously act (choosing), with an awareness that as we do so we are contributing to re/make life and life-worlds (designing).

Being in between stories is a promising framing of the existential and political condition of the planet. It also provides leverage points to resist the urge to run to the old story to hoard more (objects), retrench more into individual solutions, and secede even more from the living cosmos (into our allegedly secure, digitalized, de-naturalized, and de-communalized urban cubicles), as if this conferred genuine security and an effective antidote against the fear induced by the myths of scarcity and competition. The sense of being actively defutured surely creates real pressures to slip back into the race for individual survival, shelter, and success, but in doing so we abdicate the possibility of building collective, long-term survival and worlds that flourish. If the collapse of many socioecological systems is indeed what is at stake, posing a huge question mark on the future of the human as species and of particular human societies, this possibility should not lead to inertia but to an active ethics of co-creation of the conditions needed to navigate beyond the Anthropocenic and terricidal maelstrom of Cartesian rationality and global capitalism.

This is why actively observing how we are being made and defutured by our foundational myths becomes essential for reimagining worldmaking, personally and collectively. There is only so far you can go into redesigning design by remaining with the ontology of rearranging objects and concepts, in the hope that so many "green practices" might finally deliver us safely into the capitalistic future of ever-growing comfort and abundance. At the same time being between stories is hard and disorienting. We often feel that there is another way but lacking the words and frameworks to fully inhabit it, we feel lost. Let us remember that getting lost is part of the process—it is in fact the only way through, as Bayo Akomolafe repeatedly tells us.

WHAT IS TO BE DONE? TRANSITIONING BETWEEN STORIES

Remaking and restor(y)ing may be seen as an ontological instantiation of the well-known question of praxis—"what is to be done"?—which modern critical traditions, particularly Marxists, have long asked. We want to shift this question a bit by inquiring, what does it mean to do? And what does doing have to do with worldmaking and with what is considered to be real and, hence, possible? Can we do otherwise, so as not to deny politics its capacity to affect both the larger and smaller scales, so that we are not so quick to attach "failure" to relational undertakings?

We have often referred throughout this book to the notion of civilizational crisis and transitions espoused by some Latin American activists. Civilizational transitions involve a collective inquiry about those futures we want to cultivate in the present, being mindful that struggles over the future are also struggles over the past, and that both are fundamentally about visions of the human and about lives worth living. Thomas Berry put it thus:

> We might describe the challenge before us by the following sentence. The historical mission of our times is to reinvent the human—at the species level, with critical reflection, within the community of life-systems, in a time-developmental context, by means of story and shared dream experience.[6]

---

[6] Thomas Berry, *The Great Work* (New York: Bell Tower, 1999), 159.

Berry's five elements resonate with Wynter's accent on humans as hybrid of biology and narrative in a time-developmental context that involves some major events in human evolution, and with her call to work toward an ecumenical hybrid horizon for humans—a pluriverse. Pluriverse involves the creation of alternative stories of life and collective dreams of better futures. Recommencing the task of un- and redesigning the human thus involves re-narrating ourselves beyond the rational bioeconomic narrative, at the level of myth, not just at the level of objects, products, services, "solutions," and so forth, embedded in most approaches to the climate and ecological crises, such as "sustainability."

The realization that to have futures we need to cultivate the present is sharper than ever; at the same time, this awareness happens at a time when we—humans, the human, the planet—are being subjected to a staggering acceleration of the rate of defuturing, materially and narratively, not only by the ongoing devastation but, perhaps most importantly, by discourses of technology and the artificial. Hence the importance of honing our skills to respond to the slippages and blind spots introduced at every step of the way by the alluring patriarchal imaginations of capitalism and technology. All of this has to do with political agency at many levels. Pluriversal, relational politics is a tool, a bridge, a way of crossing over; the goal is to make life and ensure that life can be continuously made and remade.

Transitions will certainly involve a degree of convergence and articulation among transformative alternatives, meaning by this those based on relational and pluralistic worldviews, particularly those arising from below. As pointed out in Chapter 5, this might take the form of the creation of self-organizing meshworks, or networks of networks, among such alternatives; this issue is being tackled by a growing number of collective undertakings.[7] This in itself reflects the fact that there is no longer a clear understanding of what constitutes significant social transformation ("systemic change"), whether in activist or academic spaces. This is not necessarily bad news.

As this might sound naïve to many, we appeal to designer and theorist Gui Bonsiepe's pondering of the issue: "I don't know whether I am an optimist; perhaps better to use the term 'constructive pessimist'. I am aware that we are living in a period of counter-enlightenment known under the term 'post-modernism'. But this approach is not convincing. Without the term 'Utopia' you don't get anywhere (as far as design is concerned)."[8] Bonsiepe's defense of utopia is well taken, although for us it is primarily a question of thinking

---

[7] See, for instance, the Global Tapestry of Alternatives, a project centered on bringing together local and regional networks of radical alternatives (Global Tapestry of Alternatives, "Main page"). The most visible of these convergence spaces (Global Dialogue for Systemic Change; Global Green New Deal; Global Tapestry of Alternatives; Global Working Group Beyond Development; Grassroots to Global; Multiconvergence; and Towards a New World Social Forum) are gathered in the ADELANTE project, see ADELANTE, "About ADELANTE."

[8] See Lara Penin, ed., *Gui Bonsiepe: The Disobedience of Design*, Radical Thinkers in Design (London: Bloomsbury, 2021), 223.

differently about possibility, transcending the limitations of both Enlightenment and modernist counter-Enlightenment thinking, and finding multiple alternative realities here and now. Working against defuturing involves a commitment to actively participate in constructing territories of life and difference wherever we are or choose to be, in the present.

We described this as the work of healing the shadow of our culture not only by naming and questioning the dominant myths that characterize the dominant vision of the real, but also through a curious and hopeful opening toward the relationality of life. Shadow work, like moving between stories, is tricky and requires skillful navigation—witnessing the dark, the harmful, naming it as such, attempting to heal it, while understanding that light and dark are co-constitutive and that working to eliminate shadow, as one seeks to excise a cancer, might only cause it to grow.

We suggest that each social group and locality will have to come up with its unique set of strategies for transitioning, especially those of us in secular liberal societies who have lived far too long as allegedly autonomous individuals; this fiction must go, once and for all. Whether in the Global South or the Global North, in rural areas or urban territories, we are bound to reweave our relations to others based on care and respect; this reweaving needs to be genuinely relational. And while of course not everything can be relocalized, relocalization points at the need to regain the capacity for producing our own lives more autonomously.

Another way to put this is that we wanted this book to serve as an invitation to you, dear readers, to ask yourselves where in your life might you rebuild conscious interdependence? Where are there spaces for cultivating the conditions for regenerating and reentering the stream of life? Where in your life might you cultivate technologies of care, new "we's" and forms of collectivity? Which ways are at your disposal to discover your (our) historical mission, in profound acceptance that you are not an individual, while still being a self?

In Buddhism there is the notion that people are born at a particular time on earth to serve, in their unique way, according to their dharma. We may ask of each of those brave beings who are reconnecting with Earth at this point in planet-time, what is their (our, your) specific gift to the world? What challenges have they come to learn from and overcome? We need to think about these questions in concrete terms, not abstractly; no detail or mishap, or great boon, of your life is inconsequential.[9]

---

[9] Joanna Macy leads people in a powerful exercise she calls the Bodhisattva Perspective, or the Boddhisattva Check-In, see Frieda Nixdorf, "Boddhisattva Check-In (Revised)," Work That Reconnects Network, January 12, 2022, available online: https://workthatreconnects. org/resource/bodhisattva-check-in-revised/ (accessed September 13, 2022). While this can be quite triggering for many, we offer it in the spirit of invitation. The point of the exercise is to get clearer on what you in your particular incarnation and life are here to do by reflecting on the specific conditions of (y)our arrival to the planet. These include where, to what parents, what wealth, what deprivations, what gifts, what obstacles. Seeing

THE WAY IS NOT FORWARD, IT IS AWKWARD: WAYWARD LIVES, BEAUTIFUL EXPERIMENTS

Philosopher Yuk Hui has articulated the current predicament poignantly: "How should we respond to the challenge the human has undertaken to eliminate its own condition of existence?"[10] We hasten to add, however, that we are dealing here with the challenge *some* (monohumanist) humans have *unknowingly* undertaken, albeit *through their own designing*. For Hui, the simultaneous meltdown of modernity and its seeming economic and technological triumph is fostering new conditions for philosophy and thought, and the possibility of multiple cosmotechnical starting points for new world histories.[11] A revolution in thought entails a revolution in life-making. For us, this means that there are possible points of departure everywhere for reweaving thought and social life, perhaps most auspiciously in the work being undertaken at the onto-epistemic and social peripheries of anthropocentric worlds.

In contemplating the possibility that transitions and new conditions for thought are on the rise, it helps to distance ourselves from the linear thinking, single models, and patterns of control that shape most politics of social change at present. We may consider Akomolafe's admonishment: "the way isn't forward, it is awkward."[12] Awkward meaning not quite graspable from where we are now; not fitting into an easily recognizable success narrative. Awkward meaning it is not a matter of the good triumphing over bad, or of any side asserting victory over the rest. (Think of the principle of contingency: *relational politics cannot be predicted or defined* a priori. *They can only be defined in concrete instances and places once they have emerged, and often that emergence is messy and not fully intelligible.*) The "awkward way" might feel at times like going down, "backwards," slowing down, leading humble lives. It might also look like questioning the patriarchal master narratives of linear progress, perpetual growth, simple causality, prediction, logocentric rationality, uni-/monoverse, secularity, marching in unison to the drumbeat of rationality, white privilege, billionaire techno-gurus, individual success, panicked avoidance of suffering and death, and anthropocentric continuity.

More constructively, going awkward might mean flourishing in the cracks and fissures of oppressive designs and practices; attuning to the intuitive, the irrational, the feminine, the sacred, the ineffable; building rhizomes in all kinds of possible directions with like-minded experiments, concepts, and struggles; committing to place despite the pressure to delocalize and

---

all these things as choices you made as a being *choosing* to enter into the stream of life at this time can be a powerful exercise regardless of whether you believe in reincarnation or not.

[10] Hui, *Art and Cosmotechnics*, 249.

[11] Yuk Hui, "Singularity Vs. Daoist Robots: Is there another path than accelerated Western modernization?," *Noēma Magazine*, June 19, 2020, available online: https://www.noemamag.com/singularity-vs-daoist-robots (accessed January 6, 2022).

[12] Bayo Akomolafe, "Coming Down to Earth."

de-communalize; creating pluriversal kinds of collective intelligence on the heels of digitality; meditating on and organizing horizontally for the phasing out of a civilization premised on infinite growth, unbridled competition, and extractive capitalism.

Giving up on simple "forward" politics, again, is not necessarily bad news, if we opt to see—despite, and in the midst of, the horrors created by the global capitalist juggernaut—the myriad "beautiful experiments" being attempted in so many domains of life, often with great insight, passion, and commitment, by the so many "wayward lives" attempting to find their way into saner, healthier, happier worlds, whether personally or collectively but always in relation. We borrow these expressions from Saidiya Hartman's book, *Wayward Lives, Beautiful Experiments*, an original and lucid reconstruction of the lives and deeds of young Black women arriving from the US South to New York (Harlem) and Philadelphia, between the 1880s and the 1930s, only to find an equally virulent, albeit different, form of racism in what they expected to be spaces of freedom in the urban north. The book's opening paragraph goes against the grain, and it bears quoting in toto:

> At the turn of the twentieth century, young Black women were in open rebellion. They struggled to create autonomous and beautiful lives, to escape the new forms of servitude awaiting them, and to live as if they were free. This book recreates the radical imagination and wayward practices of these young women by describing the world through their eyes. It is a narrative written from nowhere, from the nowhere of the ghetto and the nowhere of utopia. [13]

As Hartman tells us, the challenge is to see how they survived, and at times even thrived, in the context of brutality, deprivation, and poverty, how their beautiful experiments in living—in between the crowded tenements and the street, the laundry work and their intimate lives—yielded lives that were painful but at times also beautiful, fugitive moments of going about as if they were free, in the mist of "the insistent hunger of the slum."[14] Theirs was a "revolution in a minor key." Hartman is painfully aware of the onto-epistemic and societal grasp on Black lives, but refuses to see in their kind of urban marronage only the horror and not the beauty, to linger on the tragedy without putting forward a compelling view of how young colored girls tried "to make a way out of no way, to not be defeated by defeat,"[15] so as to set into motion "a fierce and expanded sense of what might be possible."[16] Hartman's creative, careful, and loving unearthing of the histories of these forgotten young women demonstrates why another possible is and must be, possible.

Perhaps there is a planet B, after all: the planet being created collectively at present by the infinite number of beautiful experiments emerging from interdependence and mutuality the world over, activating their incredible potential.

---

[13] Hartman, *Wayward Lives*, xiii.

[14] Hartman, *Wayward Lives*, 84.

[15] Hartmand, *Wayward Lives*, 347.

[16] Hartman, *Wayward Lives*, 59.

Appendix: Our use of the concept of ontology

Nosotrxs no pedimos la propiedad de la tierra, nosotrxs proponemos otro arte de habitar en la tierra (we do not demand property over land; we propose a different art of dwelling on the earth).
MOIRA MILLÁN[1]

No age lets itself be done away with by a negating decree. Negation only throws the negator off the path. The modern age requires, however, in order to be withstood in the future, in its essence and on the very strength of its essence, an originality and range of reflection for which we of today are perhaps preparing somewhat, but over which we certainly can never gain mastery.
MARTIN HEIDEGGER[2]

Ontology is often described as the study of the real, of what is. In this book, we take ontology as a tool or bridge to help us move between dualist and relational life narratives and practices. Some readers might ask: "why appeal to ontology, isn't it a very Eurocentric concept?" As we mentioned in Chapter 3, we consider ontology to be a provisional category not for philosophy, of course, but in the sense that those peoples and life-worlds that do not distinguish between "representation" and "reality" or between "myth" and "fact," nor make a sharp separation between being, knowing, and doing (i.e., between ontology, epistemology, and social practice) may not need such abstraction. For those of us who mostly inhabit a One-World world, ontology helps us see where we have been and possible paths toward pluriversal configurations. Talking about ontologies also help us take other worlds seriously, including when it comes to seeing such worlds within the West itself.

Our thanks to B. Scot Rousse for his helpful comments on a draft of this Appendix.

[1] Mapuche activist.

[2] Martin Heidegger, "The Age of the World Picture," in *The Question Concerning Technology and Other Essays*, 115–54 (New York: Harper Torchbooks, 1977).

We have five entry points into ontology: First, Winograd and Flores's use of the term in *Understanding Computers and Cognition.* Second, anthropologist Mario Blaser's characterization of ontology. Third, Heideggerian phenomenology, perhaps the most influential framework on the relation between philosophy, ontology, and modernity, including for several design theorists on whom we draw. Fourth, those trends in social theory that go under the rubric of post-dualism and the ontological turn. And fifth and finally, discussions on "cosmovisions" by Indigenous and ethnic intellectuals and movements (a vernacular term that invokes concerns that could be described as ontological). We will only deal with the first three in this short Appendix (the latter two are variously discussed in the book's chapters).

As indicated in Chapter 5, Winograd and Flores define ontology simply as "our understanding of what it means for something or someone to exist."[3] They underscore the ontological character of designing by positing the need to recognize "that in designing tools, we are designing ways of being."[4] Every tool or technology is ontological in the sense that, however minutely, it inaugurates a set of practices, ways of knowing, and modes of being. We design tools, and these tools design us back. Design contributes to establish the traditions within which humans understand their structures of possibility.

Against the mind-body dualism—leaning on Martin Heidegger's understanding of the unity of being-in-the-world—Winograd and Flores uphold the primacy of practical understanding. For them, the world "is always organized around fundamental human projects and depends upon these projects for its being and organization."[5] This means that the skillful disclosing of new worlds demands pragmatic activity around a shared concern. We may surmise that when pursuing different worldmaking practices, activists and designers act as ontological disclosers in this sense.[6]

Winograd and Flores's treatment of ontology resonates with the debates over the past decade and a half in the field of political ontology, a category first introduced by Mario Blaser to refer to the investigation of how different ways of worlding come into being and relate to each other in contexts of power. As explained in Chapter 3, Blaser distinguishes three dimensions of ontology. The first refers to the premises all social groups have about the kinds of entities that exist in the real world; the second emphasizes that ontologies are not just ideas, they are embodied in practices and performed into worlds. The third stresses that ontologies are often embedded in myths and narratives that enact worlds, whether we agree with their truthfulness from the perspective of our own world.[7]

---

[3] Winograd and Flores, *Understanding Computers and Cognition,* 30; Hubert Dreyfus, *Being-in-the-World: A Commentary of Heidegger's Being and Time, Division One* (Cambridge, MA: MIT Press, 1991).

[4] Winograd and Flores, *Understanding Computers and Cognition,* xi.

[5] Winograd and Flores, *Understanding Computers and Cognition,* 58.

[6] Charles Spinosa, Fernando Flores, and Hubert Dreyfus, *Disclosing New Worlds* (Cambridge, MA: MIT Press, 1997).

[7] Blaser, *Storytelling Globalization,* 3; Blaser, "Ontological Conflicts."

We find consistency between this characterization of ontology and Heidegger's. First, from a Heideggerian perspective, the word "ontology" could mean the explicit philosophical subdiscipline that contrasts with epistemology (in this sense, ontology is the discipline he tried to reinvent in *Being and Time*). Second, it also means the understanding of being (or of "reality") that is built into the practices of a world (as when we talk about the "modern ontology"). Heidegger develops his conception of world as "a name for what is, in its entirety," which in this particular essay he also calls "a world picture" (referring to how a world's practices embody some holistic, overall coherence, or, as anthropologists might say, the whole of social life, in a non-anthropocentric sense).[8]

The fact that Blaser includes both discursive and nondiscursive elements in his definition of ontology fits well with a Heideggerian understanding. As Hubert Dreyfus emphasizes in his exegesis of *Being and Time*, an ontology cannot be reduced to a list of explicit or implicit assumptions. Ontologies are embodied in social practices; think, for instance, of the richness of child-rearing practices across cultures (Dreyfus's example) and the extent to which they reflect diverse understanding and actual ways of being a child, a society, a human, and so forth. Ethnographic accounts of "non-Western peoples" are replete with examples of incredibly diverse practices that enact equally diverse worlds.

Heidegger's reinvention of ontology aimed to provide a fresh analysis of what it means to be human, claiming that the tradition (from Plato to René Descartes, Immanuel Kant, and Edmund Husserl) had systematically misinterpreted such question because of its emphasis on theory and representation. His hermeneutic phenomenology is the most sustained attempt at arriving at an explanation of being that does not assume an ontology of intrinsically independent objects, on the one hand, and conscious, intentional subjects, on the other, but one that acknowledges the salience of involved practical understanding in everything humans do. His radical critique of the long-standing representational episte-mology cleared the ground for a reinterpretation of the multiplicity of forms of being-in-the-world. Succinctly, humans are doing subjects before they are detached knowing subjects.[9]

Being and Time purported to develop a novel mode of access to the question of being. As its author put it, "the very fact that we already live in an understand-ing of being and that the sense of being is still veiled in darkness proves that it is necessary in principle to raise this question again."[10] The insistence on the uttermost importance of preparing the ground for this question returns in his well-known ontological analysis of technology. In this essay, Heidegger develops

---

[8] Heidegger, "The Age of the World Picture," 128.

[9] In *Being and Time*, Heidegger explains this position with the help of the concept of Dasein. Dasein refers to everyday human existence; it is a conception of the self-interpreting human being, yet different from that of a conscious subject. Dasein implies an embodied, pre-theoretical understanding of its being, dependent on shared practices. From here follows an understanding of the human as always involved, "thrown into" the world, and the idea that Dasein's basic form of being-in-the-world is "dwelling."

[10] Martin Heidegger, *Being and Time* (New York: Harper and Row, 1962), 23.

a critical view of the representationalist tradition of Western metaphysics as intimately tied to the objectivizing notions of causality and instrumentality. With modern technology, this link becomes such that it cannot but become a "challenging" imposed by "man" upon nature to always be available for human purposes (in this way, the river is construed as the opportunity for a hydroelectric plant, earth is seen as a deposit of minerals, and farming as the basis of a mechanized food industry, in his examples).

Said otherwise, everything is irresistibly ordered by man as "standing-reserve" for human purposes, and nature comes to be treated as an objectifiable set of calculable forces to be unveiled through scientific research. He names this novel situation "Enframing." Not only does enframing undermine any possibility of relating to the natural world (as *physis*) in all its mystery (it blocks *poiesis*), it becomes a fundamental ontological structure for the modern age. This, for Heidegger, becomes "the supreme [existential] danger," in that it concerns man "in his relationship to himself and to everything that is ... it banishes man into that kind of revealing which is an ordering."[11] Heidegger's notion of world picture thus establishes a tight link between science and technology, metaphysics, and the consolidation of an anthropocentric and secular modernity through a representational regime that confers upon Man mastery over the world. Succinctly, "the fundamental event of the modern age is the conquest of the world as picture."[12]

Heidegger's emphasis on our constitutive thrownness is useful to problematize the human anew, for such thrownness confers upon human existence (Dasein) a primordial ontological structure based on relationality and care. There is a "solicitude" at play in human situations that arises from our being with others, that is, from the fact of relationality.[13] Today, we may argue, humans are being solicited in a fundamental sense to activate our care for a new manner of dwelling in the world.[14] The question becomes: what kinds of worlds might be conducive to a manner of being-in-the-world that is also a new mode of dwelling

---

[11] Heidegger, "The Question Concerning Technology," 26, 27. Not all is lost, for Heidegger, because there is always the possibility of other ways of revealing conducive to existentially richer ways of coming to presence on the earth (what he calls "saving power," a term he borrows from Friedrich Hölderlin). But this requires first coming to terms dialectically with the concealment induced by enframing and modern technology. As discussed in Chapter 5, Clive Dilnot expands upon the Heideggerian analysis of technology in his analysis of the artificial as a new horizon for being. For a related post-Heideggerian investigation, see Hui, *Art and Cosmotechnics.*

[12] Heidegger, "The Age of the World Picture," 134.

[13] "Because being-in-the-world is essentially care *(Sorge)*, being-amidst the available could be taken in our previous analyses as *concern (Besorgen)*, and being with the Dasein-with of others as we encounter it within-the-world could be taken as *solicitude (Fursorge)*" (Heidegger, *Being and Time*, 237).

[14] The notions of solicitude and care in today's context are being developed by Fernando Flores and B. Scot Rousse, in conversation with Terry Winograd, Don Norman, and Arturo Escobar (group conversations).

on the earth, one that reactivates the existential mandate of care?[15] Feminists and others have made critical contributions to invigorating discussions on care in this sense, returning the human to relational existence.

We believe that the ontology of enframing and its attendant political implications continue to be a pressing condition. The growing awareness of the breakdown of the dominant way of worlding is an auspicious condition for a renovated problematization of the human. Which historical background practices most shape our ways of being, knowing, and doing, both for various social groups and for the growing planetary culture? This is the question we tackled in Chapters 1 and 2 with reference to Wynter's deconstruction of "bioeconomic man."

The ontological lens sheds light onto the significance of transitioning between stories of the human and the world. Consider this statement:

> Therefore, what is necessary above all is this: that beforehand we ponder the *essence* of Being as that which is worthy of thinking; that beforehand, in thinking this, we experience to what extent we are called upon first to trace a path for such experiencing and to prepare that path as a way into that which till now has been impassable[16]

He calls this "the Turning," going beyond the current "entrapping-with-oblivion" of the human. Instead of thinking about an abstract "essence of Being," today we need to think of the multiple relational ways of being and becoming, and then ask about the paths that need preparing in this regard.[17] Pondering these paths requires dwelling in the restorative "surmounting of Enframing."[18] In these statements, we may glean the ideas of transitioning between narratives of life and the need for non-objectifying relations to knowledge, technology, and politics.

There are some other useful ideas for thinking about transitions. "Where and how it [the Turning] will come to pass after the manner of a [different] destining no one knows. Nor is it necessary that we know."[19] As emphasized in Chapter 3, this uncertainty is constitutive of relational politics and transitioning. Yet we must be mindful not to chase "after the future so as to work out a picture of it through calculation, since that would only extend what is present."[20] The risk

---

[15] Heidegger, *Being and Time*, 415. "The question arises of how anything like the world in its unity with Dasein is ontologically possible. In what way must the world *be*, if Dasein is to be able to exist as being-in-the-world?" (emphasis in the original).

[16] Heidegger, "The Question Concerning Technology," 40.

[17] We are mindful of the importance of considering not just being, but also becoming and the actual conditions for being (as recent post-Heideggerian commentary emphasizes). Later Heidegger himself gave up on doing ontology, presumably in part because he saw the whole project as inevitably tied up with the history of metaphysics; so instead he tried to do the "history of being" or, even later, "thinking."

[18] Heidegger, "The Question Concerning Technology," 41.

[19] Heidegger, "The Question Concerning Technology," 41.

[20] Heidegger, "The Question Concerning Technology," 48.

of slippage into a calculative rationality reveals the dangers always lurking within objectifying representationalism; it applies to most solutions to climate collapse, which thus become part of the crisis, as discussed in Chapter 2.

Thinking about ontology is relevant to us since it helps us outline "the ontological task of a genealogy of the different possible ways of being."[21] This notion is central to political ontology's concern with both dominant ways of worlding and pluriversal undertakings. Relevant in this regard is the fact that Heidegger connects ontology with truth. As he states, "metaphysics grounds an age, in that through a specific interpretation of what is and through a specific comprehension of truth it gives to that age the basis upon which it is essentially formed."[22]

The connection between the investigation into "what is" and truth was, of course, extensively elaborated upon by Michel Foucault. Foucault's eventual statement about the entanglement between being, truth, and power throughout his work vividly articulates the stakes. "It was a matter of analyzing, not behaviors or ideas, nor societies and their 'ideologies,' but the *problematizations* through which being offers itself to be, necessarily, thought—and the practices on the basis of which these problematizations are formed."[23] Furthermore, "there are times in life when the question of knowing if one can think differently than one thinks, and perceive differently than one sees, is absolutely essential if one is to go on looking and reflecting at all."[24] We are at one such juncture, collectively, as a species. This sort of investigation constitutes a political ontology of the relation between being, becoming, dwelling, designing, knowledge, the sacred, and politics.

---

[21] Heidegger, *Being and Time*, 31.

[22] Heidegger, "The Age of the World Picture," 115. In this passage, Heidegger talks specifically about metaphysics, not ontology, but arguably, he is using the terms interchangeably. Those interested may consult the entry on "Ontology" from the recent *Cambridge Heidegger Lexicon*, ed. Mark Wrathall (Cambridge: Cambridge University Press, 2021).

[23] Foucault, *The Use of Pleasure* (New York: Vintage Books, 1985), 11.

[24] *Foucault, The Use of Pleasure, 8.*

Index